"This brilliant book will educate, encourage, and empower
any who are attempting to reach the next generation with the Gospel."

—Dr. Bruce Larson, author of 23 books, pastor emeritus
at University Presbyterian Church in Seattle

"Ken Baugh and Rich Hurst understand the complexity of this generation's needs.
They provide an effective and biblical framework for developing them into maturity and leadership."

—John Townsend, Ph.D., psychologist, speaker,
and author/coauthor of *Boundaries, Safe People,
Hiding from Love, Raising Great Kids*, and others

GETTING REAL

An Interactive Guide to Relational Ministry

Ken Baugh & Rich Hurst

FOREWORD BY RICK WARREN

GETTING REAL

NAVPRESS

BRINGING TRUTH TO LIFE

P.O. Box 35001, Colorado Springs, Colorado 80935

The Navigators is an international Christian organization. Our mission is to reach, disciple, and equip people to know Christ and to make Him known through successive generations. We envision multitudes of diverse people in the United States and every other nation who have a passionate love for Christ, live a lifestyle of sharing Christ's love, and multiply spiritual laborers among those without Christ.

NavPress is the publishing ministry of The Navigators. NavPress publications help believers learn biblical truth and apply what they learn to their lives and ministries. Our mission is to stimulate spiritual formation among our readers.

Baugh, Ken
Getting real: an interactive guide to relational ministry / Ken Baugh, Rich Hurst.
p.cm.
Includes biographical references.
ISBN 1-57683-179-5 (pbk.)
1. Church work with young adults. I. Hurst, Rich. II. Title.

BV4446 .B38 2000
295'.25--dc21

Cover photo by Lars Topelmann/Grapistock
Creative Team: Brad Lewis, Eric Stanford, Ray Moore, Tim Howard, and Terry Behimer

Some of the anecdotal illustrations in this book are true to life and are included with the permission of the persons involved. All other illustrations are composites of real situations, and any resemblance to people living or dead is coincidental.

Unless otherwise identified, all Scripture quotations in this publication are taken from the *HOLY BIBLE: NEW INTERNATIONAL VERSION* ® (NIV ®). Copyright © 1973, 1978, 1984 by International Bible Society. Used by permission of Zondervan Publishing House. All rights reserved. Other versions used include: the *New American Standard Bible* (NASB), © The Lockman Foundation 1960, 1962, 1963, 1968, 1971, 1972, 1973, 1975, 1977; *The Message: New Testament with Psalms and Proverbs* (MSG) by Eugene H. Peterson, copyright © 1993, 1994, 1995, used by permission of NavPress Publishing Group; *The New Testament in Modern English* (PH), J. B. Phillips Translator, © J. B. Phillips 1958, 1960, 1972, used by permission of Macmillan Publishing Company; *The Living Bible* (TLB), copyright © 1971, used by permission of Tyndale House Publishers, Inc., Wheaton, IL 60189, all rights reserved; the *Good News Bible: Today's English Version* (TEV), copyright © American Bible Society 1966, 1971, 1976; *The New English Bible* (NEB), © 1961, 1970, The Delegates of the Oxford University Press and The Syndics of the Cambridge University Press; the *Amplified New Testament* (AMP), © The Lockman Foundation 1954, 1958; the *New King James Version* (NKJV), copyright © 1979, 1980, 1982, 1990, Thomas Nelson Inc., Publishers; and the *King James Version* (KJV). Scripture quotations marked (NLT) are taken from the *Holy Bible, New Living Translation*, copyright © 1996. Used by permission of Tyndale House Publishers, Inc., Wheaton, Illinois 60189. All rights reserved.

Printed in the United States of America

1 2 3 4 5 6 7 8 9 10 11 12 13 14 15 / 03 02 01 00

FOR A FREE CATALOG OF
NAVPRESS BOOKS & BIBLE STUDIES,
CALL 1-800-366-7788 (USA)
OR 1-416-499-4615 (CANADA)

Dedicated to
Frontline Ministries and The Next Level Church
and all those who reach this generation and those to follow

CONTENTS

FOREWORD

The eternal purposes of God for His church are unchanging. They have remained the same since the Day of Pentecost nearly 2,000 years ago. God expects His church to worship, to evangelize, to fellowship, to edify believers, and to serve the needs of people. These tasks are commanded by Christ in the Great Commission and Great Commandment; they are illustrated by the first church in Acts 2; and they are explained by Paul in Ephesians 4 and many other passages. They are non-negotiable. Any church that fails to fulfill these purposes is not really a biblical church.

However, the *manner* or *style* in which each local congregation fulfills God's purposes is very open to variety and innovation. While every church needs to be built on the purposes of God, every church also must express its unique thumbprint. Travel around the world and you'll quickly discover that God *loves* variety! He has created human beings, along with everything else, in an infinite number of styles, shapes, and colors. So it is natural that congregations composed of different groups of people are going to express the eternal purposes of God in different ways. There are tens of thousands of purpose-driven churches around the world using different worship styles, reaching different target groups, and ministering in unique ways.

While God's purposes for His church never change, each new generation must *rediscover* those purposes for their churches. And the methods that are used *must* change with every new generation. The Bible tells us *"David had served God's purpose in his own generation"* (Acts 13:36, emphasis added). He did the timeless in a timely way. He fulfilled the eternal in a contemporary setting. That is what this book is about. It is an effort to show how to do church with a new generation of young adults. Its goal is to take the timeless and express it in a timely fashion.

There are some values that are *always* relevant and always effective regardless of the target group you minister to. In the first message I preached at the inaugural service of Saddleback in 1980, I identified six values that we intended to build our congregation on: authentic leadership, personal relationships, humble service, life-application teaching, empowered lay ministry, and risk-taking faith. These are timeless values that appeal to *every* generation. But each new generation must develop *new expressions* of these values. *Getting Real* will show you how to do this with young adults.

I love the attitude of the authors of this book. They are willing to do *whatever it takes* to reach their generation for Christ. You don't have to agree with everything Ken and Rich have written in order to appreciate their creativity, their passion, their insights, and their commitment. So keep an open mind—and you'll learn something!

On a personal note, one of the most fulfilling parts of ministry is watching people grow up in your church family, answer the call to ministry, and be sent out to serve elsewhere. I first met one of the authors, Ken Baugh, nearly 20 years ago, when he began attending Saddleback Church as a high school student. Later I had the privilege of performing Ken and Susan's wedding and having Ken serve on our church staff. Today Ken leads a thriving ministry on the opposite coast. So it is with great joy that I endorse this book.

—Rick Warren
Saddleback Church
Lake Forest, CA
www.pastors.com

ACKNOWLEDGMENTS

This book is the result of having a loving and grace-giving God. With that in mind, we want to mention several people God used to make this book possible. First and foremost is Toben Heim, who worked so hard to get it published. Thank you! Without Kim Hurst there would be no book—her endless editing, encouragement, and working out of bugs was amazing. We would also like to thank Trevor Bron, Melissa Fulfer, Todd Phillips, Lisa Goodwin, Dieter Zander, Kerry O'Bryant, and Tim Celek for helping us understand how to reach this generation. And the people at NavPress were kind enough to believe in us, so thank you especially to Sue Geiman and Brad Lewis.

During the writing of this book, my (Rich's) dad died. So to David H. Hurst, I miss you and thank you for believing in me. Beyond my family, there are four men who have shaped my life: to my spiritual father Bruce Larson, to my friend Frank Tillapaugh, to my life friend Terry Hershey, and to my teammate and amazing friend Ken Baugh, thank you. To my pastor and teacher Trevor J. Bron and The Next Level Church, my part of this book would have been nothing without my being a part of you. Finally, to my wife, Kim, and wonderful daughters, Katy and Jessa, you make me laugh and you bless me. Special thanks to my mother, who kept praying for me when everyone else was quiet.

A number of people have greatly influenced my (Ken's) life, both personally as well as for ministry. Without their mentoring and support, I wouldn't be equipped to serve Christ in the same capacity. I am deeply grateful to these men and women who have given me a part of their knowledge, experience, and life. I would like to thank my grandfather, Floyd Rongstad, for leading me to Christ and guiding me into full-time ministry. I would like to thank Rick Warren, both as a spiritual father and as a mentor, who helped me understand how to reach seekers and build a thriving church. To Dr. Warren Herd, for teaching me about grace and believing in me during some dark seminary years; without his help, I don't think I would have made it. To Dr. Beth Brown, who helped fan into flame my passion for teaching. To Rich Hurst, my best friend, mentor, and one who has always helped me think outside the box. To Doug Kyle, who has been in my foxhole many times. To Drs. John Townsend, Leonard Cerney, and David Allen, who have helped me heal the broken places of my heart. To the Congos, McFaddens, and all those at Discovery

Bible Church who came alongside my family and helped us survive during some very rough days. To Lon Solomon and Ron Johnson, two men who have believed in my dreams to reach a generation and have given me all the resources necessary to do it. To my staff team at Frontline—Kevin, Jim, Dan, Beth, John, Wayne, Stephanie, Courtney, Cathy, Julia, Trevor, and the late Gerry Dixon—doing ministry with all of you is pure joy. Thank you for working so hard for Christ. And finally to my parents and family, thank you for your support and love. To my dear wife, Susan, my soul mate and true love—without your help, support, and constant encouragement I couldn't do life. And to my two angels, Jessica and Ariella—your daddy loves you very much. Thank you all, you have shaped my life, and I am humbly grateful.

INTRODUCTION

We recently saw a photo of a street scene in Ireland. An elderly woman, dressed conservatively in an overcoat and scarf, had stopped to talk with four young adults—three men and a woman. The young woman was dressed in a pink miniskirt and pink socks with black platform shoes. Each young man had dyed his spiked hair a different color of the rainbow. All had studded motorcycle jackets. Yet the older woman didn't seem the least bothered by their appearance. She was being as neighborly with them as she would with anyone.

> I simply say, the cross must be raised again at the center of the marketplace as well as on the steeple of the church. I am claiming that Jesus was not crucified in a cathedral between two candles, but on a cross between two thieves; on the town garbage heap, at a crossroads so cosmopolitan that they had to write His title in Hebrew, Latin, and Greek. At the kind of place where cynics talk smut, and thieves curse, and soldiers gamble, because that is where He died and that is what He died about and that is where churchmen ought to be and what churchmen should be about.
>
> —George MacLeod[1]

If such a group lived in your community, how would you respond? Would you ignore them? Would they be just an interesting bit of scenery? Or would you reach out to them? (Now that you've answered, let us remind you that people who look like this probably do live near you.)

YESTERDAY AND TODAY

Although many churches have several programs that meet the needs and likes of an average middle-aged person, they often have little that meets the needs of the average young adult. While not every church is called to start a targeted program to draw in young adults, we believe that every church is called to minister to all members of its community, including today's young adults.

In the last fifteen years, most church ministry has been aimed at the legions of Baby Boomers (those born roughly between 1946 and 1964). Just as Boomers demanded attention in the late 1970s and 1980s, now members of Generation X (or Xers, those born roughly between 1964 and 1981) are demanding the church's attention. And coming up quickly after them are the next generation of young adults, who we will refer to as the Net Gen (those born in 1981 and after). However, unlike Boomers—who got our culture's attention by their sheer numbers—Gen X and the Net Gen captivate us because they are so distinct from previous generations.

What makes these new young adults so different from prior generations? We will discuss that at length later, but now consider one key factor. These generations constitute the most unchurched and unreached people in North America. This isn't to suggest that these young adults aren't spiritual. However, they hold a very different idea of what it means to believe in God. In addition, many young adults have a less than positive opinion of the church.

That was a pretty strong statement we just made. We'll make a lot of them in this book, and before we go on, we should tell you a few things about ourselves. We're not demographers. We're not sociologists. We're ministry guys who have read a lot and observed a lot. Please read all that we say with that in mind. We will make statements and draw conclusions based on our interpretations and observations of what's going on both in our own worlds and in the bigger world. You might disagree or think we're wrong. That's okay. We strongly encourage you to read what others are saying too, and to draw your own conclusions. As you look to minister to young adults, you'll get much further ahead if you do your own research. But at least you can use our reading and thinking to jump-start your own efforts.

Now, where were we? Oh yes, many young adults have a less than positive opinion about the church. We're going to use the term "young adults" often in this book. When we say "young adults," we're talking about people roughly between eighteen and thirty-five years of age. The difficulty in designing young adult ministry programming to reach this range of people is that within this group are many subgroups.

First, as we noted above, there are two generations, Gen X and the Net Gen. Each subgroup is defined by unique circumstances and lifestyle issues, which we'll explore in chapter 2. Briefly, here are some of the identified subgroups of Generation X:

- Star Xers
- Urban Xers
- Slacker Xers
- Digital Xers
- Extreme Xers
- Underground Xers

The Net Gen is the first generation raised (and still being raised) on the Internet. Many of the young adults in this generation—the first wave are now in their late teens—have experienced life thus far in a way unknown to any generation before them. Here are some of the terms being used to describe their unique reality:

- Techno-stress
- Boundary erosion
- Space invaders
- Death of distance
- Real time
- Techno-dependency
- On-line ego
- Warp speed
- Early meltdown
- Cocooning
- Techno-families
- Global society

To grasp the differences between young adults of today and those of twenty years ago, you should realize that some demographers believe that Baby Boomers had just two subcultures: early Boomers (born between 1946 and 1957) and later Boomers (born between 1958 and 1964). Here are examples, based on a totally unscientific poll, of how two groups of children saw the world through different eyes.[2]

Thinking back to the young adulthood of Boomers, we can remember certain distinct groups—Hippies, Yuppies, DINKS, Berkeley Radicals, Acid Heads, and Reagan Conservatives are a few of the terms that come to mind. But today's young adults have splintered into many more subcultures. Ministry that reaches one group may miss the mark for another. With so many variables, it's hard to know exactly where to begin.

WHERE TO START

Here are five assumptions that will apply to young adult ministry in the twenty-first century:

1. One program will not meet all the needs of the young adults in your church. Because there are so many different kinds of young adults, there are many different needs. These include emotional, social, spiritual, educational, relational, and career needs. Any one program can meet only a few of these. To try to meet all these needs is to ensure failure. You will need to target a subgroup.

Seeing young adults as a collection of target groups is seeing them as a sociologist would. A sociologist is aware that any society is made up of subcultures (peer groups, workers in a particular profession, ethnic groups). In the same way, you'll want to look for subcultures and design ministries with their lifestyles in mind.

	Born 1946–1957	**Born 1958–1964**
TV series	*Father Knows Best*	*The Partridge Family*
Kiddie show	*Howdy Doody*	*Romper Room*
Toy	Mr. Potato Head (real potato)	Mr. Potato Head (plastic toy)
Runner-up toy	Hula hoop	GI Joe
Goopy stuff	Mud	Play-Doh
Singing family	The Everly Brothers	The Jackson 5
Teen dance	"The Mashed Potato"	"The Bump"
Transportation	Scooters	Skateboards
Monsters	Godzilla, King Kong	The Munsters
Cartoon	Mighty Mouse	The Flintstones
Comic book hero	Superman	Batman
Sports hero	Jackie Robinson	Hank Aaron
Female role model	Annette Funicello of the Mouseketeers	Stefanie Powers as April Dancer in *The Girl from U.N.C.L.E.*
Significant childhood memory	Air raid drills	No cartoons after JFK was shot

2. Not every church needs a program to reach young adults, but any church can have an effective ministry with them. Not every church is called to start a program for every age group, but every church is called to reach out to people of all ages. This is a critical distinction.

3. This generation is not "Boomers revisited." Young adulthood is not the same in every generation. Think of the difference between an eighteen-year-old in 1942 in the era of World War II and an eighteen-year-old in 1972 in the era of the Vietnam War. Although all young adults experience many of the same developmental and growth issues, each generation experiences important distinctives. What sets one person's young adulthood apart from that of a prior generation are the external factors encountered on the way to adulthood.

4. Young adult ministry is not the same as youth ministry. Most youth ministries are built on an entertainment model. The whole idea is to have fun—and the more fun, the better.

While young adults continue to love entertainment, they also value real conversation about real issues and real responsibilities. They want to be listened to and trusted. We must give them responsibility and authority in all areas of young adult ministry. Many young adults want to create their own ministries, something that reflects them. You may not be able to begin an effective young adult ministry "for them."

5. *Young adult ministry is no longer single adult ministry.* Most young adults don't want to be called singles. They dislike labels, and the label "singles" has a negative connotation to them. Authentic relationships and friendships are much more important than being single or married. Becoming family with one another and discussing real-life issues are important. Helping to contribute to a better earth is important, and so is being careful sexually. Many young adult ministries will serve both unmarried and married young adults. Most married young adults who don't have children relate well to unmarried young adults. When people in your group get married, they will hang on with your group for a period of a year or a little longer, but as their needs change, they'll move on to new ministries.

We hope this book encourages you to move forward in an effective ministry with young adults. We want to help you dream about what God wants to accomplish through you in reaching these unchurched generations. Nothing is more exciting than to be part of what will happen in the area of ministry to young adults. Your desire—shown by your willingness to wade through this book—demonstrates that you want to be a part of the team God will build to do things in a new way with these generations.

HOW TO USE THIS TOOL

This book is broken down into idea sections, each one building on the other. Here's a quick overview:

PREVIEW (WHO IS THIS MINISTRY FOR?)

Before you begin, understanding the new world and how generations are different will direct you to make good program and ministry decisions. The world is different now, and these generations are unique. This section will help you understand why.

PHILOSOPHY OF MINISTRY (WHY SHOULD WE MINISTER TO YOUNG ADULTS?) CHAPTERS 1 THROUGH 4.

Before you entertain thoughts of ministry development or devote time and energy to sorting through the myriad "how-tos," you need to spend time with the question "Why?"

Why is your church involved in ministry? What is your rationale for the types of programs you're currently providing? Ministry programs will deteriorate if they're not built on a solid philosophy. Leaders will burn out if there's not a clear understanding of why they're doing what they're doing.

A philosophy of ministry is simply a grid

to see people and ministry through. In this section of the book we will look at a suggested philosophy of ministry and six elements of a good ministry with young adults.

For a young adult ministry to be strong, it must rest on six imperatives:

1. Don't try to copy anyone else
2. Don't try to do everything at once
3. Don't be afraid to fail
4. Do evolve a structure
5. Do be needs-driven
6. Do ask questions

PURPOSE (IN WHAT DIRECTION SHOULD WE GO?) CHAPTERS 5 AND 6.

Once you settle on a philosophy of ministry, you'll have laid the foundation for what can be an effective and rewarding ministry program. Now that you know *why* and *to whom* you are doing what you're doing, you can determine a ministry purpose or vision. The prophet Habakkuk says, "Record the vision and inscribe it on tablets, that the one who reads it may run" (Habakkuk 2:2).

Your vision statement will reflect the heart of those in the ministry and the general direction you want the ministry to take. But this section is about more than a vision statement; your purpose for your ministry is driven by core values.

PREPARATION OF LEADERS (HOW CAN WE START BUILDING PEOPLE?) CHAPTERS 7 THROUGH 10.

Building a great young adult ministry hinges on your commitment to building leaders. A common thread runs through the stories about ministries for young adults that have failed: there was no direction and/or no leadership. In this section you discover principles for building a healthy ministry. Leaders thrive in the correct environment, and this section of the book will lay out the environmental conditions for growing healthy leaders.

PROGRAMMING (WHAT WORKS?) CHAPTERS 11 AND 12.

The temptation in ministry is to start with programming. But all the foundational work must occur before you ever begin a program. In this section you'll learn practical steps for developing effective worship, fellowship, and community ministry to young adults.

PLANNING (WHERE DO WE GO NOW?) CHAPTERS 13 AND 14.

This section of the book will provide a quick guide to what to do next. We can't promise every idea will work in your context, but we do know the principles here are working around the country.

PROCESS (WHAT ARE SOME HELPFUL TOOLS FOR USE WITH YOUNG ADULTS?) APPENDICES 1 THROUGH 6.

This section will give you practical suggestions

for small groups, tools for making disciples, and ideas to get everyone involved.

This book is about how to minister to and with young adults — one of the most needy yet hard to reach groups in American history. It's intended to be a practical book, filled with proven ideas. As you attempt to minister to and with young adults, you're bound to find the going hard, confusing, and at times discouraging. But while the work is hard, it's also one of the most rewarding areas of ministry in the church today. Our great hope is that you will have some of the rewarding experiences we have had.

CHAPTER ONE

POSTMODERNISM AND YOUNG ADULTS

A young pastor recently told me (Rich) that "Generation X is dead." He said he meant the term was finished—overused and no longer descriptive. In a way he's right because being an Xer is more a state of being or state of mind than having been born in a certain year. When asked why I, a Boomer, spend so much of my time and energy in Gen X ministry, my friend Trevor likes to tell people, "Rich is more Xer than the rest of us!"

The truth is, to live in this age means to some extent that everyone is an Xer. No one is exempt from the reality of change. New technologies, new communications systems, new spirituality, the new view of entertainment as the highest element in society—all of these things impact you regardless of your age. They give you an Xer experience, an experience that's not really about your age but about the new reality of postmodernism.

The Smashing Pumpkins want their latest tour to smash some Generation X stereotypes. "There is a common feeling that the world is falling apart, and we're one of the bands of our generation accused of playing into that nihilism," said lead singer Billy Corgan. "I'm sick of being accused of feeding into that." The band hopes to raise $2.3 million for local charities during its summer tour, which opened Tuesday. "As a band we've achieved our wildest dreams," he said. "What's important now is putting our values ahead of our pockets."[1]

> Refusal to consider change under the direction of the Holy Spirit is a spiritual problem, not an intellectual problem. There is a bad concept of old-fashionedness and there is a good concept. The good concept is that some things never change because they are eternal truths. These we must hold to tenaciously and give up nothing of this kind of old-fashionedness.[2]

> The term [postmodern was used] in 1969 in reference to spiritual wanderers who are looking for roots.[3]

To be most effective in young adult ministry, you first must understand the worldview held by today's young adults. Crucial to that understanding is a grasp of the differences between the tenets of modernism and those of postmodernism. Failure to appreciate the philosophical differences will often spell failure for your attempts to reach young adults. So, what is postmodernism, and what does it mean when programming for and teaching young adults?

MODERNISM

"We are experiencing enormous structural change in our country and world—change that promises to be greater than the invention of the printing press, greater than the industrial revolution, and greater than the rise and demise of communism. Our world is changing so quickly that we can barely keep track of what is happening, much less figure out how to respond."[4]

Sociologists and trend watchers widely agree that we've shifted away from a "modern" worldview and have entered a new era, an era of "postmodernism." While there's an agreement that this shift has taken place, there's little agreement on how to define or describe this new worldview. Most definitions seem to have similar elements in common, but there is an incredibly wide variety of opinions on the specific definition.

Several tenets make up a basic understanding of modernism. Postmodernism appears to be a rejection or reaction to those tenets. The following fundamental views of modernism were addressed by Thomas Oden in *Christianity Today:*[5]

1. *Moral relativism:* What is right is dictated by culture, social occasions, and situations.

2. *Autonomous individualism:* Moral authority comes essentially from within. In the end, we answer to no one but ourselves. Our choices are ours alone, determined by our personal pleasure and not by any higher moral authority.

3. *Narcissistic hedonism:* Egocentric personal pleasure is the rule. The popular ethical expression of this mindset is "If it makes you happy and doesn't hurt anyone else, then it's okay."

4. *Reductive naturalism:* All we know is what we can see, hear, and empirically investigate. If something can't be examined in a tangible, scientific manner, then it isn't knowable. It is meaningless.

POSTMODERNISM AND *THE NEXT GENERATION*

Author Stanley Grenz has found a helpful illustration of the differences between the modern and postmodern worldviews in the most unlikely of places: television's take on outer space. In his book, *A Primer on Postmodernism,* he compares the mission and crew of the original *Star Trek* show to a later incarnation, *Star Trek: The Next Generation.*[6] We've added some comparisons from the other related shows, *Deep Space Nine* and *Star Trek Voyager,* to continue the metaphor of a postmodern reality and to provide useful insights for those in young adult ministry.

> Our view of God is relative.
> Our view of religion is skeptical.
> Our view of commitment is wary.
> Our view of reality is survivalist.
> Our thinking is relational and feelings-oriented, not intellectual.
> We live in the now;
> we can't imagine eternity.[7]

Mission: The mission of the original starship *Enterprise* was to seek out new worlds and "to boldly go where no man has gone before." The emphasis was on *man,* the rugged individual, the great leader. In *The Next Generation,* the mission is "to go where no one has gone

> Not some theory but actual modern history is what is killing the ideology of modernity. I need only mention Auschwitz, My Lai, Solzhenitsyn, Gulag Archipelago, *Hustler* magazine, the assault statistics in public schools, the juvenile suicide rate, or the cocaine babies. All these point to the depth of the failure of modern consciousness. While modernity continues blandly to teach us that we are moving ever upward and onward, the actual history of late modernity is increasingly brutal, barbarian, and malignant. We see unfolding before our eyes the troubled, conflicted alliance between an optimistic evolutionary progressivism and regressive forms of nativist narcissistic hedonism.[8]

before." Notice the shift to gender-neutral language. The mission no longer assumes male leadership or dominance.

The purpose of the mission changes with the four shows. In the original, the purpose was to explore new worlds and to seek out new civilizations, but underneath that directive was the understanding that these new worlds and civilizations would be brought into "the Federation." There was a sense of conquest in their mission. In *The Next Generation,* the crew of the *Enterprise* learns from alien cultures rather than trying to assimilate them. In *Deep Space Nine,* the crew's mission is to assist another race of beings as they rebuild their society after a long occupation by foreign invaders. The theme has now shifted away from exploration of new worlds to community building and mutual responsibility. Not surprisingly, the commander's role has made another notable change, as the crew is now led by Captain Benjamin Sisko, who is black.

Finally, in *Voyager,* the mission is completely antithetical to the original. After having been pulled against their will into a far-off quadrant of the universe, the crew is now attempting to bring their ship back home to familiar territory. They are joined in their endeavor in an uneasy alliance with the crew of an enemy spaceship who are in the same predicament. In other words, rather than exploring, the crew of the *Voyager* is returning home. Rather than facing the challenges of the unknown, they are seeking a place where they can be known. Rather than seeking and conquering, they are forming alliances, relying on others. Their mission supports the idea of pluralism, implying that no one culture is superior to another. Every culture can learn from the others. Tolerance and respect are the desired values and virtues.

Crew: The crews of the four ships reveal another point of distinction. In the original *Star Trek,* the crew, comprised of people from different nations, worked together for the common good of all humanity. "The message was clear: We are all humans and we must learn to overcome our differences and join forces in order to complete our quest for certain, objective knowledge of the entire universe."[9] In contrast, the crew of the *Enterprise* on *The Next Generation* includes not only humans but humanoid lifeforms from other parts of the universe. This continues to emphasize and reinforce a basic assumption of postmodernism: that no one is capable of completing the quest for knowledge alone. The individual cannot fully discover all truth without the help of the community.

In the original *Star Trek,* Captain Kirk was the hero. No matter what kind of problem arose, no matter what the ship and crew encountered, Kirk was always the one to save the day. He always got them out of tough jams. This continued to reinforce the somewhat arrogant belief that one man can do everything by himself. In contrast, in the other shows, the captain is never the only hero. Every character has his or her moments of success. So when problems are solved and disasters are averted, it is through the efforts of the whole crew, not just one person. Once again, this emphasizes the need for community.

A particular character worth noting in the original show is Spock. Spock represents the ideal person, an ideal being. He is completely rational and shows no emotion. It is not that he lacks emotions, but he is able to keep his emotions under perfect control. Over and over again, he is rational and almost computerlike as he solves problems. His character accurately portrays modernity's belief that the answer to all the problems in life can be solved by rational expertise.

In contrast, in *The Next Generation,* a character named Data replaces Spock. In one sense Data is the perfect Spock because he doesn't have to suppress his emotions—he has none. He is not human at all but an android, a humanlike machine. Ironically, while Spock tries to rid himself of his emotions in order to be the ideal man, Data works to feel emotions so he may know better what it truly means to be human. Likewise, for the postmodern, truth is not just that which can be objectively studied but is also that which is felt and experienced subjectively.

Along these same lines, *The Next Generation* has introduced a new crew member, Counselor Troi. She has been gifted with the ability to perceive the hidden feelings of others. Once again this seems to be a direct attack on the belief that truth can be discovered only through reason and objective observation. The postmodern believes that what a person intuitively feels about any given situation is just as valid a criterion for truth as rational deduction and scientific observation.

In *Voyager* we are introduced to Seven of Nine, a crew member who was once an extension of the vast, evil organism called Borg. Seven of Nine is now fully human, her Borg implants having been removed. But she never feels quite comfortable with her new identity. She is a human, with all the rights and privileges of a human, but she's still somewhat uncomfortable with the responsibility of emotions and other human complexities.

Spirituality: This is another place where we see a changing worldview throughout the four series. *Star Trek* essentially ignored questions concerning God and religious beliefs. Once again, this was a reflection of the modern mindset. Only that which could be seen, observed, measured, or rationally deduced was true. God was systematically removed from the worldview of the modern man. *The Next Generation,* on the other hand, includes the supernatural, embodied in the character Q. The entity called Q has supernatural powers and comes and goes in the lives of the crew of the *Enterprise* without warning. "While Q has some of the classic attributes of the divine, he is morally ambiguous, displaying both benevolence and . . . self-gratification."[10]

Commander Chakotay is first officer on board *Voyager.* He commanded the Maquis ship that *Voyager* was sent to find and capture. He is of Native American ancestry and strongly believes in his spirit guide, which he often consults for advice. This mirrors postmodern society's infatuation with a smorgasbord of spirituality.

FUNDAMENTAL TENETS OF POSTMODERNISM

Just as the modern worldview has its foundational principles, so too does postmodernism. These tenets have shaped the worldview of today's postmodern young adults.

1. You can never assume that knowledge is proof of anything. There are no basic principles to base anything on.

2. Knowledge is not necessarily good. For example, knowledge led to the atomic bomb.

3. You can't find an answer to everything through history or theology.

4. It is in community—not as individuals—that we operate at the higher level.

5. Science is not the answer to every problem. Truth is not limited to facts but includes intuition.

6. Knowledge is not a neutral force in learning; it is biased by its environment.

7. The world is not necessarily getting better. There are things that can't be fixed.

YOUNG ADULT MINISTRY AND POSTMODERNISM

Is it possible to present the gospel in a way that seems relevant to postmodern young adults, given the philosophical underpinnings outlined above? Of course it is! In the same way that the gospel was relevant to Greeks at Mars Hill or to rabbinical scholars in Jerusalem—or to you where you live.

At The Next Level (TNL) Church in Denver, the pastoral team (all in their twenties) has developed a four-pronged approach to contextualizing the gospel for people their age. By putting their own spin on teaching, worship, relationship, and ministry, they've become a large congregation, attracting young adults from throughout the area to their main service (which is held on Tuesdays).

Here is their approach to each of those four areas:

Teaching: Stanley Grenz writes of the loss of a unified view of reality and says the antidote in a postmodern context is to focus on "story." Christians believe there is one unifying story, a single history, including all peoples and all times. This story is the biblical narrative of God acting to redeem fallen humankind through the incarnation of Christ.

In telling the gospel story, TNL teaches that each individual accepts what God has done by faith as a yes or no decision, not a true or false premise. In a biblical sense, *faith* is a verb, not a noun. Faith is something you do, not something you own. Truth is not a concept but a person, the Son of God. Because Jesus says, "I am the way, the truth, and the life" (John 14:6), people at TNL are encouraged either to say yes or no to Him as Savior. Similarly, TNL doesn't ask people to decide whether the Bible is true or false. After all, even the devil believes the Bible is true. Rather, TNL calls for people to say yes to the commandments and stories in the Bible, or if not, then by default they are saying no.

Worship: All people were created to be worshipers of God. Yet many modern thinkers rejected God because He couldn't be proven through the laws of science. In a postmodern environment, people discover God by worshiping Him, not by studying proofs for His existence. To facilitate this focus on worship, TNL has no worship leaders, but rather they have lead worshipers. The congregation is led into worship by the example of others on the worship team. No one tries to perform "worship" for the rest of the group.

Relationship: A postmodern evangelical community must continue to move people away from autonomous individualism. Postmodern evangelicalism will always place the individual within a community. We were created to be in relationship with God and each other, and the breakdown of relationships has been a major concern for postmodern young adults.

Jesus Himself radically redefined family in

the Bible. While He was talking with a group of people, someone came up and told Him that His mother and brothers were outside wanting to speak with Him. He turned and said, "Who is my mother, and who are my brothers?" (Matthew 12:48). To today's young adults, family members are those who relate with them in a "familiar" way, not necessarily the nuclear family.

Effective young adult ministries will be those that reach out to nonbelieving people and invite them into relationship with God, in Christ, through the Holy Spirit. They will be led by teams of people who trust one another and who have a common goal. In healthy teams, people who work in isolation are the exception, not the rule.

In a relational model of ministry, power is limitless. Each person has potential ownership and therefore the capacity to effect change. Each has the power to make decisions, have choices, give input, solve problems, plan the future, and take responsibilities.

Ministry: At TNL, the term *ministry* is used to mean each member's personal, God-given mission. The most important resource of any church is the calling of each of its members to a personal, God-given mission.

TNL believes that the best thing it has to offer as a church is the good news of the gospel wrapped in the ministry or calling of each of its people. Scripture teaches that God is not a respecter of persons. That doesn't mean everyone is the same or equal in every way. It means everyone is equally important to God. God has made each person special, and He has a special ministry calling for everyone.[11]

Four key passages in Scripture enable us to understand the significance of God's ministry call to every believer.

* Psalm 139:13-16:
You created my innermost being;
    you knit me together in my mother's
    womb.
I praise you because I am fearfully and
    wonderfully made;
    your works are wonderful.
    I know that full well.
My frame was not hidden from you
    when I was made in the secret place.
When I was woven together in the depths
    of the earth,
    your eyes saw my unformed body.
All the days ordained for me
    were written in your book
    before one of them came to be.

David didn't write this to convince us that these truths applied to him because he was a king. Rather, he is telling us what he believes to be true for everyone. God doesn't know the king or the clergyperson more intimately than He knows anyone else. Nor does God ordain the days of the king or the clergyperson and not those of the layperson. Yet the concept of "ordination to the ministry" might persuade us to believe that He does.

* First Corinthians 12:12,18:
The body is a unit, though it is made up of many parts; and though all its parts are many,

they form one body . . . . God has arranged the parts in a body—every one of them, just as he wanted them to be.

Our observation is that the Church is not using wrong resources so much as majoring in the minors. It has seized on valuable but secondary resources and inflated them in importance to the point that primary resources are all but forgotten.[12]

God knows each person equally. He doesn't know any group better than another. God ordained each person's days with the same interest and concern. Plus, He arranges an important role for each in the larger body of faith. God hasn't designed a body where the ministry of a few really counts while the majority are merely a supporting cast. All members of the body count both in who they are and what they do.

• Ephesians 2:10:
We are God's workmanship, created in Christ Jesus to do good works, which God prepared in advance for us to do.

One of the chicken-and-egg questions in the field of history is "Do people shape history, or does history shape people?" In sociology the chicken-egg question is this: "Is a person a product of his environment, or is his environment a product of him?" Perhaps in light of Ephesians 2:10 we could ask, "Did God shape certain good works to fit us, or does He shape us to fit certain good works?" Either way, there are unique "good works" that fit each of us.

While chicken-and-egg questions have no answers, we can be sure of one thing. When we see our calling in light of Psalm 139, 1 Corinthians 12, and Ephesians 2, it appears that God went to a lot of trouble to design us so that He could call us to a special ministry or ministries that fit us.

• But the clincher is in Philippians 2:12-13:
Continue to work out your salvation with fear and trembling, for it is God who works in you to will and act according to his good purpose.

A NEW APPROACH

Finally, although there are some real concerns among evangelicals about the age of postmodernism (mainly, that people no longer believe in truth), we have found that the answer lies more in the approach to truth, not in losing belief in the absolute truth. Grenz so aptly put it this way:

The gospel of Jesus Christ has gone forth in every era with power to convert human hearts. Today that gospel is the answer to the longing of the postmodern generation. Our task as Christ's disciples is to embody and articulate the never-changing good news of available salvation in a manner that the emerging generation can understand. Only then we become the vehicles of the

Holy Spirit in bringing them to experience the same life-changing encounter with the triune God from whom our entire lives derive their meaning.[13]

Our task is to make sure we are using the types of methods that are going to reach this generation of young adults. In the following chapters, we'll look at some of the methods that are working in churches today.

GETTING REAL YOURSELF

1. If you had to define the terms *modernism* and *postmodernism* each in one or two sentences, how would you do that?

2. Can you name two individuals in your life who epitomize each of these terms—someone who could be called a modern and someone who could be called a postmodern? Keep in mind your own definitions from question 1 and recall the examples and differences between these two people as you approach ministry to young adults.

3. Read Psalm 139:13-16; 1 Corinthians 12:12,18; Ephesians 2:10; and Philippians 2:12-13 for yourself. Based on these verses, how would you describe your own calling to ministry?

4. Make a list of people who need to review these verses to understand that God has called them to a unique place of ministry.

5. Do you think the message of the gospel has changed, or is it just the way we need to communicate it that has changed? Do you think past ways of communicating the gospel message are ineffective today? Why?

GENERATION X

First, let's look at some of the forces that have shaped Generation Xers, those born roughly between 1964 and 1981.

DIVORCE

Generation X is the first generation in America's history to experience the results of a rapid increase in divorce. In fact, conservative statistics estimate that 40 percent of this generation comes from broken homes. The effects of divorce are devastating to children and extend far into their adult lives.

> Whatever a person is like, I try to find common ground with him so that he will let me tell him about Christ and let Christ save him. (1 Corinthians 9:22, TLB)

Archibald D. Hart, in his book *Healing Adult Children of Divorce*,[1] identifies some of the lasting implications that divorce has on children. He notes four key areas of consequence: emotional, relational, physical, and academic/vocational.

Divorce affects many children *emotionally* in that they can have a diminished self-esteem, are more prone to periods of depression, experience an underlying and pervasive sense of anxiety, and crave entertainment—especially TV, movies, and other fantasy media—as a means of escaping reality. They tend to daydream and fantasize; they avoid risk and change; they feel paralyzed emotionally when faced with personal problems; and they often have a difficult time controlling their anger.

Divorce affects children *relationally* in that they often struggle with a deep sense of rejection, guilt, and shame. They struggle with conflict. They have difficulty communicating and find it hard to form lasting relationships. Children from divorced homes frequently struggle with loneliness; they have mood swings; and they place a high priority on going through life without getting hurt.

Divorce can affect children *physically*. Children from divorced homes tend to feel disconnected. They often feel as if they are walking around in a fog. They may have frequent headaches and other stress-related symptoms. They also have a tendency either to overeat or undereat.

And last, divorce affects some children *academically* and *vocationally* in that they have trouble making key decisions, especially regarding the larger issues in life, like marriage and career, for fear of making the wrong choice. They possess a hazy sense of self and struggle with their own identities. They often vacillate between being very serious about life or very reckless, and they often have a constant, almost insatiable hunger for feedback on performance.

> The divorce rate and the remarriage rate turned upward around 1960 and increased dramatically during the ensuing decade. By 1970, the divorce and remarriage rates were higher than any previously recorded for this country.[2]

Although many Xers are hampered by these issues, there is hope. Counseling, support groups, and understanding peers all can help them to process their pain and move them into healthier emotional patterns. However, the pain of divorce still has an effect. Just as many senior adults today are prone to save money due to their experiences during the Great Depression, and just as a victim of a violent crime never forgets, so the pain of divorce has left its mark on many members of this generation. If the church wants to reach and minister to them effectively, it must understand their pain.

ANTICHILD SENTIMENT

Growing up during the early 1970s, Generation Xers experienced a wide variety of general societal discrimination. At best these young children were considered a nuisance, a barrier to their parents' desires to "find themselves" or rise up the "corporate ladder." At worst, these same children were seen as a contributing factor to a rising population crisis that could pose a clear and present danger to the American way of life.

In 1968 Paul Ehrlich, a biologist from Stanford University, wrote what became an instant best seller titled *The Population Bomb*. His premise was that the increasing birthrates were a menace to society. Children signified a drain on national resources, food supplies, energy resources, tax funds, and employment compensation. Ehrlich also founded an organization for those who shared his concerns called Zero Population Growth, Inc., which was dedicated to spreading the news of the dangers inherent in increasing birthrates. By the 1980s, Ehrlich's organization grew to more than seven hundred thousand in membership.

> Children of divorced parents are seven times more likely to suffer from depression in adult life than people of similar age and background whose parents have not divorced.[3]

By the early 1970s, antichild sentiments were growing across the country. "In the '70s and early '80s, 70 to 90 percent of all newly constructed apartments in large cities such as Dallas, Houston, and Denver were strictly adults-only."[4] This occurred in cities across the country.

Reflecting this antichild sentiment, the movie industry responded with a mass of popular films depicting children as foul-mouthed and satanic, as criminals and whores. Such movies included *Paper Moon* (1973), *The Bad News Bears* (1976), *Bugsy Malone* (1976), *Taxi Driver* (1976), *Rosemary's Baby* (1978), *The Exorcist* (1973), *It's Alive!* (1974), *Demon Seed* (1977), *The Boys from Brazil* (1978), *The Omen* (1976), *The Omen II* (1978), and *The Omen III* (1981), to name a few. Not only did these movies depict children in a negative light, but movies made for children all but disappeared. In the late '60s to the late '70s, G-rated movies fell by 70 percent![5]

There were a number of other recommendations to deactivate the population bomb. Kenneth Bouling, an economist, suggested government regulations that would require a potential parent to first obtain a license or childbearing permit. The Nixon administration established the Commission on Population Growth and the American Future, which concluded, "Population growth is one of the major factors affecting the demand for resources and the deterioration of the environment in the United States."[6] Children were seen as public enemy number one, a lethal threat to the well-being and survival of the American people. Books, magazines, and newspapers printed a variety of topics addressing the issues with titles like *The Case Against Having Children, Life Without Birth,* and *The Baby Trap* that proclaimed the benefits and freedom of not having children. People wore buttons proclaiming slogans like "None Is Fun" and "Jesus Was an Only Child."

The Germans have a word for this prevailing anti-child sentiment: *Kinderfeindlichkeit,* meaning "hostility to children." An American term was given to the problem—"popullution." A 1971 survey indicated that two-thirds of the general public agreed that it was a serious problem in the U.S. As the authors of one book put it, babies were looked upon "like headaches, things you take pills not to have."[7]

This was the cultural climate into which Generation X was born. Is it any wonder that many of them have a haunting sense of being unwanted and unloved?

With fertile Boomers taking voyages to the interior (the inner self), the very image of more children provided widespread anxiety. Parents were shunned if they tried to bring small children into restaurants or theaters. Many rental apartments started banning children.[8]

THE MELTDOWN OF THE TRADITIONAL FAMILY

During the 1960s and 1970s, a number of issues led to major changes in family life. In 1963 journalist Betty Friedan wrote *The Feminine Mystique,* beginning a new era for women's rights that acted as a double-edged sword. One edge was a positive change in the treatment of women; the other edge contributed to the breakdown of the nuclear family as women began feeling oppressed by traditional roles. No longer was staying home, caring for children, and maintaining a household seen as a worthwhile vocation for a woman. Instead, some women saw it as a means of oppression. Friedan concluded that women had become victims of a social myth that she called the "feminine mystique," which is "a pervasive belief that women gain genuine satisfaction only through marriage and children and that all other pursuits were, in effect, sublimations of this single imperative."[9]

In 1966 Friedan founded NOW (National Organization for Women), which focused on securing equity for women in the marketplace, liberalizing abortion laws, and helping secure the Equal Rights Amendment.

A generation is shaped by the nurture it receives in childhood and the challenges it faces coming of age.[10]

Moving in a more extreme direction, in 1972 Gloria Steinem founded *Ms.* magazine, which helped to promote feminist ideals and political agendas to a broader audience. As a result of Friedan and Steinem, the women's liberation movement quickly divided into two polarizing groups. One group maintained the ideals of extreme feminists such as Shulamith Firestone, Ti-Grace Atkison, and Kate Millett, who asserted that men were out to dominate women and keep them in bondage in the role of servant. The other group that emerged was more conservative, promoting traditional roles for women yet advocating equality between the sexes and equity in the marketplace.

The conservative side of the women's liberation movement resulted in a very positive progression for the equal treatment of women, but the more radical feminist side ushered in a number of extremely destructive trends, such as the legalizing of abortion. "In 1973, in the case of *Roe v. Wade,* the United States Supreme Court ruled that a woman's constitutional right to privacy includes the right to abort a fetus during the first trimester of pregnancy."[11] In the six years following the *Roe v. Wade* decision, abortions rose 80 percent, and one out of three Xer fetuses were killed.[12]

William Dunn, author of *The Baby Bust: A Generation Comes of Age,* notes that women were discovering new roles: "The 1960s was also an era of 'isms' that altered the way many Americans live, work, play, and think. Amid the ferment of the Vietnam War protests, student uprisings, the civil rights movement, and women's liberation, women became convinced that they had more options than being homemakers and forever subordinate to men."[13]

Divorce Trends: The number of divorced women at any one time is greater than the number of men because men are more likely to remarry, and to do so more quickly, than women. About five out of six divorced men remarry [83 percent], compared to about three out of every four divorced women [75 percent].

The median age for divorce (after a first marriage) is twenty-seven for women and twenty-nine for men.

The earlier the average age of the partners at marriage, the greater the likelihood of divorce. Most divorces occur at young ages, typically twenty to twenty-four for women and twenty-five to twenty-nine for men.

The most typical ages for remarriage after a first divorce are twenty-five to thirty-four for men and twenty to thirty-four for women. For both men and women, thirty-five to forty-four is the most typical age for a second divorce.

If present trends continue, about 40 percent of Americans in their late twenties and early thirties who remarry after a divorce may expect their second marriage to also end in divorce.[14]

In addition, the downward spiral of the economy was requiring more intact families to earn two incomes. A negative result of this was an increase in day care and preschool enrollments. "The percentage of children in preschool programs rose from 27 percent in 1966 to 55 percent by 1986, or approximately five million American children."[15] The effect of day care programs on children has been the subject of much debate; however, studies have indicated that extended periods of time away from parents can be destructive to children. Psychiatrist Paul Meier notes, "Mother substitutes during the toddler years present a serious problem. Any prolonged separation from the mother during this stage can result in a loss of initiative or even the determination for survival. Many children in America are being farmed out to day-care centers, many of which are very detrimental to the child's ultimate mental health and outlook on life."[16]

Couple the high divorce rate with the fact that many were latchkey children and you get a generation who may have had more time alone than any in history. They are also the first to spend considerable time in day care. At home, they were weaned on MTV, high tech video games, and computers. They became independent at a young age. Many had to grow up fast, taking on family responsibilities or part-time jobs to help out. All this has helped them become very freedom-minded, individualistic, and self-absorbed.[17]

Another negative result of the increase in two-income families was the phenomenon of "latchkey kids." Generation X was the first generation to be identified as "latchkey kids." They arrived home from school to an empty house, made their own peanut butter and jelly sandwich, and sat down in front of their surrogate parent—the TV—taking in the violence and values of pop culture.

Pregnancy was a trap, whereby men kept women in the home, out of the wider world, and away from self-fulfillment.

—Lucina Cisler, feminist[18]

Although some of the changes in traditional family roles were unavoidable due to the increase in the number of single-parent homes and the need for economic survival, the results were extremely destructive to many Gen X children.

Through the 1970s, the number of "latchkey" children under age 14 left alone after school roughly doubled.[19]

ECONOMIC UNCERTAINTY

Xers aren't the first generation to experience turbulent economic times. However, many of them feel like their future has been destroyed by the excessive spending of the older generations.

There are a variety of current and future circumstances that have raised serious economic concerns within this generation. Some of those concerns include the following.

> To hear many Xers tell it, following Boomers into youth is like entering a theme park after a mob has thrashed the place and some distant CEO has turned every idea into a commercial logo.[20]

Higher taxes: Some experts predict that a generational civil war could occur early in the twenty-first century as Baby Boomers begin to retire.

A big worry of today's younger workers is not just the projected increase in persons 65 and older but also the proportion of that increase that will be made up of those 80 years and older. This proportion will jump from 22 percent in 1990 to 36 percent by 2050. Because the oldest-old are the most likely to have health and disability problems and fewer economic resources, younger workers worry that the fast growth of this resource-shy but needy group will mean they will pay considerably higher taxes than their predecessors, leaving them less disposable income to support themselves and their families.[21]

Decrease in Social Security benefits: The Social Security Administration predicts that between 2019 and 2036 Social Security could be bankrupt. "Throughout the 1970s and 80s, most seniors got back two to five times what they paid in. Today, a retiree can expect to get back roughly double his contribution, while a twenty-five-year old will receive, at best, only half of what she is expected to pay in her working career."[22]

> We live in the richest, freest, and most powerful country the world has ever seen. But we fear for the future. For too long, we as a nation have failed to exercise self-control. We've trashed the ethic of individual responsibility. We've exploited racial and sexual differences for political gains. Those in power have practiced fiscal child abuse, mortgaging our future, and the futures of those to come.[23]

Low-paying jobs: Many Xers thought that if they went to college and earned a bachelor's degree, they would graduate, enter a solid company, and receive a good income. Then they would be able to buy a home with a white picket fence, drive two cars, have a family, and live happily ever after. However, many face the harsh reality of graduating with tens of thousands of dollars of school loan debt and find that entry-level jobs in their chosen careers are all but nonexistent, and so they end up working at some bookstore or coffee shop just above minimum wage. Unable to make it financially on their own, many move back home just to make ends meet.

This economic uncertainty is one of the reasons this generation maintains a cynical and

17

despairing attitude. Why be motivated to do something when you realize nothing you do will make any difference in the grand scheme of things? "A study conducted by Peter Hart Research Associates discovered that nearly half of the 1,000 young adults they surveyed felt that the United States' best years were over."[24]

Many young people believe that their economic prospects are gloomy. They believe they will not do as well financially as their parents or grandparents. They know that the average income for young people, even with one or two college degrees, has declined significantly over the past generation. Many feel their chances of finding the job and salary they want are bleak.[25]

GLOBAL DISTRESS

Holes in the ozone layer, depletion of rain forests, the "greenhouse effect," war, famine, AIDS, and increasing violence all add to an Xer's sense of hopelessness and despair. Through today's media, especially computers, global information is just a channel surf or mouse click away. Within twenty minutes, an Xer can tap into all the social, political, and environmental problems of the world through sources like MSNBC and CNN. This has caused many to withdraw into a state of hedonism. Many are hardened by the global despair and their lack of ability to make any difference, so they become self-centered and single-minded, focusing instead on their own survival. "Our generation faces problems that didn't exist when our parents

were our age. It's not surprising that young adults feel hopeless about the future with so many environmental and social ailments plaguing their world."[26] (Of course, to be fair, Boomers grew up in a time when cancer cure rates were much lower, the Vietnam War was a nightly news reality, and the Cold War had them learning survival techniques in preparation for the fallout of a nuclear war.)

This generation has watched more TV, and as a result has probably witnessed more violence and murders, than any generation in history. In addition, their gloomy view of the world has been shaped by numerous negative events, such as the Persian Gulf War, escalating crime, riots, AIDS, the nuclear threat, and pollution.[27]

Young adults are also witnessing global conditions worsen: the rapid loss of species and their habitat; startling effects of accumulating toxins in our bodies and the environment; increasing depletion of the ozone layer; and elected officials pilfering young pockets.[28]

FATHERLESS AMERICA

"Fatherlessness is the most harmful demographic trend of this generation," says David Blankenhorn, author of the best-selling book

Fatherless America: Confronting Our Most Urgent Social Problem.[29] Blankenhorn notes a cultural phenomenon unique to the last few decades where the social role for men in the family system has slowly deteriorated (see following table) and left both sons and daughters without a traditional father to guide and direct them through their turbulent adolescent years.

Experts agree that fatherhood—or lack of fatherhood—dramatically affects development in boys and girls. Catholic priest Ted Dobson says:

There is a "tear" in the masculine soul—a gaping hole or wound that leads to a profound insecurity. German psychologist Alexander Mitscherlich wrote that society has torn the soul of the male, and into this tear demons have fled—demons of insecurity, selfishness, and despair. Consequently, men do not know who they are as men. Rather, they define themselves by what they do, who they know, or what they own.[30]

Blankenhorn likens societal ills of increasing youth violence, domestic violence against women, increasing child sexual abuse, child poverty, and adolescent childbearing, to the diminishing role of fatherhood:

At stake is nothing less than the success of the American experiment. For unless we reverse the trend of fatherlessness, no other set of accomplishments will succeed in arresting the decline of child well-being and the spread of male violence. To tolerate the

Percentage of U.S. Children in Various Family Arrangements[31]

Living with:	1960	1970	1980	1990
Father and mother	80.6	75.1	62.3	57.7
Mother only	7.7	11.8	18.0	21.6
Never married	3.9	9.3	15.5	31.5
Divorced	24.7	29.7	41.6	36.9
Separated	46.8	39.8	31.6	24.6
Widowed	24.7	21.2	11.3	7.0
Father only	1.0	1.8	1.7	3.1
Father and stepmother	0.8	0.9	1.1	0.9
Mother and stepfather	5.9	6.5	8.4	10.4
Neither parent	3.9	4.1	5.8	4.3

trend of fatherlessness is to accept the inevitability of continued societal recession.[32]

Their parents practiced birth control and abortion and were highly concerned about making it financially. About 40 percent of Xers are products of divorce, and many were brought up in single-parent homes. The emotional upheaval and conflict this causes helped shape their view of the family and the world. It seems to have sent out a negative message to Xers about their value and worth.[33]

Within the existing Gen X culture, many young adults struggle with their role as male and female largely due to this issue of fatherlessness. They have been cast adrift in life with few values, no role models, and little direction as to what is right or wrong. Many are confused, afraid, calloused, individualistic, and ready to try something that works. One student put it this way: "Who are we to look to? Every generation is supposed to have role models. Where are ours? Madonna? Michael Jackson? People wonder why we are so confused. Wouldn't you be?"[34]

These are just some of the forces that have shaped the young adults within Generation X. And even though these forces are debilitating, many Xers are recognizing their situation and trying to work out of it. That's where the church can help. As the church begins to understand these issues and how they affect Gen Xers, it can offer redemptive ministries that facilitate this generation's willingness to heal and move beyond their pain.

NET GEN

The Net Gen, also called Millennials or Generation Y, have been affected by some of the same forces that shaped Generation X. Yet some unique forces are also at work shaping this new generation.

THE INTERNET

The Net Gen is the first generation in history to grow up with the World Wide Web. The Internet for them is more than a source of information and recreation; it's a way of life. Many of them use it for their homework and entertainment and for building relationships via e-mail and chat rooms. No longer is having a private phone enough for adolescents; now they want and need a computer with Internet access in order to stay connected to friends as well as to maintain an academic edge. Global communications are also the norm for this generation. Pagers, cell phones, fax machines, and the emerging market of Internet video phones are becoming more and more common among young people. Being connected is a status symbol; it makes you cool.

Experts have yet to determine the long-term effects of the Internet and global communications on children. But Michelle Weil and Larry Rosen have concerns, not only about the impact technology will have on the children of this generation, but also about the impact it is having on people in our society at large. Their book, titled *Techno Stress,*[35] outlines some of the adverse effects technology can have on people. The areas of concern are the following.

Information overload: With the Internet,

the amount of information available on any number of topics is virtually unlimited. But while the information is endless, the time to process it is limited. This avalanche of information creates stress because there's not enough time to process it all.

Cyber leash: With cellular systems, pagers, and voice mail, you may feel you have no privacy. You're always on and always available. Because human beings need downtime, this results in tremendous stress.

> What's interesting about Generation Y [what we have called the Net Gen] is they not only have computers but they also have the Internet. And those who've been really immersed in that technology have a completely different way of thinking— it's more chaotic and random.[36]

Human isolation: Chat rooms and e-mail have largely taken the place of face-to-face conversation as the primary means of communication for many people today. As a result, interpersonal communication skills aren't being developed as they once were. Many communications experts believe that only 7 percent of the communication process involves actual words; 93 percent involves tone of voice, body language, and facial expression. But these nonverbal elements of communication are lost on-line.

Chat rooms are also becoming a common means of meeting people and interacting with others. People avoid human contact, and communication is becoming more and more impersonal. The human dynamic is being replaced with a mechanistic system that is slowly eroding the human contact essential to personal health.

> One would have hoped that the process of progress would have been kind to our emotional life, making it ever easier to replenish our reserves. It might have seemed reasonable to speculate that as our society improved in the areas of education, affluence, and entertainment, we would see a commensurate improvement in overall emotional well-being. Yet such has not been the case.[37]

Living at warp speed: Technology saves time in many of the routine things necessary for living. It wasn't long ago that a trip to the market to buy food could be an all-day event. Today, with grocery stores and cars, what once took a day can be reduced to an hour. Technology does save time, but people are not using their extra time for resting and replenishing their emotional batteries. Instead, they run faster and fill the time with more and more deadlines. According to Archibald D. Hart, the stress that comes with living such a lifestyle is dangerous to a person's soul and body. Dr. Hart notes, "We need to recognize that the human frame has its limits, and that we should build in adequate rest and recovery time so as to allow healing and restoration to take place. This is the problem: In short, people in our age are showing signs of physiological disintegration because we are living at a pace that is too fast for our bodies."[38]

Although everyone is affected by the stresses of modern society and technological advancements, the Net Gen is the first generation to cut its teeth on some of the most historic advancements the world has ever seen, and the harmful implications of these are still a mystery.

> I believe there really are no cultural differences—I mean, culturally, yeah. But this is a new generation, we're making our own culture and it's universal culture, and it's humanity culture. It's, like, where we as young individuals are headed, and I think where we're headed is independence. It's not about an Asian culture, an African culture, an American culture—It's all about a humanity thing here.[39]

CULTURAL DIVERSITY

The Net Gen has become the most diverse generation in American history.

The Internet is just one of the media that has provided this generation with information of every form relating to politics, culture, and religion from every country on the planet. It's easy for them to become confused simply by the overabundance of choices and information. Yet the confusion is not limited to the information alone but extends to the context and commentary interpreting it. Anyone can declare himself an expert on any issue, establish a Web site, and offer his or her interpretations of right or wrong, creating further confusion.

Ethnic diversity marks this generation as well. Racial barriers that segregated ethnic groups within America for years are not an issue with many in this generation. "We've grown up in a more eclectic world, and acceptance of this is woven into the fabric of our being."[40] With a greater acceptance of ethnic diversity comes a host of other issues, like interracial marriages, and adherence to a wide variety of cultural rituals and worldviews, just to name a few.

> Why is it suddenly okay to refuse to follow one belief system, hold a solid political stance, or choose not to adapt to one specific lifestyle? Basically because no one today is in the position to judge. Their peers, as well as our contemporaries, are also searching and surfing the Net for newfound ideologies and perceptions. The majority of youth today are what we call "free radicals," living in the age of information, swiftly absorbing and learning about any point of view that they happen to run into.[41]

As Netters become familiar with other cultures through the Internet and listen to CDs by musicians from around the world, they're exposed to ethnic diversity and cultural experiences to a greater degree than has ever been known before. They don't have a strong sense of what it means to be American, and they are seeing a movement to a one-world culture where everyone is a member of a global village. Many racial barriers break down as members of this generation view one another as part of the larger family of humanity and network across international lines via the Internet to invoke change.

PARENTAL INVOLVEMENT

While children in Generation X felt that they were rejected by society, society and parents seem to be embracing the Net Gen. By and large, Net Gen children feel valued and loved. Midlife Boomer parents who experienced the emptiness of pursuing personal freedom and climbing the corporate ladder as means of success are now looking toward investing themselves in their children. More and more parents come home from work earlier, work out of their home one or more days a week due to computer technology, and take their children to work where child care is provided in the same building. Our society is also much more supportive of having children and is affirming child raising as a significant means of experiencing self-fulfillment.

The entertainment industry seems to be reflecting this change in heart toward children with an unprecedented increase in family programming on TV and in the movies. Nickelodeon is a cable network offering programming specifically for children. Programs include cartoons such as *Rugrats* and *Jonny Quest,* game shows, and sitcoms all oriented toward kids. It even hosts "retro nostalgia" programming with shows like *The Brady Bunch, Leave It to Beaver, The Andy Griffith Show, My Three Sons,* and *I Dream of Jeannie.* The Disney Channel has also become a huge network, targeting children and their families. The Discovery Channel has great shows just for kids, helping them understand nature and animals in fun and creative ways. There is even a Cartoon Network showing cartoons twenty-four hours a day.

> This generation is a generation that is bipolar in personality. This means that youth culture is no longer programmed to believe in one voice or become reliant on one message. They absorb everything and anything they choose, mainly because there is so much out there to choose from. So, like being involved in an experiment, they taste this and that, decide they like it or not, try something else, and so on and so forth. It has nothing to do with the realities of what is good or bad (that comes after the fact), it's about reaching a heightened level. It's all about the experience.[42]

Instead of the movie industry portraying children as demonic, children today are seen as almost angelic in such movies as *The Piano* and *Angels in the Outfield.* One *Time* magazine reviewer noted the change in the media's attitude toward children when he said, "Was there ever a bad child in the world, a spiteful, stubborn, domineering sapper of his parents' spirit? There is rarely one in a Hollywood movie."[43] With all this positive attention, children of the Net Gen have developed a much higher level of self-esteem and seem to have recaptured that sense of youthful idealism and optimism that had been lost within Generation X.

The Barna Research Group did a national survey that indicated a rise in youth self-esteem, optimism, and excitement about life.

- Four out of five describe themselves as "excited about life."
- Three out of four say they are "trusting of other people."
- Three out of four claim to be "optimistic about the future."
- Two out of three see themselves as "a leader."
- Two out of three believe they are "physically attractive."
- Over half (56 percent) contend that they are "religious."
- Two out of every five admit to being "stressed out."
- Only one out of every eight suggests they are "lonely."
- A mere 12 percent use the term "discouraged" to describe themselves.[44]

The Net Gen has been marked by a radical change of heart by society. Protective minivans, "Baby on Board" signs and supportive movies such as *Three Men and a Baby* were the rage.[45]

It seems obvious that when children are loved and held in high regard by both their parents and society, they grow up with a greater sense of hope and optimism about the future.

DEVALUATION OF LIFE

When the *Roe v. Wade* decision in 1973 legalized abortion on demand, little did our society realize the chain of events that would occur as a result.

Legalized abortion has opened the floodgates to the devaluation of life. The Net Gen has been born into a society that has elevated freedom of choice over the sanctity of life. With partial-birth abortions, assisted suicides, as well as graphic violence in movies and TV, the Net Gen has become desensitized and indifferent to violence.

Armed with video-game joysticks and TV remotes—a funny word, with its false promise that it keeps you at a distance from whatever excitements it bounces you through—kids are whiplashed from one bit of blood sport to another, from South Park and Jerry Springer to Mortal Kombat on Nintendo. Ordinary kids may be a bit desensitized to violence. More susceptible kids are pushed toward a dangerous mental precipice.[46]

Mortal violence is on the rise. On March 24, 1998, at a school yard in Jonesboro, Arkansas, we witnessed a massacre. Four girls and a teacher died, and ten others were injured. The assailants were two of their classmates, ages eleven and thirteen. Late in the 1998–1999 school year, two students turned Columbine High School in Littleton, Colorado, into the site of one of the most ghastly school massacres in U.S. history: fifteen dead and twenty-three wounded. Twelve students and one teacher (plus the two gunmen who committed suicide following their rampage) died in the attack.

**School Yard Shootings:
A Deadly Record[47]**

Place	Age of suspects	Dead	Wounded
Grayson, Ky., Jan. 18, 1993	17	2	0
Amityville, N.Y., Feb. 1, 1993	17	1	1
Redlands, Calif., Oct. 23, 1995	13	1	1
Blackville, S.C., Oct. 12, 1995	16	2	1
Lynnville, Tenn., Nov. 15, 1995	17	2	1
Moses Lake, Wash., Feb. 2, 1996	14	3	1
Bethe!, Alaska, Feb. 19, 1997	16	2	2
Littleton, Colo., April 20, 1999	18, 17	15	23

Aggravated assault in America has increased from 60 per 100,000 in 1957 to over 440 per 100,000 by the middle of this decade.[48]

David Grossman, a military psychologist who trains law enforcement and military personnel about the realities of warfare, said, "Children don't naturally kill; they learn it from violence in the home and, most pervasively, from violence as entertainment in television, movies, and interactive video games."[49]

The research supports the fact that violence in the media and video games increases the violence in kids. So it seems likely that with the Net Gen being exposed to immense amounts of violence in the media, they may become the most violent generation yet.

Each of these emerging postmodern generations has been shaped by a number of forces. We must try to understand these issues if we want to minister to them in more effective ways.

GETTING REAL YOURSELF

1. Think about these two postmodern generations, and list ways you think they're similar to each other.

2. List ways you think these two generations are different.

3. Why do you think members of Generation X generally seem more pessimistic about the world than members of the Net Gen?

GEN X AND NET GEN SUBCULTURES

Jan walked into Frontline Community for the first time two years ago. Ken just happened to be speaking about the topic of hope, unaware of how the Spirit of God was working in Jan's heart.

After the message, with tears in her eyes, Jan proceeded to tell her story to Ken. She said that tonight was the night she was really going to do it—kill herself. She had toyed with attempts at suicide before, but tonight was it. As Jan was planning her departure from this world, she thought she would give God one more try and showed up at this young adult Bible study. As she was listening to the message about hope, something happened and the clouds of despair began to part, revealing the warmth of God's love. That night, instead of taking her own life, she gave it over to Jesus Christ. Since then, she has been baptized, walked with God, and become one of the key leaders of Frontline.

How many Jans in your community are longing to experience God in a way they can relate to? How many Jans could be reached for Jesus Christ if more churches knew how to build effective ministries to reach them?

To be most effective in reaching young adults like Jan, it's important to understand who they are and where they are coming from. We believe this involves targeting one or two specific subcultures within the emerging postmodern generations represented within your community. We call this targeted ministry.

Targeted ministry is not some trendy evangelistic strategy but one that was widely used throughout the New Testament era. As Rick Warren points out in his book *The Purpose Driven*

Church, Jesus, Paul, and Peter were all intentional about reaching a specific people group.[1] Jesus told the Canaanite woman that he had come for "the lost sheep of Israel" (Matthew 15:24). Another time, Jesus instructed His disciples to bypass the Gentiles as well as the Samaritans and go instead "to the lost sheep of Israel" (Matthew 10:6). The apostle Paul used the same method by targeting his ministry to the Gentiles while Peter took the gospel to the Jews (Galatians 2:7).

Within your community there are most likely many subcultures, or sub-groups. To reach each of these groups you need to discover how they think. What are their interests? What do they value? Where do they hurt? What are they afraid of? What are the most prominent features of the way they live? What are their most popular radio stations? The more you know about these people, the easier it will be to reach them.[2]

In fact, all four gospels were written with a certain audience in mind. Matthew wrote specifically to the Jews, emphasizing that Jesus Christ is the Messiah. Mark wrote to the Christians in Rome, emphasizing the present work and teachings of Jesus. Luke wrote primarily with the Gentiles in mind, stressing an accurate accounting of the life of Christ and focusing on Jesus as the perfect human Savior of mankind. And finally John focused his writing to prove conclusively to new Christians and seekers that Jesus Christ is

the Son of God and that all who believe in Him will have eternal life. As you can see, targeted ministry is a valid biblical strategy as well as an effective tool in reaching people for Jesus Christ.

They're the product of a very different type of upbringing and, as a result, are driven by different motivations. It's critical that you understand what drives these young people because this is the generation that will supply us with the bulk of our employees for the next ten years.[3]

The same principle applies to us today. To make an impact for Christ on today's young adults, we must understand the various subcultures where they live out the many forces that shape them. "Each of these unique people groups needs an evangelistic strategy that communicates the Gospel in terms that their specific culture can understand."[4] As we have read about and observed Gen X and the Net Gen, we've identified a variety of subcultures. (A brief reminder: As we've said before, we're not demographers or sociologists. We're people who lead ministries and equip others to lead ministries to young adults. So every statement we make and conclusion we draw should be seen through that filter.)

Understanding young adults' subcultures will enable you to identify which ones are most prominent in your area and will give you clues in contextualizing the gospel to reach, equip, and empower them for effective ministry.

> People like me aren't looking to avoid death. We want to cheat death and spit in its eye. We want more excitement, more sex, more fun. If you want to have fun in life, man, you can't hit the brakes and play it safe. You have to throttle up and take the risks.[5]

GENERATION X SUBCULTURES

EXTREME XERS

Marc is an example of a typical Extreme Xer, living life for the experience. For him and others in this subculture, money is just a means to an end, not an end in itself.

> I'm a graduate student at a Midwestern business school, sitting in classes to learn about things like Porter's five forces of industry, management decision trees, and financial statement analysis. I sit in an entire roomful of people, all of whom are thinking about business matters. Except for me! Try as I might to focus, my thoughts stray to a small hut on the Yangtze River, or the Taj Mahal. I take this fact as a sign that something is wrong. Just a few short weeks before graduation, I received a job offer from a major software firm that wants to pay me $70,000 a year to sit at a desk and go to meetings. It's the moment of truth.

Take the job, get the money, put some face time in, crunch the numbers, walk the walk, talk the talk, and do the death march down that same road that has scattered upon it the carcasses of billions of stuffy business people that have walked before me. Or . . . ignore everything and see the world. I looked at the one world, the one littered with the carcasses of all the stuffy business people. And I looked down the other road, you know . . . the one less traveled . . . but even scarier looking. I picked up the phone and told them I would take the job . . . after I've seen the world . . . maybe.[6]

> For most extreme athletes, busted body parts are a fact of life. . . . The threat of injury or death inherent in navigating furious rapids on a slab of Styrofoam or snowboarding down a 20,000-foot mountain fails to turn away new recruits. Quite the opposite—it's the chance of a catastrophe that makes extreme sports so enticing.[7]

Money simply enables Extreme Xers to experience life. Money allows them to feed their addiction to adrenaline. Whether it's embarking on a safari, snowboarding in the backcountry, sky surfing, bungee jumping, in-line skating down steps and steep hills at over thirty miles per hour, BASE jumping (BASE stands for jumping off Buildings, Antennas, Spans, and Earth with a parachute), or free climbing (mountain climbing with no ropes), it's the thrill that drives them. The danger is part of the fun.

> There aren't many injuries in BASE jumping. You either live or you die.[8]

If you want to reach this subculture for Christ, make sure your insurance premiums are paid up. You're going to need it!

> Frank Gambalie spent his days in an office . . . flustered by the petty stresses of the cloistered 9-to-5 routine. He started bungee jumping. "I started to use bungee jumping as a drug, as a way to clean my slate. I would jump and I'd be like, 'Problems? What problems?'"[9]

usually with *techno music* and psychedelic mood enhancers. There may be a light show, and dress is usually *Retro*. Raves are usually located at different and illegal places, such as warehouses, and are not advertised by traditional means, but by flyers and word of mouth. Directions are both secretive and cryptic to avoid authorities.[10]

> It's about nothing less than speed . . . the nastiest bumps, the steepest chutes, the tightest trees, speeds just shy of panic on the fear meter, grind on curbs, rails, ramps, half pipes, or go for fat air—it don't matter which one you choose, they're all related somehow, and they are all designed for abuse.[11]

UNDERGROUND XERS

Some people refer to this subculture as the dark side of Gen X. Much of the underground revolves around grunge bands like Nirvana, Pearl Jam, Sonic Youth, REM, Red Hot Chili Peppers, the Misfits, and Helmet. This loud music boasts haunting lyrics reflecting despair, disillusionment, and anger as it facilitates an Xer dance called slam dancing or "moshing." Here Xers run, leap, and collide in midair, simulating bumper cars at a fair.

Raves are hot for this subculture as well. A rave is:

> a huge, nomadic dance party that tends to last all night, or until the police show up,

Just as an aside, not all Gen X music is dark, violent, and throbbing. Much of it is reflective and reveals the pain this generation sees in their world and in their personal lives. Gerald C. Celente, author of *Trend and Tracking*, says: "To find out what a generation believes, 'listen to their songs.'"[12]

Many within the Underground subculture also express themselves through tattooing and body piercing. "Body piercing—dating as far back as thousands of years ago—has evolved into a twenty-first century art form which has emerged from the underground, embraced by many of this generation who desire to make a statement, show a preference, their individuality and style. In some cases body piercing is now considered a fashion look."[13] Xers are doing this for many reasons but perhaps the most significant is the desire to have some type of continuity and permanence in life. "These bodily incisions stay with us for the rest of our lives. They will be one certain source of continued identity amid the flux of identity in our simulational popular culture. They also create continuity over time. In a sense, these bodily incisions love our bodies unconditionally. They will never leave, which is blessed assurance for our abandoned generation."[14]

Techno Music: A stripped down, hard-driving music, usually without vocals, that took the funk/electronic direction of house and electrofunk to a new, sped-up extreme.[15]

DIGITAL XERS

In the early 1970s the first computer game hit the market. Called Pong, it was created by Nolan Bushnell and his new company, Atari. Today, the electronic game industry takes in billions of dollars generated from flight simulators, virtual reality games, interactive Playboy centerfolds, and role-playing games such as Dungeons and Dragons and Traveler.

For many young adults, these games provide more than fun; they provide an escape from the harsh realities of life: painful relationships, low-paying jobs, an uncertain future, and a faltering global ecosystem, just to name a few. For young adults, computers have become a vital part of their existence, an extension of who they are. For example, many Xers socialize in computer chat rooms. Here they can talk, share ideas, and play multiperson games without ever having to see or touch each other. Digital Xers live in a virtual world they can control, a world that is safe and predictable.

Retro: A prefix that can be added to any word to indicate a hop or hyped return to the past.[16]

One of the interesting elements that drives this virtual world is an Xer's ability to take on any number of different personalities. You can be a man or a woman, attribute any title to yourself, and take on any political, social, or religious form. They call these MUDs (multi-user dungeons). "They are virtual sites in which users can assume whichever identities they desire. Their identities are completely self-styled. They can also design their own virtual rooms and wander throughout the dungeon, or 'domain,' conversing with other 'people.'"[17] Instead of computers being just another tool like a typewriter or calculator, computers and the Internet have become a way of life for this subculture and an important means of community and self-exploration.

Being a performance artist, I was asked to do my poetry by a close friend who requested that I remove my piercings for the small formal gathering. I honored the request even though the piercings are now a part of me. After experiencing not having them, I will not take the piercings out again. As I think about it, taking the piercings out is like denying the truth. People are attracted to truth. People who ask or talk to me about them are more spiritual. Their spirit calls out to find out why, then they ask and learn the truth! My art is my life and my art is my expression. If one is to persecute my piercing or my expression, they are persecuting me.[18]

As secondhand clothing, grunge is appropriate for a secondhand generation—one that must pay for the excessive desires of its elders, from the sexual revolution to the national debt to easy divorce. This hand-me-down generation knows that there is a poverty in our hearts, born of our roles as both society's orphans and its cleanup crew. Grunge announces, "We are on our own." It does not rejoice at this, yet it does not despair. Grunge simply offers our own take on our reality—when left alone, as we have been, we will wear the disarray in which we live (psychologically, culturally, and fashionably).[20]

SLACKER XERS

Douglas Rushkoff, editor of *The GenX Reader,* describes "Slackers" this way:

Withdrawing in disgust is not the same as apathy.[21]

Rather than battling for scarce jobs in their "chosen" fields or stepping onto a competitive professional track, slackers opt out of "gainful employment" altogether. Whether they are victims of the post-Reagan economic fallout or willing participants in a social experiment called apathy, slackers are characterized by intelligence, cynicism, and a new bohemian irreverence for authority.[19]

The Slacker subculture has often been noted for their grunge fashion. Grunge is fashion unplugged, a way of expressing their pain of being uncared for and abandoned by society.

In a classic Xer movie, *Reality Bites,* the character Troy Dyer portrays a "Slacker." To Troy, the world is "a random lottery of meaningless tragedy in a series of near escapes . . . so I take pleasure in the details like a quarter pounder with cheese." Note that we are not using Slacker as a derogatory label. Instead, we are using it to describe a subgroup of Xers who feel slighted by the system and disillusioned by the fact that their BA degrees haven't provided the edge in the marketplace their parents said they would. Much of the angst comes from high debt due to student loans and purchases made impulsively with easily attained credit cards.

STAR XERS

In his book *Managing Generation X*,[22] Bruce Tulgan identifies a subculture of Xers who are very motivated, career-driven, and eager to make a difference in the marketplace. In fact, Star Xers look very much like young Baby Boomers in that they are activists who are vigorously involved in reclaiming the promise of an open society. Their goal is to eradicate ideologies that threaten their future and to take control of their own destiny.

Their plea is for America to adopt a new paradigm, one that will provide equal opportunity for all American citizens. Their fear is that capitalism has come to the end of its usefulness and that the horizon of human progress is limited to genetic engineering for a more perfect physical species. They ask questions like "Can we redefine progress?" and "Can we remake the American Dream?" Eric Liu, the founding editor of the journal *The Next Progressive,* states,

> I want to help America to succeed. I want to help carve out a future that is not only slightly better than what I inherited, but astronomically better. I yearn for a leader who can wake Americans from our CD-listening, cable-watching, Taco Bell-eating slumber. I want to measure progress not by the monthly economic indicators, but by my sense of satisfaction with—by my sense of a stake in—American life.[23]

The cry of this subculture isn't that of whiners blaming everyone else for the ills they have inherited. Rather, they actively spread the truth about what is and what can be done. Far from being apathetic, lazy, and paralyzed in anger, these young adults are out to make a difference in our world.

> It is our job to turn on our heart lights now. It is up to us to travel through the spirals of antiquity into the polished future of positivity. To part E heart E. It is our response ability to wake up, trip in and groove on into the light of tomorrowland's magical miracles of majesty. To be set free. To recognize our divinity and re-affiliate our affinity with the highest good of Planet E. We are the Map Makers. We are the Reality Creators. We are the Dreamers of the Dream. Here to receive the rainbow cotton candy kiss of transcendental bliss.[24]

URBAN XERS

Urban Xers experience life in a battle zone where one wrong move can bring a hail of bullets. Here, only the fittest survive. "It's a world where young people harden themselves to daily suffering and hopelessness in a brutal, nomadic, pre- (or post-) civilized lifestyle that older generations find unpleasant enough in small suburban traces, but totally repugnant and incomprehensible in its undiluted urban form."[25] Xers in this urban subculture perceive the world as an unsafe place that cares little about whether they live or die.

These are some of the subcultures where Xers live out the many forces that have shaped them. These subcultures are generalizations that don't necessarily have hard and fast boundaries.

They are merely a means of helping us begin to understand the diversity and complexity of this generation. The key to reaching the Xers in your community effectively involves your understanding of who they are and where they are coming from. The goal is then to contextualize the gospel and programs within the framework of their subcultures.

> Let no one be dismayed by the thought that there is nothing that one man or woman can do against the enormous array of the world's ills. Few will have the greatness to bend history itself. But each can do some small act, and in the sum of these events will be written the history of our generation.
>
> —Robert F. Kennedy, 1965 [26]

Dieter Zander, former pastor of Axis, a Gen X ministry at Willow Creek Community Church, notes, "If Xers really understood what the Gospel was, it would be so attractive to them, because its themes of redemption, reconciliation, forgiveness, and wholeness are the things they are seeking." [27] Our job is to help translate these eternal truths of the gospel into their language and offer ministry programs and opportunities that fit within the contexts of their subcultures.

The Net Gen, like those in Generation X, also live out the variety of forces that shaped them within the context of a number of subcultures.

NET GEN SUBCULTURES

Some Net Gen subcultures are similar to Gen X subcultures. But Net Gen also has some distinctive differences. Most members of the Net Gen abhor anything trendy and desire to be free from the mainstream influences of society, pursuing experiences where they can be true to their own unique identity.

FREE NETTERS

This subculture of the Net Gen is actually a collection of individualistic free thinkers. They are the highly alternative and artistic side of the Net Gen. They look a lot like the hippies and rockers of the early Boomer generation, placing a high value on integrity and individual expression.

> A survey conducted in September 1995 by Frank Luntz for the under-35 political advocacy group Third Millennium revealed a higher percentage of those 18–34 who believe in UFOs than believe there will be money left in Social Security when they retire. [28]

Within this group, you'll find a large variety of "spiritual and artistic soul mixed with strong, ethnic urban roots." [29] They borrow and mix a variety of cultural forms of art, music and philosophy from African Americans, Native Americans, Zen Buddhists, and other Far Eastern religions. They mix all of these various media and ideas to form their own unique expressions.

> Every age uses dress and body decoration to signal what is most important at that historical moment. Throughout most of our history that message has been, "I am rich," or, "I am powerful." If today more and more people use their dress style to assert: "I am authentic," it is simply evidence of our hunger for the genuine article in an age which seems to so many to be one of simulation and hype.[30]

One outlet Free Netters use for expression is the open microphone at an urban underground club. Here they read their poetry and play their music to express their feelings and voice their solutions to the social ills of our day. They place a high value on personal rights and preserving the environment. This subculture has contributed to the craze in e-zines (Web magazines that don't require paper), natural foods, herbs, root teas, coffee houses, and antioxidant drinks. Many are vegetarians or vegans (vegetarians who demand food and clothing with absolutely no animal materials).

HIP-HOP NETTERS
The origins of hip-hop are found in the graffiti art and break dancing scene of the South Bronx, New York, during the mid-1970s. Hip-hop has its own sound and style. It's a combination of African-American, Asian, and Hispanic urban cultures mixed to rap lyrics and sound. This group instinctively knows how to borrow "influences" to invent a "personal style." The style this group embraces reflects their interaction with the rough, gritty urban environment as well as their social status.[31] They tend to be "tribal" in that their neighborhoods ("'hoods") act as an extended family. In the 'hood a high value is placed on expressions of love and respect for each other. Each person's freedom of personal expression is also highly valued.

> We went from mother's milk to moving picture elicksure. Thanks to the after school special, our life is just a field trip. Media magic has afforded us the luxury of being aware of all inhabitants on Planet 3. Mass realization of the soul 'O' world-planet-people vibe. Connecting the dot matrix of the multi-colored rainbow love tribe. We are all the same family, phylum, class, genus, species. No longer isolated individuals on distant continents, floating anonymously through space. On this Planetary Universe-city, in our every unique diversity, we are a race of ONE. And we've only just begun, to have sum fun.[32]

The literature read by this group includes African-American books, the teachings of Martin Luther King, Jr., and Malcolm X. Magazines include *The Source, Vibe, Rap Sheet*, and *XXL*. Their preferred music is trip-hop (considered the ultimate dance music at 220 beats per minute) and reggae, and prominent musical artists include Method Man, Nas, and Dr. Dre.

Hip-Hop is one of numerous variations of rap, but actually closer to describing the B-boy culture of dance, music, art, poetry, and DJ cut and scratching. The music focuses on a dance beat and borrows breaks shamelessly from nearly every other form of music.[33]

SPEED NETTERS

This is the ultra-extreme sporting subculture. Their goal is to push all limits and break all boundaries. They feverishly pursue sports including in-line skating, skateboarding, snowboarding, mountain biking, and free climbing. Adrenaline is their drug of choice, and the more extreme the sport, the better the high. They love to create new sports like mountain boarding (skateboarding down a mountain or ski trail), in-line basketball (playing basketball wearing in-line skates), wakeboarding (waterskiing with a kneeboard), street luging (done on pavement instead of ice), and boulder biking.

Their credo is "No posers allowed." In order to be in with this subculture, you have to be one of them. They are irreverent and antiestablishment and come off as disrespectful because they think modern American culture is cheesy. For them, everything "sucks."

On the other hand, Speed Netters watch Nick at Night reruns from the 1960s and 1970s, as well as the Cartoon Network. Their affinity for commercial icons from the past like Bazooka Joe and Mr. Bubbles might be rooted in their search for security. They love hanging out with friends on the streets, going to dance parties, and living in community groups where roommates support each other like family.

The magazines read by this group include *Transworld Skateboarding, Transworld Snowboarding, Big Brother, Thrasher, Slap, BMX Bike, Powder, Mountain Biking, Surfer, Spin,* and *Snap.* Their preferred music runs from ska to jungle to rockabilly punk, with retro rock groups from the 1970s, such as Led Zeppelin, Kiss, and Metallica, thrown in.

How can you continue to justify the rape and destruction of millions of acres of forests to print newspapers when electronic, ecologically sound news and information systems are available right now . . . today![34]

CLUB NETTERS

Also called club kids, this group wants to be different, to stand out from mainstream modern culture. They use their style to shock the mainstream and be unique. They are the "skin artists" who decorate their bodies with body piercing, tattoos, body sculpting (placing metal balls in patterns under the skin), and body branding (using red hot strips of metal to form patterns of scar tissue as a type of tattoo). Their body alterations serve a twofold purpose: they provide a "rush of pain" as well as a chance to express themselves in unique ways.

Faced with the ever-growing threat of mainstream mediocrity, some of us are taking control of our own bodies and express our personal freedom with ornaments. Piercing, tattoos, brands, and scarification marks us as unique individuals and shows our defiance of a society that wants everyone to look and think the same. Extreme body ornamentation announces our knowledge that we are in control of our own society and our own generation.[35]

Obviously, each subculture has its own form of expression, language, and musical tastes that make reaching them for Christ exciting and challenging. As we have worked with targeting subcultures within our own ministries and countless others across the country, one of the difficulties we have noted is that these young adults don't necessarily stay in just one subculture all the time. By day, a young woman can work for a congressman or senator on Capitol Hill looking like a Star Xer, but at night she will take to the club scene, moving into the Underground. The question is, how do we hit these moving targets for Christ?

One of the keys is to target one main subculture that seems most represented within your area, and then you will reach two or three. But you cannot target all the subcultures because they are so diverse and have very different tastes, especially in music.

When Frontline first started, the staff at the church put together a number of focus groups who met to brainstorm ideas and gather opinions on how best to reach their subcultures for

Christ. While the focus groups were a great idea, what we didn't realize at that time was that the five to eight people who made up the focus group represented five to eight different subcultures and couldn't agree on any one thing. The type of music that one preferred was nauseating to the others. The types of programs that seemed cool to one person were cheesy to another. In our initial ignorance, we launched our first service and tried to incorporate a number of different styles, hoping to make everyone happy. Instead, we made everyone mad.

> If at all possible, I would like to live my life to the fullest with the biggest adrenaline rush possible. When you feel a surge of endorphins running through your blood, through your head—I don't think anything can top it. Life should be just one big adrenaline rush. . . . I want to say I did most everything—and did it with pursuit of adrenaline—natural, untainted adrenaline.[36]

The fatal error when trying to build a ministry around the targeting concept is to try to please everyone; you just can't do it. To fix the problem, we took some time to think through who we were as a ministry team (what subcultures we most represented) and which subcultures were most represented in our area. When we determined that Star Xers were our main people group, we implemented strategies and programs that would reach them. After this, things really took off. But we learned a hard lesson: you can't please everyone.

Certainly, if Jesus were walking the earth today, He would be concerned about all the lost. Yet we can't help but wonder if He would be most passionate about reaching these young postmoderns. We agree with Dieter Zander, who said, "I think [Jesus] would say, 'I know what you're going through. I've been there . . . the kind of love you're looking for is found through me. Delight yourself in me and together we're going to see things happen.'"[37]

These young people are our future. They matter to God. May God help us as the body of Christ to understand them, to love them, and to implement effective strategies for reaching them with the gospel. We can't expect them to come to us or to embrace our traditions. We must go into their world, with the gospel contextualized to their cultures and language. These generations are a mission field right in our own backyard. With that in mind, we must find effective ways to reach each of the people groups within this generation of young adults for Christ.

GETTING REAL YOURSELF

1. As you've observed the young adults around you, what have you noticed about their lifestyles? For example, are they like Marc (the Extreme Xer who could have earned $70,000 a year right out of college), or more like others who work at a bookstore or a coffee shop earning $6 an hour? Thinking through the young adults you know might provide good clues to those your church can serve.

2. Make a guess. When you think of the young adults that live around you, which subculture do you think they're a part of?

3. Take a field trip to a local mall or another place where young adults gather. Don't be obvious, but observe groups of young adults and see if you can determine what subculture they belong to by what they wear, how they talk, or the music they listen to.

CHAPTER FOUR

MODERN GENERATIONS

According to the book *Three Generations,* Scripture uses the word "generations" in three different ways: to refer to an age group in a family, a period of time, or a group of people connected by their place in time.[1] As we look at modern generations, we'll use the third definition: a generation as a group of people who are connected by their place in time with common boundaries and common character. Those common boundaries and character can help to build an effective young adult ministry—or they can act as obstacles.

No generation stands alone. Each generation has been affected and shaped by previous generations. To effectively reach young adults, church leaders must understand the other generations active in the church. In many churches the oldest generation typically holds the key to financial funding, while members of the next generation are usually in positions of power.

As is the generation of leaves, so too of men:
At one time the wind shakes the leaves to the ground
but then the flourishing woods
Gives birth, and the season of spring comes
into existence;
So it is with the generations of men, which
alternately come forth and pass away.
—Homer, *Iliad,* Sixth Book

One generation passeth away, and another generation cometh:
but the earth abideth forever. (Ecclesiastes 1:4, KJV)

I will make thy name to be remembered in all generations.
(Psalms 45:17, KJV)

In this chapter we'll look at the characteristics and values of each of the modern generations in an attempt to properly frame young adults within the context of the other adult generations in the church. This will be a sweeping overview of the modern generations to help you better understand how each generation can help the next.

There is a mysterious cycle in human events. To some generations much is given. Of other generations much is expected. This generation has a rendezvous with destiny.

—Franklin Delano Roosevelt, 1936

BUILDERS

For two people who really hate lumping everyone into generalities . . . well, that's what we're going to do here. We're putting two generations together into what we're going to call Builders. First are the GIs; approximately 30 million of them were born prior to 1925. Members of this generation include George Bush, Johnny Carson, Jimmy Carter, Billy Graham, and Oral Roberts. Next, there's the Silent Generation; 30 million of them were born from 1925 to 1942. Members include Colin Powell, Jerry Falwell, Robert Schuller, and John Updike.

There's a third group that some demographers link to Builders, and we will too: the War Babies, who were born from 1940 to 1945. (Some classify those born after 1942 as part of the Boomers; nothing's black and white.) The War Babies represented 6 percent of all Builders. Members of this group include Paul McCartney, Diane Sawyer, Barbara Streisand, Ted Koppel, and Jesse Jackson.[2]

FORCES THAT SHAPED THEM

However you classify Builders, the people of these generations have some things in common. In their early lives, Builders experienced a slower rate of change than did following generations. For many, it was a time when families met around the dinner table. Mom cooked. There was no pizza delivery or McDonald's drive-thru. Items were purchased for their value, not because they were trendy. People fixed things that were broken. They believed in God, country, and family. Most people were loyal, faithful, and dependable, and they were survivors. Life centered around family, school, and church.

WORSHIP AND FAITH

This adult group feels a strong allegiance to institutions. In the church this allegiance is evident as denominational loyalty. Traditions provide a sense of security for these adults, so new forms of worship styles and music are discomforting. This group came of age before television was prevalent, and therefore they rely on literature or the spoken word for information. (With later generations, we see books and sermons give way to hands-on experience and visual presentations.)

On the other hand, this is a caring, doting generation. These adults have seen tremendous change in their lives (from the beginning of air travel through the space shuttle flight of their cohort John Glenn), and they have learned to be flexible, especially in their effort to understand younger adults. Grandparent love is different from parental love. It is usually softer and more understanding. Remember that this generation wants to be involved with the young people in their churches. At The Next Level Church (TNL, which we referred to earlier, is a Gen X church near Denver where the average attendee is 26 years old), it is not unusual to see Xers sitting next to their grandparents during the service.

Forces That Shaped Builders

The stock market crash of 1929
The Great Depression
The New Deal
Rural lifestyle
New technology: the automobile, radio, television, telephones
Pearl Harbor and World War II
The Korean War

The group is a great volunteer pool, with 31 million over 65 years old, many still healthy and wanting to help the future generations reach people for Christ. They still hold the purse strings as the biggest givers in the church. While Boomers may make the spending decisions, the money they spend belongs in large part to Builders.

Characteristics	*Core Values*
Hard workers	Responsibility
Intolerant	Patriotism
Private/cautious	Loyalty
Respectful	Dependability
Stable	Frugality

As you form your young adult ministry, be sure to develop an advisory board of Builders who want to help. Meet once a quarter with them, asking for help and advice. You will be pleasantly surprised at the assistance you get.

Because they still have ownership of the church, you need them if you are going to accomplish any of your goals in young adult ministry. They need to understand that this new generation demands new methods to reach them. As young adults themselves, Builders didn't need all the bells and whistles—sound systems and computerized equipment for video and production—but with a better understanding, they'll work with you to get the equipment you need for your ministry.

This group has a strong sense of obligation to serve, and if you don't ask them to help, you will lose the opportunity to enlist the best support system available to you in the church. Their commitment to missions lends itself to helping you create mission and service opportunities with young adults. Because they are strongly committed to denominations, you won't want to downplay the importance of this allegiance.

They know there is a real value in being a part of changing and updating something (like young adult ministry) rather than criticizing it.

Forces That Shaped Boomers

The Cold War
Television
Rock-'n'-roll
The space program
The civil rights movement
The Vietnam War
Kent State shootings
Political assassinations
The energy crisis
Watergate

BABY BOOMERS

Born between 1946 and 1964 (depending on whose research you use), this was the largest generation in U.S. history until their kids came along. This generation experienced the beginning of the postmodern cultural shift. They were the first generation to be raised, by and large, by absentee fathers, with television taking the place of a second parent. Their grandparents were not able to mentor them on life skills and making a living because Boomer children were raised away from Grandma and Grandpa's influence. Raised with great opportunity, they came into adolescence at a time of unprecedented economic growth in America. Yet they were also the first generation raised with the constant threat of nuclear war.

This generation is currently in the driver's seat of churches and will be for the next twenty years. Because of this, anyone working with young adults must plan to work closely with Boomers.

WORSHIP AND FAITH

Many in this generation were raised by a surrogate parent—television—and this had a great influence on their worship patterns. As children, when they got bored, they just changed the channel. In choosing a church, they want the same ease and convenience of scheduling and programming. If they don't like what one church offers, they have plenty of other churches to choose from.

Characteristics	Core Values
Multiple choices	Tolerance
Immediate solutions	Idealism
Future-oriented	Adventurousness
Mobile	Women in
Suspicious of	leadership
institutions	People not
	programs
	Live to change
	the world

This generation still wants to change the world no less than they did in the pivotal 1960s. In a worship context, one result is the dramatic growth of megachurches. "To be a megachurch, a church must have a minimum of 2,000 members. In 1970 there were only ten such churches. Today, 300 megachurches with a combined membership of over 1 million people operate in the United States."[3]

Yet, despite the rise of megachurches, pollster George Barna tells us that church attendance is down 34 percent overall. This means that we can't depend only on the church growth movement to reach greater numbers of people—something we need to bear in mind as we develop new programs.

This generation is very action-oriented in ministry and all other areas of life. This explains their interest in short-term missions, while their suspicion of institutions is perhaps responsible for their reluctance to join or even donate to traditional mission agencies. Their attraction toward immediate solutions can be seen in the way the self-help movement captured their attention.

As they first arrived into adulthood, this generation wanted flexible church programs to meet their changing lifestyles. This generation demanded "excellence" in worship. Churches like Willow Creek quickly discovered how they could reach people with an emphasis on high-quality worship music. Church parlance changed too, with Protestants following their Roman Catholic counterparts in demanding modern, everyday language in worship services.

As this group moved into church leadership, they put their mark on evangelism, calling it by a new name: targeted ministry. Following a trend that had started a little earlier, churches became increasingly segmented to focus on certain demographics: nuclear families, extended families, peer groups, white- and blue-collar workers, ethnic groups, and so on. This trend continued within each church, with more and more programs designed for certain types of people. Youth and children's ministries were now joined by ministry to unwed mothers, street people, addicts, the divorced, and so on.

> Their surrogate parent was the television set. Parked in front of the glowing blue tube for an average of four hours a day, a quarter of their waking hours, Boomers became the first video generation. Bored? Just change the channel.
>
> — *Time*, 1986

Builders and Boomers still hold keys to succeeding at reaching new generations. To be effective with young adults, we need to forge partnerships with leaders from these modern generations. Several years ago, I (Rich) was at a young adult leadership meeting, with many very talented young adults leaders. I was sad to listen to the energy they had behind comments about older generations. Here's one I heard too often: "They just don't get it."

I wanted to say, "It is us that had better get it. We talk about community, but only for those who are the right age." Several of the keys to reaching young adults are held by Boomers and Builders, and we can learn a great deal from them.

GETTING REAL YOURSELF

1. Think about the descriptions of Builders and Boomers in this chapter. Do you agree that they generally describe the members of these generations? Make a list of the words you think most clearly describe these generations.

2. Can you name two individuals in your life who epitomize each of these generational groupings? Can you think of a Builder you know and a Boomer you know? Keep in mind the terms you listed in question 1 and recall these people as you think about the present population of the church.

3. Can you think of anyone else who needs to read this section to understand the unique roles and thoughts of Builders and Boomers?

4. As you think about the church and the message of the gospel, what methods do you think were effective for reaching these generations? Do you think these traditional ways of communicating the gospel message are still effective today? Why or why not?

CHAPTER FIVE

RELATIONAL MINISTRY

When it comes to building an effective young adult ministry, you have to begin by understanding how young adults react to the traditional church mindset about ministry. Where Boomers and the prior generations usually responded to the *doctrines* taught in churches, young adults are more interested in *relationships* exhibited there. In teaching Christian tenets to this group, you need to begin with relationships.

The Bible deals primarily with relationships
and only indirectly with doctrine.[1]

Young adults are interested in genuineness, not in theories. The Bible read as stories about real-life people who had real-life encounters with God is very different from the Bible taught in many churches and seminaries. Perhaps the real test of your "orthodoxy" is found in your relationships, not in what you believe or do not believe. In the wonderful work *The Message,* Eugene Peterson says, "The Word became flesh and blood, and moved into the neighborhood" (John 1:14). All of relational ministry is captured in the Incarnation.

Young adults want answers to real-life questions and real-life problems. This may be why most young adults find the answers they're looking for in their music. Music conveys truth to them in a way traditional religion does not.

However, author Bruce Larson says in *No Longer Strangers:*

When we operate within a framework of a relational theology, we see that the good news is relevant in two dimensions. First, there is the fact that in Jesus Christ we need no longer be strangers but can belong to a community of people who are seeking a birthright, a home, and a relationship through God's love and grace. This changes our goals. We are not trying to make people believe "the right things" so much as enabling them to experience a relationship with God and with one another. Second, our ministry becomes different. We are no longer teachers, but those who through the rediscovery of the principles of relational theology may enter into relationships with others and bring them to life.[2]

This is how we would also define relational ministry.

FOUR PRINCIPLES OF RELATIONAL MINISTRY

Relational ministry is the term we use to describe the concept that all matters of faith are, at their essence, matters of relationship: the Father's relationship with the Son, the Son's relationship with us, our relationship with one another, and so on. Because of the longing of postmodern generations for meaningful relationships, this relational view of ministry speaks to them in a way that more traditional ministries have not.[3]

When applied to church life, these principles can bring an individual and group to life.

1. DON'T TEACH PEOPLE ABOUT CHRIST; DISCOVER CHRIST WITH PEOPLE.

A young adult recently challenged me (Rich) by asking, "Do you want to help my generation discover the word about Christ, or do you want to help them discover the Christ of the Word?" This is process evangelism at its best.

In process evangelism, the conversion experience takes place over a longer period than we have tended to expect from our technique-oriented evangelistic strategies of the past. In process evangelism people are convinced of

the reality of God's love not by propositional arguments or one-time evangelistic rallies but by a daily, consistent, practical demonstration that Christianity works and that God's love is real. In process evangelism pre-Christian people discover the reality of God and the love of God in the transparency of love of God's people.[4]

Most young adults won't have a Damascus Road experience like Paul the apostle. But as we come alongside and help them discover the authentic Christ, they'll experience Jesus through our lives and stories. When you show people your life and struggles, the gospel is authentic.

Young adults don't want to be told anything, particularly what to believe and how to live. But they do want to connect with others. When they see common ground, they can identify. Young adults need to understand that their leaders are on the same path we're urging them to try.

What does that mean? It means that, as a young adult leader, you want to experience Christ with young adults—not just tell them about Christ. It also means that all of your leaders are to make this their priority.

2. PEOPLE SUPPORT THAT WHICH THEY HELP TO CREATE.

There are two ways to develop young adult programs. One is to say, "Let's start a group for people in their twenties," and then sit back and hope people will come. The other is to involve young adults in every part of the process, from conception through execution. Surprisingly, many churches never stop to ask people in their twenties what they'd like in a program. This could be why so many programs fail.

The difference between these two methods is the locus of power. The second gives young adults the power to decide what they want to build for God, or to discover what God wants them to build. This method assumes that the Holy Spirit works through every generation. When we begin to live out this assumption in community, we discover a whole new kind of leadership—one that empowers people to live out their faith and to discover how to use their gifts fully.

Recently, I (Rich) was asked to help a church start a young adult ministry. It would have been easy for me to make a few phone calls, gather together those who expressed an interest, and say, "Okay, this is what we're going to do to get this thing started." Instead, I met with an interested group and opened the planning process by asking, "What would you like to do to reach people like yourselves?"

By putting the ownership of the group in the hands of those in the target audience, you show your willingness to abide by these assumptions:

Young adult ministry is not crowd control. Young adult ministry isn't just another variation of church-sponsored entertainment. Success in young adult ministry is not based on whether people have a good time.

Young adult ministry is not leadership techniques and program maintenance; it is people building. We often think that if we read the right books or attend the right seminars, we will add enough good techniques to our repertoire to have a great program. But our goal in young adult ministry is building people, not programs.

That means we build relationships and create the environment where people will grow.

Relational ministry is not autocratic. Autocratic ministry assumes that our job as leaders is to "teach right beliefs" and change those who believe differently. An autocratic leader will want others to follow his or her ideas and vision. Relational ministry, on the other hand, encourages group members to determine their own ministry direction. It doesn't matter if a person is responsible for setting up chairs for a meeting or being part of a leadership team.

> It is truly exciting to see how God, the great communicator, is trying to teach His people new ways to listen to Him and new ways to communicate one with another so that we may no longer be strangers.[5]

As a ministry leader, if you don't understand this second principle, you'll easily become driven by your own ideas and tasks. As Eugene H. Peterson says, the result is to be "preoccupied with shopkeeper's concerns—how to keep the customers happy, how to lure customers away from competitors down the street, how to package the goods so that the customers will lay out more money."[6]

If you don't learn to empower people to create, you will find yourself driven to do everything yourself. You'll have an endless need for more volunteers, and eventually become the preoccupied shopkeeper.

But when you base your young adult ministry on relational ministry, you don't worry about what tasks to undertake. You don't worry about how to get better at doing ministry or how to be a better shopkeeper. Instead, you concentrate on encouraging others to be responsible in pursing the ministry God intended for them. You make choices based on effectiveness, not efficiency; on people development, not task accomplishment.

3. DON'T GIVE MINISTRY JOBS TO PEOPLE; INSTEAD, HELP PEOPLE DISCOVER THEIR CALLING.

The greatest outcome of the Reformation was that the Bible was given back to the people of God. Perhaps it's time for a second Reformation, where the people of God get ministry back as well.

I (Rich) met with a very gifted leader recently who said her job was to motivate people. I corrected her, "No, your job is to create an environment where people want to get involved."

Because we have a hard time understanding this concept, we often have a hard time training and equipping people for ministry. The role of a leader is not to motivate someone else but to create environments where people can discover what God has called them to do. We all understand our responsibility to help others hear their call to Christ, but when it comes to helping them with their call to ministry, we stop short.

Today's young adults understand that each of us is called to ministry. Young adults will bristle if you expect them to "help you with the ministry." On the other hand, they will respond enthusiastically to efforts to help them discover their ministries.

I (Rich) was at dinner with two sharp young women from our young adult ministry.

As the evening came to a close, they finally asked why I had wanted to have dinner with them. I said I wanted to get to know them.

"You don't have a job in the church you want done?"

"No," I said.

They laughed, looked at each other, and said, "Wow!"

Why do you think they expected me to have some job for them to do? The answer is easy: they had learned that when pastors meet with you, they want something—usually for you to do a volunteer job.

As the conversation continued, I asked a few questions. I asked them to describe the best experience they had ever had with God. They related that when they were in college they had gone on a short-term mission trip to Costa Rica. They described in detail how the trip had changed everyone's life.

After they were done talking about their experience, I said, "There's one thing you can do for me."

They looked at each other again and said, "We knew it."

I said, "I think you should lead a group from our young adult ministry on a short-term mission trip to Costa Rica." The two young women turned to each other; they couldn't believe their ears.

"Really?" they said.

I have never seen two people more excited.

Over the next nine months, they found an agency to work with, advertised the trip, chose the participants, trained the team, and took them to the Costa Rican jungle. As the team's leaders, they assigned jobs to everyone once we got to the work site. To everyone, that is, except me. They were afraid to give me a job.

"What's my job?" I asked.

"The only job left is for someone to dig the hole for the outhouse. Six feet down, three feet by three feet wide." They were the team leaders; I was a team member. I dug the latrine.

4. CHURCH IS FOR EVERYONE.

Through the rediscovery of a biblical relational model, we're beginning to understand something about church community. Church is for everyone, not just the few who look, act, and speak a certain way. Those who want to reach young adults will seriously address the need to reach out to the people who are disenfranchised and people who have struggled with the traditional church.

Many young adults feel cheated, unwanted, unimportant, and treated as nonplayers when it comes to the church. Frustrated young adults are starting their own churches in an attempt to lead the way they want to. If the rest of us want the richness that young adults can bring to our congregations, we must make our churches the kind of places they can call their own.

The 1990s seem to have brought us to a new level of separation and misunderstanding between the generations. Those wanting to reach young adults and build a happy marriage between the local church and young adults need to understand that the gospel is for everyone and every generation. All of us have a deep need for a relationship with God, and we all stand before God equal and in equal need. When the church allows young adults to belong in their own way, it authenticates the New Testament.

We are called to community with others seeking a relationship with Jesus Christ. "This changes our goals. We are not trying to make people believe 'the right things' so much as enabling them to experience a relationship with God and with one another."[8]

Christians are not meant to take the place of the Holy Spirit and become super-detectives, ferreting out people's sins and weaknesses and underscoring them. When we employ this kind of strategy, it is no wonder people fail to discover the grace of God in and through us. Our task as Christians is far easier, more exciting, and more rewarding than that. It is to live out a style of life that will allow people to discover their worth, their strength, and their uniqueness, and to communicate how much God intends to do with them and for them.[7]

I (Rich) used to consult for churches, and I would agree to show up every few months to help them as they started a young adult program. This worked quite well in the 1980s, but as I approached the late 1990s, I began to notice that this method didn't work anymore. My teaching hadn't deteriorated, and my leadership techniques and goals were very much the same. What was different was that young adults no longer needed someone to tell them how to live; they wanted someone to live it with them. That was much more authentic.

The goal of our ministries should be to create an environment where people can experience the grace and redemption of a loving God. We want people to experience the power of the resurrected Christ and the relationship that He offers us. However, unless we approach relational ministry correctly, we'll run into roadblocks.

What are the obstacles to effective relational ministry?

OBSTACLES THAT HINDER RELATIONAL MINISTRY

1. WE ASSUME EVERYTHING CAN BE FIXED.
If we think everything can be fixed, all we have to do is find the solution. And if we just find the solution, we can fix this whole thing in no time at all. A church that approaches young adult ministry with the attitude that there is a problem to be fixed will alienate the very people it seeks to attract.

Have you ever heard (or even made) this statement? "Our church needs to do something for young adults." This statement could be translated, "Something in our church needs to be fixed." If you already have a young adult group, maybe you have asked yourself this question: "How come all the neurotics are in our group?" Which means what? "If we could get the right kind of people in this group, we'd have something special. If we could just get rid of the neurotics—or fix them—we'd have a healthy group."

My point is simply this: not everything has a fixable solution to it. Keep in mind two words: *journey* and *destination*. The Bible is all about the journey. There is a destination—heaven—but the rest is all journey. Your life is a journey. Unfortunately, a lot of the language from the pulpit is about destination: "When you arrive . . ." "When you get your Christian life in order . . ." "When you get married . . ." But life is a journey. Paul told Timothy to make sure his "progress [was] evident to all" (1 Timothy 4:15, NASB).

2. WE ASSUME THERE IS ONLY ONE APPROACH.
Several years ago, just after finishing work on the book *Giving the Ministry Away,* I (Rich) had a leadership retreat with the lay leaders of our young adult group. As I got ready for the retreat, I grew increasingly excited about presenting the book's contents to the group. I was going to take them through the manuscript, which was a story written about them, and I wanted to do it formally. Friday night I made the announcement: "Let's meet in the living room and get started."

Someone interrupted, "Rich, can you hold off on the living room thing and the lecture? Some of us don't really know each other that well and we'd like to talk about our faith stories with each other. Can we just sit around in a circle, the ten of us, and talk? You know, 'This is where I met Christ, and this is what it's meant to me. This is some of the trauma, and this is some of the good stuff I've gone through. This is my faith-journey experience.' Can we do that instead of a lecture, Rich?"

So I responded, "Sure, we can do that. Tomorrow we can do the lecture. We can do the faith-journey thing tonight. No big deal."

What a powerful experience it turned out to be! We stayed up until one in the morning talking about our faith experiences. The next morning I was even more charged.

"Let's get together and have lecture number two in here. I can skip lecture number one." Again someone said to me, "Hey, Rich, Laurie brought some construction paper and some glue and she thought it would be fun if we made some masks. Remember, you mentioned that we should bring our ideas to this retreat. She thought it would be fun for us to make masks to let everyone know how we're doing right now, how we're feeling."

"Okay, we can get to my stuff right after that little exercise." We made the masks. Some had smiley faces, some had sad faces, some had scared faces, and we talked about that. It was a powerful time of learning about how people were doing.

After that activity I said, "In a few minutes we have to meet for lunch. But after lunch we need to get started on my lectures because I have a lot of answers for us. I can skip lectures one and two, but not lecture three, because it's on team building."

Again. "Team building. Ooh, Mark thought it would be fun if we did a team-building exercise in the woods." We blindfolded some people in our group and helped them walk over obstacles. We had to work as a team. It was a powerful experience.

That night I wanted to do the lecture on conflict resolution. The team said, "Wait a minute. You know, we've been talking, and George brought up the movie *The Mission*, and we'd like to watch a movie and relax tonight, and talk about the movie afterward." And someone else said, "Yeah, the movie has a whole section on forgiveness."

So we watched *The Mission*. The team

members realized they needed to forgive each other and pray for one another; they wept and they cried; they laughed and they cried; and they held each other.

I've never worked with another team like that team. We shared experiences on our journey; we didn't just worry about arriving at the destination.

3. WE MISUNDERSTAND SUCCESS.

What's the number-one question people ask you about your ministry? How many attend? How many people are on your mailing list?

I (Rich) was in a group one time with some young adult leaders and we were supposed to talk about how we were doing. One woman looked at me and said, "I don't care how you're doing; how many people are on your mailing list?" I couldn't help myself, and I said, "Just over 50,000. How about yours?"

We misunderstand success when we see it in terms of numbers. Let me give you an example of what I mean. Several years ago, when I was doing a short-term mission training session at an urban church in Seattle, I had split the group into teams of three and given each team an index card with instructions. One card said to walk around the neighborhood asking for directions to the police station, the hospital, and the post office, using only the language they speak in the country you're going to.

Another card said, go down and clean up a part of the Ave. (The Ave is a busy street near the church teeming with all kinds of activity, not all of it wholesome.) The card specified that the team was to head to a certain block where "skinheads" hang out. They began working as instructed, and soon the skinheads asked them what they were doing.

"We're on a little mission trip, and we're cleaning up your cigarette butts as part of an exercise." Before they knew it, the skinheads were cleaning with them. The next time they saw them coming, the skinheads said, "Here come those mission people again. Get down and start cleaning up your butts."

Another card said to share your faith with someone on the Ave. The three women who had that card saw a man sitting on the sidewalk begging for money. So they sat down on the pavement and asked him his name.

"My name's Robert," he said. Noticing his obvious speech impediment, twisted facial features, and filthy clothes, they asked him to tell his story. Robert said, "Well, I'm on disability, and it's not quite enough to make ends meet. At the end of each month I run out of money. So I have to beg for money for food."

Curious, they asked, "Robert, have you ever had a paying job?"

Robert replied, "I've never been able to get one. I think I frighten people with my looks."

The young women looked at each other and got an idea. While two stayed and talked with Robert, one walked to all the fast food places within a few blocks of Robert's post on the sidewalk. She asked if there were job openings and soon returned with a handful of applications. The three women quickly quizzed Robert and filled out the applications, including the facts that he had no job experience and no high school diploma.

They then returned to a pizza place less than a block away where they had been told there was an opening. One of the young women spoke to the manager. "I've brought a friend of mine in for the job opening you told me about. Here's his application. He has a speech impediment and is difficult to understand. If you'd like to interview him right now, I'll stay and interpret if necessary."

The manager looked at the odd collection of people and said, "I'll give him an interview tomorrow. I'm looking for a busboy."

They met Robert there the next day and waited nervously as he went in for the interview. When he came out, he proudly brandished his new uniform. "I got the job! I start tomorrow!"

One day I was in my office at the church, sitting with my friend Terry, when Robert barged in as he did every Tuesday. That Tuesday he had a lava lamp. He said, "Look! I got a lava lamp at a garage sale and I just wanted to show you." I said, "That's great!" And he walked out.

My friend, Terry, asked, "Who's that?"

I replied, "That's Robert."

Terry asked, "Does Robert come to your young adults group?"

"No, Robert's never been to our group." I then told him the story of how these three people, and a few others now, met with Robert on a regular basis and cared for him, made sure he had his needs met, and made sure he had someone to talk to. And every Tuesday he just kind of barged into my office.

"Well, does he come to your church?" Terry asked.

"No, Robert wouldn't feel comfortable at church, I don't imagine," I replied.

The point is that Robert never showed up

on the tally sheet. Robert never came to the young adults group. Robert never came to church. But let me tell you, Robert knew what it meant to be embraced by the body of Christ.

If you are in a setting where your ministry is judged by numbers, try to include "a memo from below." In other words, write the story of someone who has been changed through your ministry and add it to the "numbers" sheets that you send in to your ministry headquarters. Remind others that success is more than numbers on the tally sheet.

4. WE ASSUME THAT PEOPLE WILL VOLUNTEER. An Episcopal rector told the story of having to find housing each year for a visiting college choir. Every year he'd stand before the congregation and say, "Good morning. Glad you're here to worship with us in the house of God. We're excited about celebrating the Eucharist today. I have a few family announcements today for you, and so if you're part of the family, this is for you. If you're not, just listen and see if it's something you'd like to be a part of.

"In six weeks the college choir will be back. We're excited about them coming, and we need homes for them to stay in. If your home is available, please call the church office tomorrow."

How many calls the next day? Zero.

The next week he tried again. "Good morning. We're glad you're here to worship with us. We're excited about worship today. I have a few announcements. We have a need for some homes for the college kids to stay in. Now, if you love Jesus, we want you to call the church office tomorrow."

One or two calls came in.

The next week, he's at it again. "We have a few announcements for you as a church family. If you want to go to heaven, we want you to call the church office tomorrow and volunteer your home."

And year after year, he was on the phone up until the last minute trying to find homes.

Finally, one year he changed course. He thought to himself, *If I really believe that the people are the ministers, why don't I treat them that way?*

So that year he stood up six weeks before the choir's arrival and said, "Good morning. We're glad you're here to worship with us. We have some family business, and if you're a part of the family, this announcement's for you. The college choir is coming in six weeks, and we need homes for them to stay in. We have taken the liberty of assigning kids to families in the congregation; you can check the list and find the name of the student you'll be hosting. Now, if there's some reason your home is not available, please call the church office tomorrow."

Here's the point of this story: we assume people are irresponsible, and so we treat them that way. People aren't irresponsible. Asking for volunteers, however, is the wrong way to tap into that responsibility. Choose people, lay your hands on people, give them assignments, and believe in them. Believe the best for them. When you say you're going to start a meeting on time, start it on time. When you say you're going to do something, do something. People aren't irresponsible.

5. WE HAVE A FAULTY PERCEPTION OF LEADERSHIP.
I (Rich) have often imagined a conversation in

which the Father quizzes His Son about His leadership team.

"Jesus, how are You doing at choosing leaders?"

"Father, You haven't been to Galilee lately; there's not much to choose from. I've found a guy who cusses all the time, and another who steals a lot. I found these two dysfunctional boys that go everywhere with their mother . . ."

Of course, such a conversation never would have occurred. Our perception of leadership is very different from Jesus' perception. Jesus saw people for who they would become, not for what they were at that time—that cusser, that thief, those dysfunctional boys.

We have a faulty perception of young adult leadership. We assume people can't be in leadership until they've arrived. Again, that's destination, not journey.

Several years ago I (Rich) was working with our leadership team to choose new members. The group wanted to choose a guy named Matt, and they asked me to call him.

I called him on the phone. "Hi, Matt. You've been chosen to be on the leadership team. Do you accept?"

"Oh no," Matt replied, "I'm not even sure what I believe right now." He then went on to talk with me about the struggles he was facing and how they were affecting his faith. But after our talk, he agreed to try working with the leadership team.

Fast-forward two years. Matt, who by then had grown by leaps and bounds as a believer and a leader, had just returned from a trip to Russia. As he stood before the biggest Rotary Club in America, the club that had funded his trip to Russia and enabled him to work with other teachers, he said, "Thank you for giving me the money to go to Russia and share my faith over there."

Jesus sees people for who they will become. Paul told the church at Philippi that he hoped they would "shine like stars in the universe as you hold out the word of life—in order that I may boast on the day of Christ that I did not run or labor for nothing" (Philippians 2:15-16).

Who are your stars? Which of your disciples is holding out the word of light? Who is it in your ministry that you are helping to learn to teach? Who is it in your ministry that you are helping to learn to heal?

We have a faulty perception of leadership. Once, a young man named Steve was chosen to be on one of our leadership teams. His reputation with women was well-known. When I met with him, I said, "You've been asked to be on the leadership team, and I want to give you a chance. I know you're struggling in relationships, but I'm going to believe God's future in your life. I'd like a six-month commitment that you will have godly relationships. I'll tell you what I'm going to do: I'm not going to sleep around either. Will you make that commitment with me?"

Steve looked at me like I was nuts. "But you're married," he correctly observed.

"Sure I am. So what? Let me tell you a story." I then told him of the time a guy had come into my office complaining about our views of extramarital sex.

"You know, I'm so sick of you married guys telling us single guys that we can't sleep around!" he said.

After we talked for a while, I brought up the name of one of the beautiful women in the group. I said, "Do you know Sue? Isn't she great-looking?"

"Oh yeah," he replied.

I responded, "I've been thinking about asking her to go out to dinner with me."

He said, "Wait a minute! You can't do that; you're married!"

I snapped back with all the drama I could muster, "I'm so sick of you single guys telling us married guys we can't do anything!"

Steve agreed to make a six-month commitment to leadership and godly behavior. He followed that up with another term. Today, he's a pastor. Had we not believed in him, had we not given him an opportunity, who knows what his journey would have been?

GETTING REAL YOURSELF

1. Review the obstacles that hinder relational ministry. Do you think your ministry or church is guilty of any of these?

2. As you think about the leaders you work with (or the leaders you dream of working with), can you imagine ways to experience leadership together rather than you trying to "teach" or "impart" your knowledge of leadership. Write down any hands-on exercises—formal or informal—that you might do together.

3. How would you define success? Why is it so easy for churches—okay, all kinds of organizations—to get caught up in defining success by numbers? Can you think of ways success is defined in Scripture?

4. Could you write a success story (a "memo from below") about someone whose life has been changed by your ministry?

CHAPTER SIX

THE CHANGING CHURCH

For the church to effectively reach today's postmodern generations, it will have to embrace some strategic changes. Yet "change" and "church" can be mutually exclusive terms. The tendency of many churches is to settle in, get comfortable, and create "sacred cows" that over time become ineffective in discipling believers and reaching the unchurched. Many churches have embraced safety, security, and comfort instead of taking risks and stepping out in faith.

> There is nothing more difficult to undertake, more perilous to conduct, or more uncertain in its success than introducing change. Resistance to change is universal. It invades all classes and cultures. It seizes every generation by the throat and attempts to stop all forward movement toward progress. Many well-educated people, after being confronted with truth, have been unwilling to change their minds.[1]

Our goal in this chapter is to challenge you to ask yourself, "Why do we do what we do?" instead of settling for "We've always done it that way before." The critical concept to embrace as you move into the uncertain waters of change is to remember that "there is no methodological mandate in Scripture, just a Great Commission. The message is everything, the methods are incidental."[2]

We believe that one of the major challenges for the church heading into the twenty-first century is to implement the absolutes of the Christian faith with strategies that will effectively reach the emerging postmodern generations. The resistance to embracing changes will most likely have a lot to do with letting go of traditional methodology in favor of a more flexible approach.

Of course, we know that the message of the gospel is eternal and unchanging. We're not advocating changing the message, only the methods. The apostle Paul said in 1 Corinthians 9:22, "Whatever a person is like, I try to find common ground with him so that he will let me tell him about Christ and let Christ save him" (TLB). The changes that we're suggesting will help you find the "common ground" necessary to reach and minister to young adults effectively.

The world is undergoing sweeping changes. The old generation, the old leaders, the old perspectives and paradigms and ways of doing things are passing away. A new generation is emerging, and that generation is reshaping the world in profound ways. A new generation of Christians is arising around the world, and they are asking, "How do we meet the challenges of this new world? How do we carry the changeless Story of God into a rapidly changing world?"[3]

EIGHT CRUCIAL SHIFTS THE CHURCH MUST MAKE

1. WE NEED TO CHANGE HOW WE TEACH.
The new goal is to create a *learning* environment rather than maintaining a *teaching* orientation.

As we noted in chapter 2, Generation X and the Net Gen have been raised in a media-saturated environment that has accustomed them to small bits of information in rapid-fire succession from a variety of media. This onslaught of information comes primarily from cable TV and the Internet. Today, information is readily available and it has created in these generations a voracious appetite for more and more data, as well as an ability to assimilate that data in a short time span.

Xers want so many answers to so many questions from so many sources in such a hurry because our learning and communication skills were shaped by the forces of the information revolution.[4]

Having grown up in an information-saturated society, young adults have learned to assimilate information differently than previous generations did. That means that in the church we must change our teaching styles from a lecture-dominated format to a more varied approach. Our goal should be to communicate the Word of God by using a variety of media in creative ways that facilitate life change, not just the accumulation of more information. This is done primarily by means of video, drama, dance, music, and storytelling that emphasize both the journey and the destination.

The overarching goal for the church of the next generation is to create a focus on learning environments instead of classroom environments. A learning environment includes a variety of teaching media aimed at reaching a maximum number of individuals who learn differently. Some people learn better through pictures and illustrations, some through music, others through verbal communication. The goal is to create an environment in which learning is customized to an individual's learning style(s).

> My daily grade school homecoming was a five-part ritual: ride the school bus home, let myself in, lock the door behind me, grab some cookies and milk, and park in front of the television.[5]

Content is still important. But instead of disseminating information to be memorized or believed, we need to help young adults interact with the content of the message in real-life situations so that they leave better equipped to live out their faith in practical ways. Stories are key in making this connection. Stories help young adults go beyond mere retention to application of truth. (Pardon our aside while we make an admission: Stories are tough. We would have liked to fill this book with stories to illustrate every point we're trying to make, but it's not always that easy. Still, we encourage you to use stories as often as possible to help young adults apply their faith in their day-to-day lives.)

An easy way to visualize what we are talking about is to look at the table on the next page. Here we take a variety of church models and suggest that the experiential model is the most effective for communicating the gospel to postmodern generations.

Therefore, the learning environment that is most effective for a postmodern generation is more process-oriented. It integrates faith and practice into the journey of life and enables the learner to interact with the truths of the gospel through a variety of creative forms, placing a heavy emphasis on the arts.

2. WE NEED TO CHANGE HOW WE LEAD.

The new goal is to move toward an "I'll do it with you" model of leadership.

Like many Boomers, young adults simply don't respond to authoritative leadership that barks out orders, demands results, and micromanages tasks. While young adults need direction, they prefer guidance within the context of a relationship. Therefore, in order to lead today's young adults, we must continue moving toward a more relational style of leadership.

> The modern world is dying. A new postmodern world is emerging, and people today already look at the world through postmodern eyes. While the gospel message has not changed in two thousand years, our way of communicating that gospel must change if we are to be effective as we approach the beginning of a new millennium.[6]

Another word for relational leadership is *mentoring*. The biblical image of a leader is that of a servant, not an authority figure. Leaders of postmodern ministries need to see themselves as mentors. Let's define mentoring so that we know what we're talking about.

Mentoring
A mentor, as defined in the dictionary, is "a

Modern/Traditional Model	Modern/Seeker Model	Postmodern Model
Goal is knowledge transfer	Goal is obedience/change of behavior	Goal is integration of faith into real life
Focus on Bible knowledge	Focus on life skills and application	Focus on living out biblical knowledge in the context of community
Content/doctrine/beliefs	Felt needs/ministry/maturity	Faith as a journey and life change as a process
Church-based	Home-community-based	Service-based
Sunday only	Seven days a week	Journey of entire life
House curriculum only	Best available + other	Life experiences/God stories

wise, trusted advisor . . . a teacher or coach." You might think of mentoring as training a person within the context of a relationship. This is just what Jesus did. The key to mentoring in a church context is not just to model how to accomplish tasks and reach goals, but how to do that in a way that strengthens relationships among team members and facilitates the process of becoming more like Jesus Christ. A good mentoring relationship creates a safe place that encourages risk-taking, offers unconditional support, provides feedback on performance, and gives rewards and verbal encouragement at key growth points.

Mentoring is being effectively used in the corporate world largely because the skills necessary to succeed in the marketplace today are constantly in flux and need to be sharpened or changed on a regular basis. Training isn't static anymore; we must adapt to change and take a more flexible approach.

Keys to Mentoring
As a mentor of young adults, you need to keep ten key things in mind.

1. *Accept them.* Young adults have lived much of their lives being judged by their performance or lack thereof. If you want to endear yourself to members of these generations, you need to model unconditional love and acceptance.

2. *Love and care for them.* Nurture is a key ingredient to becoming whole and healthy people, yet it is one of the developmental necessities that

many young adults grow up without. Nurture is simply caring about people because you really love them and value them, not just because of what you can get out of them.

> Good leaders communicate a clear vision and articulate a precise direction. Good leaders provide performance feedback, inspire and encourage, and when necessary, discipline. Good leaders also mentor. Mentoring is the part of a leader's role that has growth as its outcome.[7]

3. *Support them outside the ministry.* Spend time with young adults on their turf, visit them at their work, take them out to coffee or lunch. Invite them over to your house to watch a movie or just hang out. To develop trust and confidence, young adults need a lot of time, more so than other groups, due largely to the neglect they experienced in childhood.

4. *Don't pamper them.* It's true that young adults crave love and concern, but they don't want to be babied. They prefer to be seen as self-starters, independent and self-motivated. The trick is to show them that you really care without overprotecting them.

5. *Keep your hands off, but be available.* Young adults need a lot of freedom and ability to do what they are asked to do. Don't micromanage them. Don't control them. Instead, guide and direct them. Build into their learning environment frequent pit stops where they talk with you to make sure they are staying on track. The key is to empower them to make decisions, then step away and coach.

6. *Affirm them.* Sincere words or appropriate expressions of affirmation go a long way with this generation. However, if you tell them you love them, you'd better mean it.

7. *Explain why.* Young adults have received a bum rap in that many think they are always doing things their own way. Young adults will do it your way if you explain to them why and if you ask for their honest feedback. If you listen to and value their opinions, they'll work hard.

> Leadership skill sets are shifting from training or growth skills to reproductive or multiplication skills. Leadership is more relational and experiential than organized and intellectual. The role of church leaders is to equip the saints for ministry rather than to get them to help staff do ministry. Power is diffused rather than concentrated and the leader's role is based on influence rather than position. Proclamation comes from the demonstrated power of a changed life, and the leader's right to be heard is earned through service and the story of his or her own life.[8]

8. *Equip them.* Much of the help young adults need is in developing a stronger set of interpersonal skills. Many defenses get triggered in team environments, and that can sabotage the whole process. The best way to equip them is to spend time with them in which they can watch you in action and see how you

respond to different obstacles and situations. Modeling the proper means of working through problems and dealing with difficult people will help them learn there is more to accomplishing a task than just accomplishing the task; there are people and feelings that need to be considered.

What gets these folks up in the morning is very different from why Baby Boomers woke up. They are not interested in climbing the conventional job ladder. Offer them an extra $10,000 per year, and they won't necessarily hop jobs. What's critical to Gen Xers is feeling they have an impact on what the business is doing. Titles don't matter to them, but job responsibilities do. They really want to feel as though they are contributing.[9]

9. *Set specific standards.* Young adults need to know what is expected of them, even though the leader doesn't necessarily have to set those expectations. One of the best ways to implement specific standards is to have them write out their own ministry job description and set their own standards. Young adults are often much more concrete and even stricter with themselves than you might be. Allowing them to set the standards (with you guiding the process) takes you out of the dreaded authority position and places you into the more influential coach position.

10. *Make teamwork fun and rewarding.* Be creative in putting together a team environment that's fun, challenging, and exciting. Take your team out to play laser tag or see a movie.

Violating these ten principles will add frustration and create an environment that will demotivate young adults and cause them not to want to be involved in ministry.

3. WE NEED TO MOVE FROM AN INWARD FOCUS TO AN OUTWARD FOCUS.
The mandate of the New Testament is to "go"— go out and impact your community and world for Jesus Christ. We all know and agree with the Great Commission, but how is that reflected in our ministries? One of the key issues in ministering with postmoderns is to tap into their desire to serve and help in the community. The church must encourage ministry to move outside its walls.

Chaos or disorder become the source of new order instead of something to be avoided. Chaos is desirable because it is the start of something new. Organizations, over time, do not have to wind down and go out of existence if they embrace chaos and learn new ways to achieve old things.[10]

When we allow young adults to take their passion for Christ to the streets, amazing things happen. Mike came to me one night after the service and said, "Ken, do we have a ministry to children with AIDS?"

I said, "No. What do you have in mind?"

Mike went on to describe to me his passion to work with children with AIDS and their families. I asked Mike if he knew what needed to be done, and he said he would find out. Not long after that initial conversation, Mike came back to me and shared his plan.

From that conversation, our ministry to children with AIDS was born. Each month we had young people going down to Children's Hospital in Washington, D.C., to work with these kids. That Thanksgiving we made sure that we provided some turkey dinners to the families from our annual Turkey Outreach.

Then, during the Christmas season, the hospital administrator said to Mike, "Another organization usually provides the children with Christmas gifts each year. However, this year they are unable to help. I hate to even ask you this, especially after your group was so generous at Thanksgiving, but do you think your group could help out in some way?"

Mike said, "Well, I don't know, but I'll find out."

So Mike told me the story and asked me what we could do. I asked Mike to put a plan together and get back to me. After Mike and his team thought about it, they decided to organize the receiving and distributing of gifts in the same way our church does for Angel Tree.

That week at the service I got up before our young adults and told them the situation. I asked that each of them take an angel off the tree in the lobby and bring the gifts back to the church over the next few weeks. That night, all two hundred angels were taken. Over the next few weeks the gifts started coming in. They brought action figures, remote-controlled cars, dolls, games, trucks. Our halls looked like a

Toys-Я-Us store! In fact, so many toys came in that the children had gifts throughout the whole rest of the year.

Not long after that, the hospital administrator came back to Mike, but this time with a different request. "Mike, every year we take the children with AIDS and their families away on a retreat to our camp in upstate New York. We were wondering if you'd be open to being the chaplain for our camp this year."

So Mike, who began with a vision to help children, became a spiritual leader for the sick children and their families. He led morning Bible studies, prayed with people, and pastored them all during that week. Amazing! You just don't know what will happen when you allow your people to take their passion to the streets.

Young adults want to make a difference in their community. They're not sure about changing the world, but they sure want to make a difference one life at a time. If the church will provide the freedom and opportunities for them to act, amazing things can happen.

4. WE NEED TO MOVE FROM MODERN APOLOGETICS TO POSTMODERN APOLOGETICS.

Postmodernism presents many challenges to the church, not the least of which is in the area of our approach to apologetics. One of the tenets of postmodernism is the tolerance of multiple paths to God. To postmodern ears, the Christian concept of "one way through Jesus Christ" seems arrogant. But the orthodoxy of Christian faith demands that we adhere to the absolute truths of God's Word. So how do we effectively use the tools of apologetics in a postmodern context?

The answer lies in moving from a modern approach to a postmodern approach. As we noted earlier, the modern worldview upholds the scientific method over faith in things unseen. In the modern mindset, if you can't taste it, touch it, see it, smell it, measure it, and test it in a laboratory, it's invalid. Within the modern mind, there's no tolerance for faith. Reason and logic prevail, and the establishment of something as true has been limited to only those posits that can be proven using some type of logical formula. To combat this modern mindset, the Christian community responded very effectively with what we call modern apologetics.

> Xers themselves insist they are anything but the "slackers," "hackers," or uncaring, body-pierced youth portrayed in mainstream media. They are boldly proving that today's young adults have purpose, determination and a plan for changing the face of America, one neighborhood at a time.[11]

To put it simply, modern apologetics uses historical evidence and archeological artifacts to prove the validity of the Christian faith. Books like *Evidence That Demands a Verdict* and *More Evidence That Demands a Verdict* by Josh McDowell, *Reasons to Believe* by R. C. Sproul, *A Case for Faith* by Clark Pinnock, as well as a host of others, provided the Christian community with sound arguments to prove the Christian faith.

> Service leaders agree they're experiencing significant increases in young adult volunteers. According to a 1992 survey by Independent Sector, an organization that monitors volunteerism and philanthropy, almost half of eighteen to twenty-four year olds volunteer, a figure which has been climbing steadily since 1988.[12]

However, as we continue to move into a more postmodern worldview, the modern approach is no longer the only means of proving something. For postmoderns, personal experience is just as valid as hard-core evidence. Apologist Alister McGrath notes these changes:

There has been a general collapse of confidence in the Enlightenment trust in the power of reason to provide foundations for a universally valid knowledge of the world, including God. Reason fails to deliver a morality suited to the real world in which we live. And with this collapse of confidence in universal and necessary criteria of truth, relativism and pluralism have flourished.[13]

In postmodern thinking, if I experience something as true, it's true for me, even though I might not be able to prove it to you by some logical means. As a result of this validation through experience, the rational apologetic that has served us so well in the past is becoming less and less effective within a postmodern context. We need to develop a new apologetic that convinces postmoderns. The apologetic that will be effective in today's context is one that demonstrates the reality of our faith within the context of relationships among believers and one that is demonstrated through service to our local communities.

One of the greatest evangelistic strategies—and one that the church has largely neglected—comes from the mouth of Jesus Himself: "Your strong love for each other will prove to the world that you are my disciples" (John 13:35, TLB). Here, Jesus gives us a clear means of relational apologetics as we love each other within the context of the church and as the unchurched see the reality of our faith lived out.

Unfortunately, much of what has shaped the attitude of postmoderns against the church are the scandals and fighting they have seen within the church. Gustavo Gutierrez, a Catholic Peruvian theologian, notes: "The church cannot be a prophet in our day if she herself is not turned to Christ. She does not have the right to talk against others when she herself is a cause of scandal in her interpersonal relations and her internal structures."[14] If the church wants to reach postmodern young adults, we must begin living out our faith within our biblical communities that reflect the heart of Jesus.

The other way we live out a relational apologetic is through service evangelism. (In chapter 12, we've provided a number of service evangelism projects for you to implement, but here we would like to unpack the philosophy behind them.) The concept of service evangelism is nothing new. The Salvation Army and others have been doing it for years. However, what we're proposing involves some new twists.

> Biblical communities are simply congregations or small groups where believers live out the *"one another"* commands found in the New Testament.

Steve Sjogren, pastor at the Vineyard Church in Cincinnati, Ohio, has been influential in our thinking in this regard. Steve has built his church from zero to more than five thousand simply by going out into the community and serving people. When Steve first arrived in Cincinnati, he started going to local bars during the day and asking the managers if he could wash their toilets. Now, if I'm an unchurched person and I hear that a pastor is cleaning toilets in a bar, I'm just a little intrigued. Over the years, Steve and his congregation have touched more than a million people within the greater Cincinnati area by serving them in a variety of ways.

At Frontline where I (Ken) serve, we have adapted and used this model with great success. The basic premise is quite simple: Go out and serve in your local community by washing cars, raking leaves, shoveling snow, giving out gift certificates to a local ice cream shop on a hot summer night, or handing out free ice-cold Cokes in front of a stadium on a hot summer day. When asked what you're doing, respond by saying, "We're just sharing God's love in a practical way."

The Church, surprisingly, may find itself in a position to teach Xers something of utmost importance: countercultural witness in the name of faith. For example, at its best, it can teach concern for the poor and excluded, care for immigrants, and economic justice for all. Our generation, which so frequently takes ironic stances as it reappropriates the materialism it has been given, might even reject such materialism in favor of a countercultural witness if the Church toward which it is so skeptical inspired it to do so.[15]

What we've found is that when you go out to serve others in the name of Christ, it takes them by surprise and you find them asking you about Jesus. When you approach a person with a modern apologetic statement like "Jesus is the only way to God," it raises a lot of questions like "Well, if there is a God, why is there evil in the world?" or "What about the native in some distant land who has never heard about Jesus Christ—is he going to hell?" or "What about dinosaurs and the Bible?" or "How can you say that there is only one way to heaven?" just to name a few. Instead, when you're serving someone, the genuineness of your actions demands a different set of questions like "Why are you doing this?" or "What's in this for you?"

Rather than being defensive about difficult questions, service evangelism creates an environment where the person being served asks you why, providing a great opportunity for you to share your "God story." The bottom line for many young adults is that they are tired of all the lip service, clichés, and pat answers they have seen and heard from some Christians. They want to see us live out the reality of our faith first. They want to hear our God story, where we admit, like the blind man Jesus healed, "I don't have all the answers, all I know is that I was blind, and now I see" (see John 9:25). Serving in the community creates credibility among the unchurched, and with that credibility established, they'll raise questions with an open spirit.

This doesn't mean that modern apologetics have to be discarded. Instead, modern apologetics takes on a more effective role in the discipleship process. Postmodern apologetics start the process as we demonstrate the reality of our faith within our own internal relationships within the church and build relationships with the unchurched through acts of service.

I love the story of Paul Yonggi Cho's church in South Korea. Dr. Cho told his small-group leaders to identify one person at their workplace that they could serve in some simple way—things like holding the elevator, carrying something when another's hands are full, getting coffee for a co-worker. The results were astounding. On average, it took only four months from the day the group leader identified a person to serve until the time that person received Christ and became a part of the local church. The church was seeing ten thousand conversions *a month* from Buddhism to Christianity simply by looking for opportunities to serve others. Relational apologetics work!

5. WE MUST MOVE BEYOND COMMITTEES TO RELATIONAL TEAMS.

Traditionally, task accomplishment within a church was done through committees. However, to accomplish tasks effectively utilizing the gifts and skills of young adults requires a different approach: relational teams. A committee makes decisions; teams produce results. Committees have countless meetings; teams have strategic meetings that target goals, brainstorm potential barriers, and discover effective means for breaking through them. Committees focus primarily on tasks; relational teams focus on accomplishing tasks within the context of developing healthy relationships among team members. We examine the elements of relational teams and their importance within the broader context of young adult ministry in chapter 9.

6. WE MUST MOVE AWAY FROM A CULTURAL THEOLOGY OF THE CHURCH TO A RELATIONAL ONE.

Maybe you've heard the cliché "People don't have a problem with Jesus; they just don't like His friends." This cliché is definitely true for young adults. Many of them have inherited the anti-establishment and countercultural mindset pervasive among Boomers during the 1960s, and they have projected this attitude toward the church largely due to the hypocrisy they have seen. We talk of love, yet we "shoot our wounded." We talk of brotherhood and family, yet we live out a prac-

tical racism. But perhaps the greatest source of anger toward the church from many young adults is their perception that the church has domesticated Jesus. Nowhere does this feeling come out more plainly than in music videos.

> The team is a basic unity of performance for most organizations. It melds together the skills, experiences, and insights of several people. It is the natural complement to individual initiative and achievement because it engenders higher levels of commitment to common ends.[16]

The band Soundgarden wrote a song called "Black Hole Sun" in which they pit Jesus against their perception of the established church. The video of the song makes the point even clearer.

> In one revealing scene, a minister in a white tuxedo bends down delicately, displaying the leash that he holds in his hand. A young lamb waits with gentle expectation, tethered to the other end. In slow motion, the preacher reaches out a hand that holds a baby bottle, squirting a milky, creamy substance. After he places the bottle in the lamb's mouth, the tiny animal sucks the mystery liquid.[17]

Tom Beaudoin, in his book *Virtual Faith,* gives us his interpretation of this music video. "Perhaps more than any recent generation, Xers see behind the curtain; they scoff at the minister's pretense that this Lamb of God is on a leash. As if Jesus and His message can be reduced to such simpleminded domesticity."[18]

In another scene in the same video, "an elderly man rests on hands and knees like a domesticated animal, poised in front of his television, observing the face of the bearded minister. This is the image of the televangelist with whom Xers are familiar. The steady fall in the 1980s of preachers—victims of sexual scandal and monetary mismanagement—is a standard part of the Xer grudge against religious institutions."[19]

Tragically, it seems to many young adults that instead of the church being a place to encounter God, it has been reduced to parks and recreation for the suburban middle class. As George Barna says so well: "Americans are seeking first and foremost a deity who will handle their consumer-driven wants, needs, dreams, hurts, and disappointments."[20] But in order to bring young adults into the church, we must replace our culturally derived theology of the church with a Christological theology that unleashes the radical, countercultural example of Jesus Christ. We need to help young adults see the church not as an institution but as the body of Christ and the primary vehicle by which God communicates His redemptive message to the people of the world.

7. WE MUST MOVE FROM UNINTENTIONAL TO INTENTIONAL MINISTRY.

Effective ministry is intentional ministry; it doesn't happen by accident. Too many churches take a ready-fire-aim approach. They shoot an arrow at the side of the barn and then run up and draw a bull's-eye around it and declare, "That's where we wanted to hit it." For an effective ministry with postmodern generations, that type of approach won't work. In order to be intentional, it is critical that you have alignment within four key areas as seen on page 69 (adapted from *The Power of Alignment*).[21]

Imagine a ministry where every participant shares a common vision of the purpose, core values, and goals of the ministry. Imagine a group of believers working together in such a way that they all know their unique role and how they contribute to accomplishing the so-called "main thing" of your ministry. Imagine being on a team where everyone genuinely cares for each other and works together to accomplish key tasks that really impact the lives of others. Sounds too good to be true, doesn't it? Well, it's not; it's the result of alignment.

Alignment is the integration of strategic tasks, core values, relational teams, and the kingdom of God. Notice that the circle representing "The Main Thing" is divided into four quadrants. Quadrant one (Q1) is composed of the elements that make up the kingdom of God. These elements are the Great Commission (which gives instructions on what to do in the kingdom of God) and the Great Commandment (which tells us how we are to build the kingdom within the context of relationships).

Quadrant two (Q2) consists of the relational teams that execute the strategic tasks. Relational teams are equally as concerned with group connectedness as they are with the completion of strategic tasks.

Quadrant three (Q3) consists of the core values that shape your ministry. Your core values determine what you believe about ministry—what you do in ministry and why you do it. They help you stay focused and intentional.

Quadrant four (Q4) consists of the strategic tasks that you will use to flesh out your core values and build the kingdom of God.

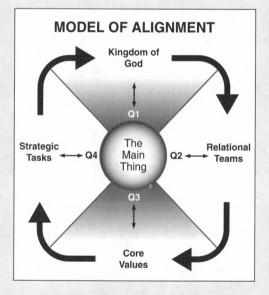

MODEL OF ALIGNMENT

"The Main Thing" is the overall goal of your ministry. Notice how accomplishing the Main Thing—your ministry's overall mission—involves each of the four quadrants.

Alignment is one of the most powerful tools you can use in transitioning from doing ministry by chance to doing ministry on purpose.

8. WE NEED TO MOVE FROM BUILDING PROGRAMS TO EQUIPPING PEOPLE.

The old model for young adult ministry centered on programs. If you wanted to do a young adult ministry, the first step was to build a program. We'd like to suggest a different model—a people-equipping model. Ephesians 4:11-12 says, "It was he [Christ] who gave some to be apostles, some to be prophets, some to be evangelists, and some to be pastors and teachers, to prepare God's people for works of service, so that the body of Christ may be built up." The apostle Paul is very clear. The job description of pastors is to equip people to do the ministry, not build programs themselves and then recruit volunteers to help out. The following chart can

People-Driven Ministry	*Program-Driven Ministry*
Leadership	Management
Effectiveness	Efficiency
Spontaneity	Structure
Discernment	Measurement
Dreams	Program needs
Causes	Effects/symptoms
Release/empowerment	Control
Role of pastor: mentor	Role of pastor: program director
Transformation	Transaction
Investment	Expense
Principles	Techniques
Synergy	Compromise
Abundance	Scarcity
Relational teams	Committees
Journey	Destination

help you understand the distinctions between a people-driven and a program-driven ministry.[22]

The people-driven ministry model builds healthy young adults who in turn build a healthy ministry. It unleashes people to live out their God-given dreams in a variety of ways that facilitate life change in others, glorify Jesus Christ, and build the kingdom of God.

These eight changes are just a few of the key strategies that we feel are necessary to build an effective ministry with postmodern generations. Our hope is that this thinking will move you forward as you contemplate needed changes in your church. "Life is change. Growth is optional. Choose wisely."[23]

GETTING REAL YOURSELF

1. It's a simple question: Do you think the church needs to change in order to reach young adults?

2. How does your own church need to change?

3. Do you think the changes we've outlined are just semantics, or do you think they're real? Why do you think that?

BIBLICAL FOUNDATIONS FOR LEADERS

By this point you're starting the seventh chapter of the book and probably brimming with ideas. It's time to start your young adult ministry, right? Not quite yet. Your leadership team is vital to the success of your ministry, and you must make sure both you and they understand their important roles. The common thread that runs through all the stories we've heard of failed young adult programs is the lack of leadership. And failed leadership often stems from a misunderstanding of the biblical basis for the ministry.

Does the Christian faith have the resources to face the postmodern challenge, withstand it, even learn from it?[1]

How can you build a biblically sound ministry? You start by choosing capable leaders who understand God's purpose for their leadership. What role do leaders play in the ministry? What specific jobs do leaders do? Which is more important: "doing the job right" by yourself, or teaching others to do the ministry? An understanding of biblical principles will answer these questions for your leaders and clarify for them their vital role in the success of the ministry.

To get a better view of leadership, consider the following verses:

He [Christ] gave some as apostles, and some as prophets, and some as evangelists, and some as pastors and teachers, for the equipping of the saints for the work of service, to the building up of the body of Christ; until we all attain to the unity of the faith, and of the knowledge of the Son of God, to a mature man, to the measure of the stature which belongs to the fullness of Christ. As a result, we are no longer to be children, tossed here and there by waves, and carried about by every wind of doctrine, by the trickery of men, by craftiness in deceitful scheming; but speaking the truth in love, we are to grow up in all aspects into Him, who is the head, even Christ, from whom the whole body, being fitted and held together by that which every joint supplies, according to the proper working of each individual part, causes the growth of the body for the building up of itself in love. (Ephesians 4:11-16, NASB)

Intimacy is at the heart of competence. It has to do with understanding, with believing, and with practice. It has to do with the relationship to one's work.[2]

These verses show us that our job as leaders is to "equip the saints" (the Christian members of our group) so they can do the work of service. What a common mistake it is for leaders to do the work of service while the other members look on, unequipped to participate in their own call to ministry!

FIVE PRINCIPLES FOR GODLY LEADERSHIP

The following principles will help your leaders incorporate the biblical doctrine of "equipping the saints" into your young adult ministry. All of the principles have practical applications that will act as a guide for how to properly manage your young adult min-istry. There will always be new gurus and new ideas for leadership and management, but these principles are ageless and act as the foundation for practical programming for the renewal and growth of your members.

1. THE STARTING POINT OF MINISTRY IS GOD.

Too often, ministries start when people see needs and start programs to meet them. But the Bible makes it clear that the starting point of all ministry is God. God's dream for each Christian is to be an extraordinary human (Ephesians 5:18-20; 1 Peter 2:21; 1 John 3:16). Any kind of Christian growth is totally beyond the realm of human effort. Jesus said, "Apart from me you can do nothing" (John 15:5).

Ministry and spiritual growth are things that God does by means of the Holy Spirit (1 Thessalonians 1:5). What does this mean? It means that as a leader you recognize it is ultimately God who instigates spiritual growth in your life and in another person's life. The key is to *be* the people of God before you *do* the work of God.

Before we do any kind of ministry, we must submit ourselves to God and understand that our identity is wrapped up in Him. The ultimate responsibility lies not in what you do, but in who you are connected to. As a Christian, you have no choice whether or not to be a minister; we're all ministers (Ephesians 4:11-12). The choice comes down to how you support your ministry. Paul supported his ministry by making tents. Some of us will support our ministry by receiving a salary from offerings and tithes, while others will "make tents" in nonchurch jobs.

Your leaders need to know how important it is for them to connect with God. Their growth is from God the Holy Spirit. We get ourselves into trouble when we start to believe that our success in young adult programming is all about our creativity and planning. Christian growth begins with God. Your cleverness, your creative use of video, even your funny stories have little to do with how much others grow in Christ. The best you can offer is to help people understand how to be connected to God and rely on Him.

compass *n.* an instrument for showing direction

— *Webster's New World Dictionary*

2. THE COMPASS FOR MINISTRY IS THE BIBLE. The Bible is God's Word to us—period. "All Scripture is inspired by God and profitable for teaching, for reproof, for correction, for training in righteousness" (2 Timothy 3:16-17, NASB). It is the encouragement for Christian faith and practice.

The Bible was never meant to be just a book of doctrines. It's a book of stories about real-life people and their encounters with God. By recording their struggles, the Bible encourages us to live in a committed relationship with God. We strive to follow their example where appropriate, and to follow God's commands where so directed.

Seek the LORD while He may be found;
Call upon Him while He is near.
Let the wicked forsake his way,
And the unrighteous man his thoughts;
And let him return to the LORD,
And He will have compassion on him;
And to our God,
For He will abundantly pardon.
"For My thoughts are not your thoughts,
Neither are your ways My ways,"
declares the LORD.
"For as the heavens are higher than the earth,
So are My ways higher than your ways,
And My thoughts than your thoughts.
For as the rain and the snow come down from heaven,
And do not return there without watering the earth,
And making it bear and sprout,
And furnishing seed to the sower and bread to the eater;
So shall My word be which goes forth from My mouth;
It shall not return to Me empty,
Without accomplishing what I desire,
And without succeeding in the matter for which I sent it."

(Isaiah 55:6-11, NASB)

Because the Bible is the basis for Christian practice, it should serve as the guide for our methods of ministry (2 Corinthians 1:12). In the same way, the Bible helps us distinguish between absolutes and nonabsolutes. Absolutes are biblical principles that do not vary with time or culture. Nonabsolutes are the specific applications that may vary with time or culture. For example, the Bible says, "Christians should gather together" (see Hebrews 10:24-25); it does not say "Christians should gather together on Sunday mornings, wear suits or dresses, and sit in pews." The absolutes are eternal and unchanging, but we should have great freedom to change the nonabsolutes depending on the need of a particular situation.

> Resist the temptation to establish rules and to design "boxes" for people's spiritual lives. Resist the temptation to do the Holy Spirit's work for him. Hands off! Let him change them, remold them, reshape them, activate them. Get them to know him and he'll do the work in them.[3]

3. THE PRIME FOCUS OF MINISTRY IS PEOPLE, NOT PROGRAMS.

God created us for relationships, not tasks; Christ died for people, not programs; the church is not a building or a program but God's people on earth. Programs can't exist for their own sakes; they must only exist to bring people into relationship with God. It's tempting to think that ministry is about getting things done. Wrong. We do ministry so that people will grow in Christ and so that their relationships with each other will grow. Our goal is to encourage people in their journeys at all times. The decisions we make will at all times be in the best interest of people, not programs.

> For God so loved the world that He gave His only begotten Son, that whoever believes in Him should not perish but have eternal life. (John 3:16, NKJV)

The first words of Jesus' public ministry were "The time has come . . . the kingdom of God is near" (Mark 1:15). Throughout His entire earthly ministry, Jesus relentlessly proclaimed the kingdom. He even told His followers to seek the kingdom before their own basic needs.

> So then, just as you received Christ Jesus as Lord, continue to live in him, rooted and built up in him, strengthened in the faith as you were taught, and overflowing with thankfulness. (Colossians 2:6-7)

The most telling passages indicating the priority of the kingdom are found in the opening and closing chapters of the book of Acts. The opening chapter sums up Jesus' post-resurrection ministry with His disciples by simply stating that He spent forty days speaking to them about the kingdom (1:3). (Don't forget that Acts 1 describes the prime time of Jesus' ministry. It answers the question "If Jesus had just one more opportunity to teach, how would He use it?" The fact is that He didn't zero in on church growth; rather, He taught about the kingdom.)

Later, at the conclusion of Acts, Paul is under house arrest in Rome, where for two years "boldly . . . he preached the kingdom of God" (28:31).

Between the events of Acts 1 and those of Acts 28, Christians planted a lot of churches. Because the church is the primary vehicle of God's work on earth, it would be difficult to overstate its importance. And that is exactly the point. The church or the program is the vehicle; the kingdom is the objective. The kingdom is about people and relationships.

> Mere change is not growth. Growth is the synthesis of change and continuity, and where there is no continuity there is no growth.[4]

4. THE GOAL OF MINISTRY IS GROWTH.

It's been said that the church today is six miles wide and a quarter-inch deep. Young adults are tired of what they perceive as inauthentic faith. To overcome that perception, effective young adult ministries attempt to encourage a deeper faith in people—not just others—but ourselves as well.

In the Great Commission passage of Matthew 28:19-20, the process of encouraging others to deeper faith is called disciple making. One sign of someone becoming a disciple is that he or she begins to live by the principles of the Bible. That process begins and ends at different places, but here are the elements that stand as part of the journey.

> They accuse us of arrested development because we have not lost a taste we had in childhood. But surely arrested development consists not in refusing to lose old things but in failing to add new things?[5]

A progressive commitment to Christ, evident day in and day out: This is what Jesus referred to when He said we would have to "take up [our] cross daily, and follow [Him]" (Luke 9:23, NASB).

A progressive commitment to the family of God: "If anyone does not provide for his own, and especially for those of his household, he has denied the faith, and is worse than an unbeliever" (1 Timothy 5:8, NASB).

> A tree doesn't grow because it adds rings: a train doesn't grow by leaving one station behind and puffing on to the next.[6]

A progressive commitment to the body of Christ: "While we have opportunity, let us do good to all men, and especially to those who are of the household of the faith" (Galatians 6:10, NASB).

> And we proclaim Him, admonishing every man and teaching every man with all wisdom that we may present every man complete in Christ. And for this purpose also I labor, striving according to His power, which mightily works within me. (Colossians 1:28-29, NASB)

A progressive commitment to evangelism: "You shall receive power when the Holy Spirit has come upon you; and you shall be My witnesses both in Jerusalem, and in all Judea and Samaria, and even to the remotest part of the earth" (Acts 1:8, NASB). An effective young adult ministry will be committed to mission and have a concern for all people, which is a natural byproduct of loving God and often happens spontaneously. A young adult ministry will then draw the alienated and postmodern person to its accepting, reconciling warmth, and when the people of God are sent out into the world, they will be what C. S. Lewis calls "a good infection for Christ"[7] and attract people to Him.

5. THE ENVIRONMENT FOR MINISTRY IS TEAMWORK, NOT INDIVIDUALISM.

Jesus said the world would know we are His disciples if we love one another (John 13:34-35). He also said the world will know He was sent by the Father when it sees the unity of the believers (John 17:23). Nowhere do we see this played out better than in Acts 2:42-47, where the people were so committed that they gave and shared freely of everything they had (money, land, food, and so on).

> When we make the choice to work toward people-oriented ministries, we build teams in which everybody has a role. When we focus on building successful programs, only the few superstars have roles, while the rest watch.[8]

We have repeatedly referred to the concept that "everyone is a minister." Many churches write this on their banners or in their bulletins, but few live it out. So let us say it again: Ministry is not just for the few but for everyone. God has gifted every Christian (Romans 12:3-8; 1 Corinthians 12:7-11; Ephesians 4:11-12). Being committed to team ministry, we acknowledge that God has called some to leadership. We recognize there will be a first among the equals, but our emphasis is on the equals, not the first.

> For just as we have many members in one body and all the members do not have the same function, so we, who are many, are one body in Christ, and individually members one of another. (Romans 12:4-5, NASB)

CHAPTER EIGHT

THE TARGET

It's Tuesday night just after 7:00 and the warehouse-turned-sanctuary is nearly full. The early birds are milling around sipping lattes while a musician checks sound levels for the concert he'll give later in the coffee bar tucked into the lobby.

Out in the surrounding business park, Day-Glo-vested traffic attendants—many sporting berets, pierced eyebrows, shaved heads, and various other fashion statements—are squeezing cars into every available parking spot. By 7:17, when the weekly worship service starts, there will be 1,500 or so of the devoted and the curious—and almost no one over thirty—ready to participate in TNL's two-part service: an hour of standing and singing followed by an hour of sitting and listening to a twenty-seven-year-old preacher.

We've mentioned it before: this is The Next Level Church, a ministry targeted at Generation X (yes, the generation reputed to have short attention spans), started by Xers for Xers, although anyone is welcome. In less than four years, the former young adult Bible study has grown to include small groups, a children's ministry, local and international missions, and Christian education opportunities.

The leaders of TNL are grateful for the rapid growth of their ministry, but not altogether surprised. Before this ministry began, the leadership team studied all the ministries they could so as to learn how best to target their ministry at the group they wanted to reach. Every aspect of the ministry, from the unconventional Tuesday night time slot to the coffee bar to the mission program, is the result of targeting.

Targeting is a process that allows a ministry team to make sure its programs will be effective and that they will hit their intended mark. Other organizations have used names like the "planning grid," the "ministry growth strategy," or the "planning arrow." We've chosen to use the image of a bull's-eye to indicate that there are several layers that precede the ultimate goal of making disciples of postmodern young adults.

(Okay, okay. We've talked about developing people, not programs. But you knew we'd eventually talk about young adult ministry as a program, didn't you? Well, you were right. But whenever we use the word "program," think back to the times we've talked about alternatives to programs because that's more what we mean. "Program" is just a convenient label for your people- and relationship-oriented ministry.)

> If you aim at nothing, you will hit it every time. If you aim at everything, you hit nothing.

INTENTIONAL MINISTRY

You have a choice in how you program your ministry. You can take a "blast" approach, aiming at everything and often hitting nothing. Or you can be intentional. When I (Rich) first started in young adult ministry, I read books and other ministries' newsletters. I decided we should have a large group meeting, singing, a message, small groups, and outreach to the unchurched.

Without realizing it, we had taken a "blast" approach, and before long, everyone was burned out. Only twenty-five young adults attended regularly. We tried to do everything all at once and ended up not doing anything very well.

The better way to pursue ministry is to take a targeted approach and zero in on specific, well-designed goals. To target your approach, you take time to find out what you do best and invest your time, people, and resources there.

In the young adult ministry I just mentioned, we decided to continue our main meeting but we dropped most of the other programs. We simply didn't have enough people. We hung on to small groups because they created community. By focusing on just those two things, our ministry became intentional and began to grow.

Unintentional ministry can lead to an overly busy leadership staff. Urgent matters take up disproportionate amounts of time. An unfocused ministry will often shift its attention away from the Head of the Church to one of its members, often the highly visible pastor. On the other hand, intentional ministry allows people to recognize the needs of those around them and carefully aim their ministry at meeting those needs, rather than spraying a blast of programs and hoping some people find them meaningful.

THE TARGET

How can you learn to be intentional in your planning? How can you make sure your programs are hitting their mark? In the next several pages we will describe how targeting can help you plan and execute your ministry goals. As you proceed through this material, imagine a bull's-eye target with nine levels of concentric circles.

BULL'S EYE
SET GOALS
IDENTIFY YOUR RESOURCES
IDENTIFY THE OBSTACLES
DREAM TOGETHER
IDENTIFY YOUR OBJECTIVES
IDENTIFY YOUR MISSION
IDENTIFY YOUR CORE VALUES
PRAY

LEVEL 2: IDENTIFY YOUR CORE VALUES

Core values are the guidelines that determine your ministry's direction. Stephen Covey, author of *First Things First,* calls core values a compass that gives you a "true north." Don't be surprised if your programs, staffing decisions, budget determinations, and many other areas of your ministry fall into place once you have established your ministry's "true north." Your core values will become clear to you when you have assessed which of the community's—or world's—needs you feel most passionate about and equipped to address.

Understanding How to Pray

- Ask yourself what needs exist in the world around you.
- Ask yourself what it is that makes you weep, like Nehemiah did. What is it that makes you angry and makes you want to do something to change it?
- Make a commitment to pray about these things.
- Research the contributing factors and related issues.
- Talk to friends about your concern.
- Gather together others who are interested in the same issues and then pray together.

You know you're weak in this area if . . .

- your leaders are never quite sure why a ministry exists.
- your leaders are not sure what needs are being met.
- your leadership structure is unclear.
- people feel confused about their role in this ministry.

LEVEL 1: PRAY

The first step in establishing an intentional ministry—the outer ring of the target—is prayer. The book of Nehemiah provides a biblical model for intentional ministry. In one of the opening passages, the author describes how Nehemiah wept when he heard about the condition of the walls of Jerusalem. He was moved by a need. The best ministry comes from the heart, whether you feel moved by some person or some project. Intentional ministries will be conceived through many means. But they share the characteristic of being born from a deeply burdening need.

The Mission Team: A Continuing Saga

Once upon a time there was a young adult ministry whose members had a small problem. Each person in the group got two weeks of vacation a year but had no one to spend it with. Even those who were roommates didn't generally have the same vacation schedule. They decided they wanted to plan a group vacation. With no specific ideas in mind, they set out to plan a vacation that would seem worthwhile to the young adults in the group.

A team of six was formed to explore the idea. At the first meeting, they decided not to make any plans at all but to use the time to pray and worship God. The prayer meeting turned out to be a great time of fellowship, and another was scheduled for the following week.

Week after week they, a group of ever-better friends, met and prayed about their "vacation." Soon details began to emerge from their prayers. They became increasingly burdened with the sense that their vacation should mean something to God's kingdom. Soon it became apparent that this "vacation" was turning into a ministry of its own.

continued . . .

I (Rich) was once asked to come in and work with a young adult ministry in a local church. I agreed and asked to meet with the young adults themselves. When we met, I asked a simple question: "What does your ministry exist to do? Why do you have this ministry?" The room was silent. They were not sure why they were meeting.

The next day I met with the leadership team and we debriefed the previous night's meeting. I asked what needs they felt were

Understanding How to Identify Your Core Values

- Ask questions or do surveys.
- Meet with people and ask them what their needs are. For example, ask a single parent to lunch to learn that person's spiritual, social, educational, and relational needs.
- Search the Internet.
- Drive around your community and see what needs exist.
- Have a professional survey done that shows the demographics of your church's community.
- Look at the U.S. Census Bureau statistics for your area.
- Ask a clerk or official at City Hall what needs you might address in your city. Many city governments have volunteer coordinators or at least a listing of organizations that regularly need volunteers and other help.

You know you're weak in this area if . . .

- your ministry is too "me-focused." You are interested only in meeting, not in meeting needs.
- the people involved in this ministry say their own needs are not being met.

being addressed in the group. Again, they were not sure.

Then I changed course and asked them what their own needs were. They listed social needs along with a need to understand the Bible and be challenged to live according to its direction. I pointed out that their own needs were probably the same as the needs of their peers in the group. From there, we had a fruitful discussion that helped them identify their ministry's particular role and the needs they felt called and equipped to address.

In any ministry, the driving force is the desire to meet certain perceived needs. Needs are the catalysts that propel you toward intentional and effective ministry. (Of course, an urgency to meet needs is not enough to sustain or properly direct your ministry. The shortcut between identifying a need and starting a ministry outreach is littered with failed programs.)

Needs are the "why" of ministry. Once you know the needs you want to address, you can clearly identify a special role for your ministry and the core values that will steer your programming. Take time to assess these needs thoroughly. Divide the process into physical needs, relational needs, spiritual needs, and community needs. Some of these will overlap; the important thing is that you list as many needs as you can identify.

A word of caution: Be sure you don't identify the needs of a group without talking with them and involving them. Be sure to conduct research among those you hope to reach.

In addition to meeting with the people who

The Mission Team, *continued . . .*

As a result of their prayer sessions, the friends decided to go on a short-term mission trip. They formed a core team and listed all the needs they felt moved to address. The team began to grasp the role of the short-term mission by observing the following needs:

- Young adults want to test whether they have a genuine call to the mission field.
- Young adults want to build relationships with each other and with other peoples of the world.
- Christians need a challenge to be wise stewards of their time, money, and energy.
- The gospel needs to be shared.
- World poverty needs to be addressed.

Once the team knew the needs that moved them, they could assess their values. Based on the above, they came up with the following core values:

1. *Relationships:* Our ministry should focus on healthy relationships with other people and with God.

2. *Discipline:* Our ministry should challenge members to grow in the spiritual disciplines of stewardship and service.

3. *Evangelism:* Our ministry should teach people to be passionate about spreading the gospel and addressing human suffering.

continued . . .

are part of the ministry, you can also meet with other pastors and ministries in the area or make calls around the country to similar ministries. Even if you have a young adult ministry with hundreds of people in attendance, you still need to ask how you are doing at being intentional in all aspects of your ministry.

LEVEL 3: IDENTIFY YOUR MISSION

When NASA launched the space shuttle with John Glenn aboard, it did so to accomplish a specific set of purposes. Some shuttle missions involve launching a satellite, starting a second vessel on its way toward some distant planet, or carrying hundreds of scientific experiments to be conducted in the absence of gravity. Whatever the reason, each shuttle is launched for the purpose of accomplishing a certain mission—an intentional mission. NASA typically refers to the "shuttle's mission" when discussing a particular voyage.

The same is true in launching an intentional ministry. You shouldn't take off until you have determined your specific mission. A mission statement should tell people where you are headed.

Understanding How to Identify Your Mission

- Make sure it's easy to understand! Do not make your mission statement long and complex. Do not use big words that no one can understand. And do not use language that's understandable only in your church community. For example, avoid words like "redeeming" and "fellowship" or phases like "share the gospel" if they are meaningless to your audience. Instead, try "lovable," "friendship," and "telling people the story of Jesus Christ."
- Make sure it is *your* mission, not someone else's. You might be tempted to use someone else's statement. If you've seen one you like, why not copy it? If the ministry you're going to do is in a different setting and you are different people, how can you borrow someone else's idea?
- Make sure you believe it. Don't use a statement just because it sounds good. Make sure you understand and believe it.
- Change it when *you* change! Don't feel like you can never change your statement. It's meant to serve you, not box you in. When you decide you want to try a new direction, rework your statement. That way you are being thoughtful and intentional about what you are going to do. Be sure to do this with other team members and help everyone stay informed.
- List all the needs you identified earlier on a large sheet of paper. Using these words, write two sentences that describe what you intend to do. Start the sentences with "Our passion is to . . . ," "We intend to . . . ," or "We exist to . . . "
- Take your time. Get away with your leaders for a day or weekend to a relaxed setting and thoughtfully prepare your mission statement.

You know you're weak in this area if . . .

- the ministry has no clear direction.
- those in leadership cannot articulate the focus of the ministry.
- observers of your ministry cannot immediately identify the needs you are attempting to address.

continued...

How does a mission statement do this? You should be able to state—in a broad sense—what your mission is all about in a single sentence. This lets others know where you are headed and helps keep you on track. It keeps you from becoming tempted to always put your attention on what seems most urgent. It also gives you permission to say no to any direction that may not be appropriate to accomplishing your overall mission.

Your mission statement should also tell people who you are. In addition to your purpose, it should state the reasons you feel called and qualified by God to address these needs.

Finally, your mission statement should reflect your overall purpose for existing as a ministry. If you are in ministry to build people (not programs), your mission statement should clearly state how you plan to serve people.

LEVEL 4: IDENTIFY YOUR OBJECTIVES

Now you're ready to aim your ministry toward a more specific set of objectives. Objectives need to be broad enough to permit flexibility in designing your ministry yet identifiable enough to provide guidance. For example, in the early sixties, President John F. Kennedy announced that the United States was "going to the moon." Most people didn't care if it was the dark side or the light side; they just wanted the U.S. to get there! You can use this same principle with your objectives. An intentional, focused ministry starts by aiming at broad objectives first.

One of the objectives in your ministry might be "leadership training." This objective isn't specific. It can be measured. It is broad enough to allow your leaders to participate in and develop many specific ministries that would constitute leadership training, but at the same time it provides an objective for your ministry so you won't be pulled off the course that has been set. With leadership training as an objective, you can ask yourself at each juncture, "Will this new program train leaders?"

Understanding How to Identify Your Objectives

- Have multiple objectives. If you have only one target, you fall out of balance and fail to address some important needs. When you aim toward several related objectives, you're less likely to develop tunnel vision. We suggest you have no more than five objectives and no fewer than three.
- Objectives must maximize your resources and your efforts. For this reason, don't be random in choosing objectives.
- Objectives must be born out of your stated mission. They cannot be abstract. These are commitments through which the mission will be carried out. It is through the objectives that we can measure our effectiveness.
- Objectives should be functional. These objectives must be specific enough to take you somewhere. They must be intentional enough to keep you motivated. Objectives, like far-off galaxies, must cause us to dream about how we will reach them.
- Start with only a few objectives, then add more later.
- Avoid dangerous objectives. For example, avoid being too self-centered in the selection of objectives and aiming only to meet your own needs.

Objectives should tell you where to invest your time, energy, and resources. They define where you are going so you can concentrate your efforts. They can also give you a way to measure what has been done. Objectives are critical for focusing an intentional ministry.

You know you're weak in this area if . . .

- the ministry tries to do everything.
- few people feel the ministry addresses their particular needs.
- you are tempted to add new programs without considering how they fit your overall mission.

The Mission Team, *continued* . . .

The team planning the short-term mission program came up with these objectives:

1. Locate possible sites in Central America or the Caribbean.
2. Locate possible sites in the U.S.
3. Develop an appropriate evangelism program.
4. Choose mission partners who will help us address world poverty issues.
5. Choose partners who will give us opportunities to develop relationships with the people where we go to serve.

continued . . .

You'll want to identify several objectives for your ministry.

LEVEL 5: DREAM TOGETHER
In his book *Young Adult Ministry,* Terry Hershey wrote about the importance of the dream session. This is a time when those putting together the ministry can be creative and let themselves imagine what could be someday. This is a time when you can look beyond the targets, peer down the journey before you, and try to picture unthinkable destinations for your ministry.

Ask yourself this question: "If nothing were impossible, what would I like to see happen with this ministry?" Don't worry about whether the dreams are feasible or even rational.

Even though there are few rules to holding a dream session, there are some guidelines:

First, each dream should be measurable. "I want the people in this church to be appreciated" is a good dream, but it isn't measurable. "I would like to see people involved at all levels of church leadership" is a measurable goal.

Understanding How to Dream Together

- Set the ground rules for a dream session: There is no such thing as a bad dream or idea. No one can say, "We tried that before."
- Take a night or longer and pray about the dreams and think them over.
- List dreams on a large sheet of paper and post them on the wall so everyone can keep dreaming about them.

You know you're weak in this area if . . .

- the people involved in the ministry feel that no one cares about their ideas.
- leaders go elsewhere to have their ideas implemented.
- nothing new ever happens.
- your programs seem old-fashioned and don't reflect current trends.

Second, because these are dreams, don't stop to discuss or rationalize. Many dreams are squelched by negative comments. The four words "We can't do that!" can cause a dream to be lost forever.

The Mission Team, *continued* . . .

The short-term mission team held a dream session and came up with three pages of dreams. They wanted to send evangelism teams to Russia and medical teams to Mexico, as well as doing all kinds of local service projects. On and on the list went. They reminded themselves that there is no such thing as a bad dream. A dream session is the time to create vision, not evaluate feasibility. That can be done later.

continued . . .

Remember, people's ideas are inexhaustible; there's no limit to how creative people can be. But when someone says, "That idea won't work," only the most committed dreamers will continue to dream. The rest of us find our flow of ideas comes to a halt. The conversation ends. Remember, there is no such thing as a bad dream or idea.

I (Rich) was recently asked to sit in on a team meeting for a ministry. The leader started the meeting by saying, "Let's just dream for a while. What could we do to turn this ministry around?"

One person said, "We can't do anything—it won't work. No one in the church will let us do anything."

Another person responded by exclaiming, "They never let us try anything new!"

The Mission Team, *continued . . .*

The short-term mission planning team identified the following obstacles to watch for:

1. The quality of each trip will be compromised if we attempt too many trips each year.
2. Trips will suffer if we don't find people to take ownership.
3. We might not raise the money needed to finance the trips.
4. Poorly selected team members might diminish the quality of each team and the program as a whole.
5. Mission agencies may not want short-term teams working in their areas.

Some of these obstacles presented more challenge than others, but each one helped the team think before acting. This process gave them a chance to address any potential problems.

continued . . .

you can avoid them, but other times you must meet them head-on. In planning your target, you must consider the potential obstacles that might adversely affect your plan.

Understanding How to Identify Obstacles

- List all potential problems you may encounter from outside your ministry.
- List all restrictions your church may give you.
- List people who may pose potential problems.
- List any legal limitations.

You know you're weak in this area if . . .

- the ministry is constantly involved in dealing with obstacles that arise but weren't foreseen.
- people in leadership become frustrated and begin to feel that the ministry is destined for failure.

Wow! Can you imagine being on that team? This is a place where people have allowed themselves to become victims. They'd forgotten that we all have power in our ability to imagine how to do things. Don't let others stop you from dreaming.

LEVEL 6: IDENTIFY THE OBSTACLES

As we attempt to meet needs in ministries, we inevitably will run into obstacles. Sometimes

LEVEL 7: IDENTIFY YOUR RESOURCES

The next step in the target process is to identify those resources available to help you in your mission. Typically, people and organizations already exist that can offer great resources.

There are all kinds of resources you can tap into, including financial, people, prayer, spiritual, and practical. Once you've identified the obstacles to your ministry, and then list all the resources that already exist or can be developed, how you can overcome the obstacles becomes more obvious.

Understanding How to Identify Your Resources

- Identify the experts you can call upon.
- Identify resource agencies.
- Identify untapped resource people in your church.
- List the programs or procedures already in place in your ministry or church that will facilitate this mission.

You know you're weak in this area if . . .

- valuable time and energy are wasted "reinventing the wheel" rather than being spent on gleaning the insights learned by others in the church.
- a very small group of experts are involved, leaving them overtaxed while other experts are underutilized.

The Mission Team, *continued* . . .

When the mission team started their short-term ministry, part of their planning was to identify experts already in their midst. They discovered that some of them had been on mission trips before. Their experience represented a vast resource. Those persons, in turn, pointed the team toward agencies in the U.S. and contacts in foreign countries. It also didn't take long to find people in their midst who spoke other languages and who were willing to help prepare the teams to communicate in different countries. In the end, the team realized that the high impact of the short-term mission program is due in large part to many wonderful people in their own church body.

The team also discovered several other resources during the process of establishing its short-term mission program. It learned some creative ways to raise money. Other churches offered themselves as resources. They found that the library, the airline company, pharmaceutical companies, area hospitals, and countless other sources had knowledge and resources that were helpful.

continued . . .

LEVEL 8: SET GOALS

This next stage is crucial to your ministry's success. The right goal at the right stage of your ministry's development will help you achieve your purpose and your dreams. If you try to achieve too much too fast, the result is usually burnout. If you move too slowly, frustration and a loss of interest can result.

Your goals are different from your mission statement or your target areas. Your mission statement is your purpose; your targets are the general direction of your ministry. You accomplish your mission statement and fine-tune your targets as you realize your mission goals.

Here's an example. I (Rich) was in Atlanta working through the target process with the head

The Mission Team, *continued* . . .

The short-term mission team listed the following mission goals and named the individuals responsible to see that they were carried out. (Note: Just because a person is assigned to an area, that didn't mean he or she was to accomplish the goal alone. Instead, he or she was responsible to get the group together to do it, or to choose a team of people who would be responsible.)

Short-Term Goals:

1. Pray regularly (Jamie).
2. Meet with resource people (Jamie and Polly).
3. Hold a dream session (Jamie and Polly).
4. Choose a leadership team (Trevor, Jamie, Polly, and Rich).

Mid-Term Goals:

1. Pray regularly (Jamie and Polly).
2. Have biweekly leadership team meetings (Rich, Jamie, and Polly).
3. Gather information about potential sites for the trip (Amy, Jerod, and Jamie).
4. Choose a potential site (whole committee).
5. Send two people to check out the mission site (Polly and Jamie).
6. Begin to select participants (Jerod, Jamie, and Amy).

Long-Term Goals:

1. Pray regularly (Jerod and Rich).
2. Train the participants (Kim and Jamie).
3. Send participants on short-term mission.
4. Evaluate the experience (whole team).

of a national organization. As we worked on the mission statement, he handed me a file that contained several mission statements from other Christian organizations. Some were wonderfully written, but what struck me was that none included any organizational goals to go along with the mission statements. I wondered how these organizations could gauge their success without measurable goals. Mission statements are only a part of the process; you also need goals. Goals put the "feet" to the mission statement.

Understanding How to Set Goals

- Make sure your goals are specific enough to accomplish.
- Make sure you give your team plenty of time to accomplish the goals.
- Attempt to accomplish only a few goals in each phase.

You know you're weak in this area if . . .

- the ministry tries to accomplish too many goals in one term and therefore fails to set or meet other goals.
- goals are listed but no one is named to have the ultimate responsibility to see that the goals are met and/or tasks are completed.

Evaluate and renew or revise your ministry's goals every year. You might also split them into short-, mid-, and long-term goals. Short-term goals are those you intend to accomplish in the next ninety days. Mid-term goals are those you intend to accomplish in the next six to nine months. Long-term goals are those you hope to complete in a year or longer.

LEVEL 9: BULL'S-EYE!

Congratulations! You're ready to implement your ministry! You are now intentional about what you want to do. Refer often to everything you've developed to get this far; it can provide direction and focus for your ministry and keep you from being distracted. But the target is only as good as your commitment to use it and keep it updated with new dreams and new directions.

Troubleshooting

Q. What if we don't meet all of our goals?
A. That's okay! You may choose to push them to the next term, or you may have determined that they are no longer important. Remember that goals, like every step in the target, are meant to guide you, not condemn you.

Q. What if the group changes leadership drastically during the process?
A. Make sure all incoming leaders understand the "target" and that they agree with the direction of the mission. If one or two new leaders are brought into an existing team, have the existing leaders explain each step of the target to the newcomers. Not only will this educate the new leaders, but it will affirm for existing leaders the process they undertook to arrive at their current ministry. Whenever you have a major leadership change—in other words, if more than half of the leaders are new—you should hold a leadership retreat to work through the "target" process again with all existing and new leaders. The new target should reflect the input and personality of this new group of leaders.

Q. How do we update our target?
A. The answer above gives good advice for updating your target in the case of new leadership team members. But even in the absence of leadership changes, your target may need periodic revisions. The important thing to keep in mind is that developing a target is always the result of teamwork, never just one person's wishes. Whether you are reevaluating something as minor as short-term goals or as major as your mission statement, the entire team needs to take part in the process.

Q. What if our mission statement is not the same as that of the church we're a part of?
A. A distinctive mission statement is fine as long as it is not in opposition to the mission of your parent church. Often, the mission statement of a young adult ministry is more specific than the church's. If your statement contradicts the church's, you need to go back and rework it after discussing the differences with the church leadership.

1. If you listed the core values of your current young adult ministry—or one you're dreaming of starting—what do you think those might be?

2. If you had to write a mission statement for your current ministry—or one you're dreaming of—what would it be? Remember, all a mission statement consists of is a sentence or two that tells people where your ministry is headed.

3. If you had to pull together leaders right now for your ministry, who would you choose? (Remember, leaders aren't going to be perfect. Jesus chose blue-collar workers, commercial fishermen, ranchers, and IRS agents to be His leaders.)

4. Put into your own words what you think it means to have an intentional ministry.

CHAPTER NINE

DEVELOPING CORE TEAMS

Bob and Scott were staff pastors at a community church. Each was in charge of a successful area of ministry: Bob with youth, Scott with singles. Over coffee, the two lamented their church's lack of a viable program for young adults, and they decided they were just the two to address the problem. After a little more discussion, they decided what they wanted and who they wanted to reach. They wanted a group to reach people in their twenties; they wanted a "cutting edge" ministry. They put together a band, got some videos, and rearranged one of the rooms in the church to look like a coffee house. They put out some cool flyers and a few weeks later kicked it off. It was a miserable failure.

Not willing to give up, they asked for volunteers to help them in the new outreach. As people signed on, they were given a part in Bob and Scott's plan. Within a few months, the young adult outreach was dead and buried.

Bob and Scott's approach to young adult ministry was wrong-headed in several ways. Of course, the most obvious is that they didn't involve young adults in any meaningful way. True, they did involve others, but only after they had decided they knew what the young adults at their church wanted and needed. Their approach was a waste of time and a waste of God's call on the lives of the young adults in their church.

> The moment we begin to see others in terms of what they can
> *do* rather than who they *are*, we mutilate humanity and
> violate community.[1]

Effective leaders in business, if they are to build their organizations for the long term, must have the capacity to cultivate the next wave of leaders, or their contributions are unlikely to last much longer than their physical presence within the company.[2]

Your young adult ministry should rely heavily on young adults who volunteer to lead it. But these volunteers shouldn't be there simply to accomplish your goals. Instead, they will have their own ideas, their own talents, and their own call to ministry. Your job will be to develop those ideas and talents, and form a team that will work together to accomplish God's purposes for your young adult ministry.

The goal of this chapter is to help you build effective core teams. Core teams are groups of people who trust each other and share their strengths to reach the common goal of a successful ministry.

To function best, your core team members need to be well-informed, motivated, relational, and rewarded. Let's look at each of these briefly.

Well-informed: Enthusiasm wanes quickly when team members aren't kept informed about their role. Make sure they always know the answers to these important questions:

- What are we supposed to do?
- How do you want it done?
- Why am *I* doing it?
- Who is in this with me?

Accept people where they are. Do not expect perfection from them. Don't let your love and acceptance hinge on their performance as Christians.[3]

You need to communicate effectively *what, how, why,* and *who* if things are going to happen in a way that builds people, teams, and ministry. This requires clear communication. Create an environment where people know what is expected of them.

Motivated: Fortunately, you can provide much of that motivation by making things fun. Face it, no one likes everything they do; there's always a little dirty work they would rather not do. For that reason, it's important to build fun into your ministry.

Relational: It's also your responsibility to create an environment where people make good decisions. To get to this point, you have to personalize your relationship with each team member so you can learn the best way to encourage each one. Remember, what motivates one may not motivate another.

Rewarded: Even with leaders who volunteer their time, you get what you "pay for," so be sure to reward your team members for their good work. Be creative in your rewards.

All work and no play makes Jack a dull team member. Here are some ways that your young adults ministry team can have fun together:

- Play laser tag before an important meeting.
- Go out to eat together.
- Have an art night: draw pictures, finger paint, make clay figurines.
- Go boating.

TEAM LEADER FUNDAMENTALS

As leader of the team, you also have certain responsibilities:

You must be willing to give up control. People need to be set free to pursue their own mission or ministry call. That means you need to get out of the way.

You must be willing to do the same things you expect them to do. Don't ask anything of a team member you wouldn't do yourself. Be a model.

You must be secure in yourself. Be willing to let others get the credit. As the famous story goes, when Quincy Jones gathered dozens of celebrities to record "We Are the World" for charity, he advised everyone who entered the recording studio to hang their egos at the door. Your own security will also create an environment where failure is not fatal! Remember, failure is never a person; it's always an event.

You must have a desire for others to succeed. You must want people to "win." Give others credit. Let them know their growth as a person is more important to you than the success or failure of the job they do. This attitude is what separates people-oriented leaders from program-oriented leaders.

You must be willing to invest your time. This way of doing ministry can be very time-consuming. This approach takes more time at first, but later on, as your leaders are empowered to carry out their own dreams for ministry, you'll find yourself spending less of your time and energy.

Effective rewards:

- Send volunteers to seminars.
- Work side by side with them.
- Run interference for them.
- Be willing to take appropriate risks with them.

EIGHT STEPS FOR BUILDING A CORE TEAM

1. *Be selective about your leaders.* You'll be spending an awful lot of time with them, so choose them well. Do not ask for volunteers!

95

Carefully choose those who will best accomplish the goals and abide by the stated philosophy of your ministry. That doesn't mean you should choose people just like you. Aim to balance your team with people who have different skills, gifts, temperaments, and personality traits.

Make sure team member job descriptions address the following questions:

- What is the position title (that is, team member, facilitator of team, and so on)?
- What is the purpose of this position?
- What will this person be doing? What are the specific responsibilities?
- Who does the team member report to, and who does he or she receive information from?
- Who does the team member work with most closely?
- What gifts and skills are required?
- What are the expectations of the team member (that is, lifestyle, time commitment, and so on)?
- What is the term of service for this position?
- What are some measurable goals during this term?
- When and how will we evaluate this job description?

2. *Discover each person's strengths and build on those.* In addition to providing team balance, capitalize on people's strengths by placing them where they will shine, not simply where you need a warm body. Use testing instruments (like spiritual gift surveys and temperament analysis tools) to assess where best to place each person.

3. *Encourage your core team members to invest in other people.* Just as you have set the example of developing their gifts and strengths, they should be developing others as well.

As you rollerblade alongside your team member or sit across the table with a cup of coffee, ask questions like these to find out his or her dreams:

- What do you like best in the ministry?
- What do you like least in the ministry?
- What would you like to do more of?
- What would you like to do less of?
- What are some of your personal goals?
- What are some skills you would like to develop personally, as well as in the ministry?
- What kind of recognition, acknowledgment, or rewards are the most meaningful to you? How do you feel when you don't receive them?

4. *Give each person a specific job description.* This critical component enables the team members to carry out the philosophy of ministry.

5. *Meet for lunch, dinner, and other relational times.* Use the time to ask questions that will help you understand them and their dreams.

6. *Set a time frame.* We recommend six-month to one-year commitments. If the leader is in the right place, he or she can renew the commitment for up to two years.

7. *Affirm team members publicly.* Celebrate successes. Make sure you give credit and affirmation in front of the rest of the group.

8. *Hold team members accountable and ask them to be accountable to each other.* The goal is not to police one another's behavior but to hold one another accountable for what each has agreed to do.

ONGOING DEVELOPMENT AND FINE-TUNING

Once your core team is in place, your energy will shift from creating to sustaining and improving. The first step—after the procedures outlined above are implemented—will be the development of your team's philosophy of ministry, the guiding principles of your ministry.

DEVELOPING A PHILOSOPHY OF MINISTRY

A philosophy of ministry statement helps the core team members understand why things are done a certain way, why you're expending energies in one area and not in another. The philosophy of ministry is closely tied to the mission statement. Remember that the mission statement tells people who you are, and where your ministry is headed. It helps keep you on track. A philosophy of ministry directs the ways you will attempt to accomplish the purposes of the mission statement.

Briefly, as you shape your philosophy of ministry, you'll want to answer these questions:

- What role does God have in this ministry?
- What role does Scripture play in the ministry?
- What role do people play in our ministry?
- How is the ministry carried out?

DEALING WITH DIFFERENCES

No matter how wise, how well-chosen, how wonderful your core team members are, conflict is

Good Team Members Will:

1. Always be willing to do more than your share.
2. Refrain from saying uncomplimentary things about other team members behind their backs.
3. Accept reality: All members do not have the same duties. Not everyone on a team can do the same things.
4. Participate in team activities even when it is inconvenient to do so. When you agree to be a team member, you agree to be connected and accountable to your teammates. This isn't always convenient. Make every effort to be a team player.
5. Confront conflicts. Every team will experience conflicts. It's a normal and healthy part of team development. But when those conflicts remain unaddressed, they become destructive. When you commit to resolving conflicts, it strengthens team relationships.
6. Be there. Don't be late or absent for trivial reasons.
7. Be involved, concerned, and active in your own personal growth. Team development and personal growth cannot be separated.
8. Contribute to the personal growth of other team members whenever appropriate by sharing resources and information.

likely at some point. The following principles of conflict resolution will help you in those times.

- Hear feelings, not words. Attempt to be empathetic.
- Be congruent, in touch with your feelings and therefore responsible for them.
- Avoid "you" messages that can cause others to become defensive. Use "I" messages.
- Be ready to forgive and to ask for forgiveness. Real empathy will bring genuine apologies and repentance that will soften hearts and free you up from the slavery of bitterness, hostility, and vindictiveness.
- Be responsible for personal change.
- Stay with one issue at a time.
- Call "time" when the discussion becomes destructive. The person who calls time is responsible for arranging a new time (preferably within twenty-four hours) to discuss the matter further, once the feelings have been tempered.
- Stay with the here and now. Avoid bringing up the past or referring to the future.
- Don't use the words "never" or "always." Avoid generalizations.
- Avoid remarks that have nothing to do with the issue; they are only designed to hurt. Attack problems, not people.
- Approach the one you have a conflict with. If that person is unable or unwilling to work with you to resolve the issues, meet with a neutral referee (someone both of you agree on). If things still aren't resolved, then approach the other person with a group.
- Above all, be loving. Demonstrate a godly love that is accepting, supportive, and caring.

One of the most helpful things to remember in resolving conflicts is to learn to clarify. Most problems arise out of misunderstandings. Once we clear up misunderstandings within the team, moving forward becomes easier.

DEALING WITH UNMET EXPECTATIONS

While the ideal team is one in which people trust one another to reach a common goal, sometimes the system breaks down. There are some common reasons why teams fail:

- Team members do not understand what they are supposed to do. (We operate under presumed rules and understandings.)
- The team has never developed an agreed-upon common goal. (Some want social interaction; others want spiritual content.)
- There are circles and cliques where fighting exists. (This was the problem Paul was addressing in the letter to the Philippians.)
- There are interpersonal problems and team members do not know how to deal with them or where to get help.
- Some team members are intimidated by the leader and consequently become passive.

Sometimes the good work of the team is threatened by the team's leader (you or someone selected by you). This kind of threat can take many forms:

- The team leader is threatened by the success of his or her team members.
- The leader is ambitious and wants to win at any cost.
- The leader shows disregard for the feelings or needs of team members, destroying the motivation of the team.
- The leader has an inability or unwillingness to delegate. This sends the message that team members are not trusted to do the work.
- The leader criticizes others to make himself or herself feel or look good. This doesn't motivate anyone; it just destroys all respect and trust toward the leader.
- The leader betrays a teammate by going around his or her back or betraying a confidence. This removes any trust that may have been there.
- The leader has no vision for the future. If a leader can't see past today, then that leader will have difficulty leading the team toward anything.
- The leader displays arrogance or a cool personality. You'll build an effective team by letting your teammates know that you care about them, not that you care only for yourself.
- The leader does not invest time training others. As a leader, you are to build up the body by training and equipping others to minister.

- The leader sees people as commodities. If you see people as a way to get something, they will know it and want nothing to do with you.
- The leader is lazy. A leader who wants others to do the work and then takes the credit himself or herself is bound to fail.
- The leader doesn't ask for help. The leader is allowed to have needs. As a leader, you provide the model for your teammates. That means being honest enough to seek the help of others.

Key Questions for Existing Teams

- What's our goal? (This question can be easily answered if the team has worked through the target material in chapter 8.)
- Are people supporting our efforts?
- Do team members feel supported in their efforts?
- Are people complaining about our ministry?
- Is there a lack of interest in what we are doing?
- Are decisions made that cause confusion?
- Are people having unresolved conflicts with each other?
- Are people taking risks and are they being imaginative?
- Are we moving ahead, maintaining, or melting down?

FINAL THOUGHTS

This chapter is written as though the reader does not already have a leadership team in place. But that won't always be the case. Perhaps you don't have a blank slate; your core team is already in place. Should you start rebuilding a new team, or should you work with the existing team members? Let's look at the factors involved in your decision.

New teams: If you develop a new team, you have a great opportunity to start off on the right foot. Perhaps you have never had a leadership team, or the past team has served its entire term and you are now filling their positions. Having a new crew of leaders is a wonderful time to introduce new concepts in young adult ministry leadership.

Existing teams: Now that you've read the material in this chapter, you must decide if the group of people in place can adapt to the requirements and goals outlined here. If not, perhaps some of them will need to be replaced.

Key Questions for Paid Staff

- How do I decide who will do what?
- How do I interface our philosophy with our church's philosophy?
- What do I do when I inherit a core team that has a negative attitude?
- How do I report to the senior pastor?
- What are the best ways to use my position to affirm lay leaders?
- What size should core teams be?

If you need to replace your leadership team, don't expect a huge fight. It's likely that those you think are poorly suited for the new leadership structure won't be interested in their new positions.

Key Questions for Lay Leaders

- How many positions do I need?
- How do I relate to church staff members?
- How do I get church support?
- What do I do when the church doesn't support me?
- What do I do when people don't follow through?
- How do we maintain accountability with our leadership and the church?
- What size should core teams be?
- How do I lead as a lay leader?

FINAL CAUTIONS ABOUT BUILDING CORE TEAMS

Building a team doesn't happen by accident; it happens because someone makes a choice to do it. To change from the "Lone Ranger" model of ministry to the team model is a choice. Here are a few guiding principles:

• Change is hard work. It will take time. When you make up your mind that this is the way to do your ministry, everyone involved must agree on the steps to get there (the senior pastor, a committee, church elders, and so on).

• There are no magic answers. There will be times when the teamwork model does not seem to work, but it sure beats the alternatives (personality-driven ministries, top-down control from outside the group, and so forth). Don't let setbacks and failures stop you.

• The people who are in power must support change. To bring about change in any organization, you must have the support of those in positions of power.

• Give yourself credit when you bring about change. When a group of people begin to work together as a team, reward each other. Celebrate your success as a team.

• Ownership enhances commitment. People support what they have helped create.

• Don't hesitate to ask for help. There are good consultants and others who are ready and willing to help you develop team ministry.

As you use the team approach, you can develop a group of people who get to know one another and who learn how to deal with conflict. You will discover that using this style of ministry will lead to environments in which people feel they can share their dreams and fears. They won't feel used.

GETTING REAL YOURSELF

1. As you read through the responsibilities of core team members, do people naturally come to mind who are fit to serve as ministry leaders? Make a list of people and spend some time praying about them and for them before you approach them about serving.

2. Do you have a conflict with someone in your ministry that you need to confront right now? If you've already confronted that person and the conflict isn't resolved, can you think of a neutral party who can help mediate the conflict?

3. As you think about the responsibilities of being a team leader, do you think you're the best-equipped person in your group to do the job? Or is someone else more naturally gifted to lead your team?

4. As you read through the list of negative leadership qualities on page 99, do you see any that you're guilty of ? What steps can you take to overcome these negative traits? Make a list and commit them to prayer each day.

CHAPTER TEN

ENVIRONMENT FOR YOUNG ADULT MINISTRY

Have you ever wondered why so few young adults with expertise in technology have a vision for technology ministries? Or why young adults who know how to read seldom think about literacy ministries? Or why bikers rarely consider their passion an opportunity for ministry? Or how about Christian snowboarders—have you ever met a Christian who connected her passion for boarding to a ministry calling? Why is that?

Leaders must be environmental change agents.

—John Maxwell[1]

THE ESSENTIAL TRIAD

A complete young adult ministry consists of what we call the essential triad. It includes these concepts:

- Worship—a vertical dimension expressing devotion to God.
- Edification/nurture—a horizontal dimension expressing commitment by Christians to build up one another in the faith.
- Mission/outreach—a horizontal dimension expressing commitment by Christians

to communicate the gospel to those outside the faith.

Of course these three overlap, and it could be argued that everything a Christian does is potentially an act of worship. Yet we would say that these three categories encompass a complete ministry. But if you think about worship, nurture, and outreach, and the way a lot of churches actually do ministry, it's usually pretty obvious that little time is spent on outreach.

In other words, most ministry activities are vertical (worship) and horizontal (nurture), but there's a catch: they are done *by* the ministry *for* the ministry. With few exceptions, one part of the essential triad (mission) is missing.

However, the typical young adult ministry has enormous potential to impact its culture. Why? Young adult ministries are populated by people who are committed to God and want to make a difference for Him. And there's the culture, hemorrhaging from crisis after crisis. Yet it seems agonizingly difficult to connect the two.

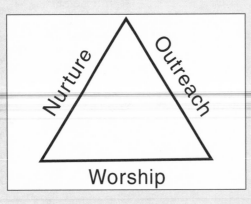

"WANT-TO"

Recently I (Rich) have watched laypeople who minister with passion. They invest their lives in ministries relating to rave dances, whiz kids, people in prison, unwed mothers, internationals, people who are physically impaired, and so on. They pay a

price in time, money, pressure, study, and numerous other areas. Sometimes they know their spiritual gift set, but most often that doesn't even occur to them. And in most cases, they haven't spent much time pondering their temperament profile. They come from all kinds of backgrounds and have a wide variety of discipleship and small-group experiences. But they have just one common denominator: they possess what I call "want-to"—a deep, God-given desire to do a special ministry. Actually, what I'm describing is ordinary people responding to their ministry callings.

Yet all of us know that most Christians are not conscious of God's call to a particular ministry. People rarely possess a ministry passion. That raises a question. What would it take for the average believer to feel a passionate call from God to a particular ministry? If we answer that question, we will unlock the ministry vision of a new army of ordinary Christians.

Ultimately, motivation for ministry is an issue of the heart, and the heart is God's territory. But cultivating the heart to respond to God's leading necessitates a joint venture between the church and God. The church creates the context for the Spirit of God to work. Paul describes God's calling this way: "Work out your salvation with fear and trembling; for it is God who is at work in you, both to will and to work for His good pleasure" (Philippians 2:12-13, NASB).

First comes the challenge to work out our own salvation. Then follows the promise that God will work in us. Another way we could think of this same verse: "Pay attention to all of your life, including God's call to ministry. And do so with serious concern. Because God will give you the desire to do what He wants you to do. And He will even enable you to do it in a way that pleases Him."

CLOSED SYSTEMS

Motivating people for ministry is the most persistent challenge leaders of young adult ministries face. The reason it's so tough is that churches by nature operate within closed systems. In a closed system, structures and mindsets are static.

Here's an example. Once, my friend Frank was in Canada, where he briefly visited a Hutterite community. The young man traveling with him was raised a Hutterite. As they drove into the community, the young man told Frank they were arriving during nap time and only one person would be awake to greet them. Sure enough, that was true. Later, Frank described this community's lifestyle as "frozen" in time. A successful Hutterite community shapes those in it down to the smallest detail by resisting change in both the way people think and the way they live.

That's what any closed system does. It shapes those in it to fit the system. There is no room for individual initiative or uniqueness in a closed system. Communism is the great twentieth-century experiment with a closed economic and political system.

On the other hand, an open system is continually being shaped and reshaped by its participants. Of course, a ministry with an open system will still possess absolutes in both faith (belief) and some practices (behaviors). But how faith and practice play out in life's arena is determined by the individual. While Christians are not free to violate the absolutes, they are encouraged to pursue God's unique calling in their lives. In an open system, the sky is the limit for everyone when it comes to personal ministry.

"How are Christians motivated for mission?" is a tough question. Or the flip side of the query asks, "What are the motivation killers in the local church?"

- Guilt motivation
- "Ought to" or "duty" motivation
- Big-event motivation
- "Let's take this city for Jesus" motivation
- Loyalty to a particular tradition, church, or denomination motivation
- "Let's build the best church in the city" motivation

But many ministries have been operating within a closed system for so long that we take it for granted. That's important to realize because the things that have the greatest influence in shaping our lives are often the things we take for granted. Most of what we do in life we take for granted. We assume the sun will rise in the east and that we can count on gravity. Taking things for granted is not bad; in fact, it is necessary. The problem arises when we take the wrong things for granted.

The book *Calling*[2] lists six issues that can create an open system. If we can encourage young adult ministries toward a mindset change that moves them away from a closed system, the potential for mission and ministry will be unlimited. If you let yourself dream a little, the possibilities are downright exciting. So it's important to evaluate how your young adult ministry is faring in these six areas.

1. KINGDOM-FOCUSED

The kind of church young adults want to participate in is kingdom-focused, not size-focused. Many young adults in your community don't care about big churches. Unfortunately, many churches taste success (growth) without engaging young adults in ministry. Churches often grow using techniques from the business world. But remember that business is also failing to capture the hearts and minds of young adults. Church growth doesn't very often mean community impact. And that is often the very thing that young adults want.

Young adults do not see the advantage of building bigger churches, just as many subcultures of young adults don't see the advantage of building bigger businesses. The exceptions to this are "Star Xers," who seem to want a career-driven lifestyle. But if you want to reach the majority of young adults, your ministries have to be kingdom-focused. Remember, Jesus uttered the word "church" only twice. His primary focus was on building the kingdom of God.

What is a kingdom-focused ministry? It is one that helps young adults see how to submit their lives to the lordship of Christ. This process of developing committed disciples takes more time than getting a group of people to commit to building a superstructure and program. It takes time to commit to them personally.

2. LAY-FOCUSED

Young adults also want their churches to be lay-focused. The traditional church generally has a pastor or small group of leaders who dispense a vision, and everyone else follows. The focus is on the pastor or leaders. In a good young adult ministry environment, the emphasis will be on each member of a ministry. This allows the ministry direction to be led by the dreams and gifts of the young adult. In the old model, the pastor or leaders dole out a little new information every week. But in the real world many young adults have more information than their pastor or leaders do. They need leadership from pastors, to be sure, but they don't need to rely on pastors for information.

Traditionally, when we said someone was a minister, we meant that he or she was paid and had probably trained formally for "ministry." When we said that someone was a "layperson," that generally meant he or she was helping the minister. But what if we acted as though we really believed that every person in a church body is called to ministry? What if we believed God had gifted everyone for a role in every ministry?

We must redefine what partnership means in the church. To be lay-driven means there is a partnership among God, the clergy, and lay-people (in Scripture, the layperson is the *real* minister).

3. MESSAGE-FOCUSED

I love a magazine advertisement I saw for Bethel Seminary. The top half of the page, with the picture of an old Coca-Cola bottle, said, "That was then." The bottom half, with a photo of all the different Coke products now—regular Coke, Diet Coke, Cherry Coke, big Coke bottles, little Coke bottles, caffeine-free Coke, and so on—said, "This is now." The next month the same ad ran but with different pictures. The top half of the page, the part that said "That was then," had a photo of a Bible. The bottom half, the part that said "This is now," showed the same Bible. I think that's a great illustration of Paul's words:

> Though I am free and belong to no man, I make myself a slave to everyone, to win as many as possible. To the Jews I became like a Jew, to win the Jews. To those under the law I became like one under the law . . . , so as to win those under the law. To those not having the law I became like one not having the law . . . , so as to win those not having the law. To the weak I became weak, to win the weak. I have become all things to all men so that by all possible means I might save some. I do all this for the sake of the gospel, that I may share in its blessing. (1 Corinthians 9:19-23)

Do you realize the Bible contains no real methodology for "doing" church? Did they have Sunday school in Philippi? Did the church in Antioch have evening services? Did churches in the region of Galatia run AWANA programs? Did anybody hold fall or spring revivals? And who among them conducted confirmation classes?

While we have just incidental references about how New Testament Christians did church, we do know a lot about what they believed. The message was everything; how it was communicated didn't matter much.

However, these verses do tell us one thing about the apostle Paul's methodology: it was extremely pragmatic! If it worked, he did it; and if it didn't work, he didn't bother.

The approach today is very different. Sometimes it seems we can get away with heresy more easily than we can fool around with the way we do church. We become emotionally attached to methods. Sunday school began because Sunday morning was the best time to train people in Christian basics. Few young adult ministries that I know of meet for Sunday school, yet churches fight over continuing Sunday school for young adults. If the apostle Paul were to decide about having Sunday school for young adults, I'm sure his first question would be about its effectiveness. (Just a note, though. That's not to say that Sunday school won't ever be an option for young adult ministry. As young adults start families, a small-group time or Bible study time during an hour when child care is provided may end up being perfect—never say never!)

The criterion for methodology in an open system is simple: Methods must not violate the message. As the familiar saying goes, "We must do everything possible, short of sin, to introduce people to Christianity."

Second, we must experiment with our methods until we find out what is effective. In 1 Corinthians 9, the apostle Paul says he stretched his methodology across the entire cultural spectrum (those with the law and those without the law—that means everybody). We're free to do the same.

Earlier in the book, we described The Next Level, a young adult ministry that meets on Tuesdays at 7:17 P.M. People sit all over the place, some even right on the stage. Some lie down. Not all the band members wear shoes. The teaching pastor has a shaved head and wears an earring. Will that work everywhere? No! But it works where we are, and we are reaching people for Christ.

4. ENTREPRENEUR-DRIVEN

Young adults also want a ministry that allows entrepreneurialism. A new day has dawned for leadership. Building the pyramids required a handful of people to think and about forty thousand "grunts" to do the work.

The days of the pyramids are far behind us. Today we build "information superhighways." And just as the interstate highway system revolutionized automobile travel, so the information superhighway is revolutionizing access to information. The ability to lead is linked to the ability to access information.

Millions of church people possess both the life experience and the ability to access the information they need to launch significant mission enterprises. But they lack opportunities to lead. Tom Peters, management guru and author of *In Search of Excellence,* says he would like to see every person in a given company be his or her own entrepreneur. Translate that idea into the life of the church, and it means that every person would have permission to design and direct the mission project God has placed on his or her heart.

The profile of leaders in an open system looks very different from the manager-leadership profile that, until recently, dominated business, education, and the church. We no longer live in frontier towns where the pastor had to interpret the outside world for his congregation because he was one of the few people who could read. These days, young adults can access information needed for ministry as readily as the pastor.

Managers, as opposed to leaders, love information for the sake of having information. How many issues have been tabled at ministry meetings for lack of information? Leaders, on the other hand, access information for action. Leaders know that if someone possesses a strong enough desire, he or she will find the information necessary to do the job.

The most important information today's leaders need is to know that others are not dependent on them for information. But people do need leaders to create structures where available information can be used.

As a pastor, I (Rich) was seldom the sole leader. Other staff and laypeople were capable leaders in their areas of responsibility. They made the decisions necessary to lead their areas. If push came to shove, I sometimes needed to exercise the responsibility of my position. But those times were rare.

5. SPECIALIST-DRIVEN

Since the industrial revolution, the impact of tedious, routine work has been well documented. The idea that "jobs are not big enough for people" is bad news because most people's primary source of identity is their job. When you meet someone new, you're probably more likely to ask, "What do you do?" than "What are you?"

Yet the Christian community has always contended that what we are is more important than what we do. According to the Westminster Catechism, the highest calling for humankind is simply to walk humbly with God and to please Him. Jesus said that the first commandment is to love God with all your heart, soul, and mind.

Church history, beginning with the New Testament, reveals a tension between Christians who have emphasized *being* and those who have emphasized *doing*. Compare the apostle Paul's statement with the apostle James's declaration:

It is by grace you have been saved, through faith—and this not from yourselves, it is the gift of God—not by works, so that no one can boast. (Ephesians 2:8-9)

What good is it, my brothers, if a man claims to have faith but has no deeds? Can such faith save him? . . . In the same way, faith by itself, if it is not accompanied by action, is dead.

But someone will say, "You have faith; I have deeds."

Show me your faith without deeds, and I will show you my faith by what I do. (James 2:14,17-18)

I think most of us are looking for a calling, not a job. Most of us, like the assembly line worker, have jobs that are too small for our spirit. Jobs are not big enough for people.[3]

Martin Luther disliked James's emphasis on doing so much. He called the book of James a "right strawy epistle" and placed it as the last book in his translation of the Bible. While most theologians find harmony between Paul and James, tension between doing and being continues.

The post-World War II generation was not the first to produce parachurch ministries. The monastic orders of the Middle Ages were the parachurch organizations of their day. Some orders—the Benedictines, for example—emphasized "being" by retreating from a corrupt world to concentrate on worship and nurture. Others—the mendicant or begging orders like the Franciscans, for example—emphasized "doing" by staying among the poor as servants.

Parachurch movements gain their identity through what they do. Their names—Prison Fellowship; Young Life; International Students, Inc.; Promise Keepers—often tell their story. Churches tend to isolate themselves from the world to concentrate on being the church.

6. EMPOWERMENT-DRIVEN

The church, unlike a business, assumes that God is the boss. That's the easy part. But answering the question "How does God delegate His authority, and to whom does He delegate it?" is comparable to crossing a minefield.

Young adult ministries must often face questions about who God has delegated His authority to. When I (Rich) asked a team of young adults to start a ministry that would be totally lay-driven, they took the challenge with great enthusiasm. They chose who would do the teaching. When I told the church staff who the young adults had chosen, they immediately said no. The teacher was not acceptable to them. I went back to the team and said, "I'm sorry, but you can't have him teach." They were angry. I had told them it was their ministry and that I was there only to be a resource. But it turned out my statement was untrue. I had given them responsibility, but I had not given them the authority.

Young adults need and deserve the authority that goes with the responsibility. They want to be able to decide what has to happen and how to get it done.

GETTING REAL YOURSELF

1. If you had to put the concept of closed systems and open systems into your own words, how would you define each of these terms?

2. With your definitions in mind, would you describe your church as closed or open?

3. Can you think of a church in your community that seems closed and behind the times? Can you think of one that is open to new ideas and seems to be on the bleeding edge of ministry? What makes those churches different from each other?

4. Think of the six mindset issues of a church operating under an open system: kingdom-focused, lay-focused, message-focused, entrepreneur-driven, specialist-driven, and empowerment-driven. How would you rate your young adult ministry in each of those areas?

5. As a leader, do you give people authority to go along with the responsibility they take for areas of ministry?

CHAPTER ELEVEN

TRANSFORMATIONAL COMMUNITIES

Janet finally got her dream job. The only problem was she had to move three thousand miles away from home to take it. As she packed her things, she thought about the friends and family she would miss. She thought back on some tough times she had gone through recently and how a few of her close friends from high school had really helped pull her through. *Those kinds of relationships are hard to find, and it will be difficult without them,* she thought. Since her parents divorced fifteen years ago, Janet has found it difficult to connect with and trust people; she has a pervasive sense of aloneness and gnawing fear of being rejected. But, as quickly as these thoughts came, they diminished as she began thinking about finally finding a job that was meaningful, one where she felt she could really make a difference.

> Next to physical survival, the greatest need of a human being is psychological survival . . . to be understood, to be affirmed, to be validated, to be appreciated.[1]

Loneliness had of late become an emotion I had stopped feeling so intensely. I had learned loneliness's extremes and had mapped its boundaries; loneliness was no longer something new or frightening—just another aspect of life that, once identified, seemed to disappear. But I realized a capacity for not feeling lonely carried a very real price, which was the threat of feeling nothing at all.[2]

It only took a couple of months in her new city until Janet's feelings of being alone and isolated started bothering her. She had been pretty busy for the first few months on the job. Finding an apartment, setting it up, registering the car, getting insurance—all took up much of her free time, not to mention the long hours at her new job. But now that she was starting to settle into a routine and the newness and excitement of her new life was subsiding, she realized that she was going to have to take the initiative to meet some new people. While her fears of being hurt by people were paralyzing at times, she knew she needed to make new friends.

She heard about a church in her area that a number of young adults attended. So she decided to go. The night she walked into the church, she was amazed at the number of people her age and all the friendly smiles she received. A young woman named Marcy came up to her, started some small talk, and then introduced Janet to a couple of her friends. When the service began, Marcy asked Janet to sit with her. During the message, the speaker talked about how God created us with an internal need for close relationships and how we can't make it alone in life. A young woman spoke about how her small group had recently helped her through a very difficult time in her life as she had been seriously contemplating suicide. She said her small group helped save her life. After the service, Marcy invited Janet to join them in their small group on Wednesday nights. Though hesitant, Janet agreed to try it.

Relationship, or bonding, is at the foundation of God's nature. Since we are created in his likeness, relationship is our most fundamental need, the very foundation of who we are. Without relationship, without attachment to God and others, we can't be our true selves. We can't be truly human.[3]

Three months have gone by and Janet is experiencing the fulfillment of being connected in community with others. The women in her group, even within this short amount of time, have become her best friends—almost like her family. Her fears of rejection and abandonment still linger, but in the safety of her group, she is able to share her true self. When she talks about her fears, dreams, and failures, the others embrace her. Home is still three thousand miles away, and lifelong friends can never be replaced, but Janet has found some shelter by connecting with other believers and is coming to understand the power of community.

How many people have experienced the power of community—really connecting with a few others in such a way that they know who is behind the mask? A community is a place where people know your fears, failures, and dreams but love you anyway. Why is this important? Because that's when life change happens.

The Bible exhorts us strongly to connect with other believers for a variety of reasons. In Genesis 2:18 God says, "It is not good for the man to be alone." Hebrews 10:25 says, "Let us not give up meeting together, as some are in the habit of doing." Paul exhorts us, "Carry each other's burdens, and in this way you will fulfill the law of Christ" (Galatians 6:2). James 5:16 reveals the power of confession: "Confess your sins to each other and pray for each other so that you may be healed." Biblical community is powerful; it's life-changing and healing. And it's a requirement in the body of Christ.

There are more than fifty "one another" commands in the New Testament that you can't obey unless you are in relationship with other believers. Every believer is to be actively involved in a ministry of caring for each other. When you see the number of references to this in the New Testament, its importance begins to sink in.

The Bible also contains dozens of other verses that exhort us to love our neighbors, to build up the church, to be like-minded, and to do good to

The "One Anothers" of the New Testament

- "Be at peace with each other." (Mark 9:50)

- "Wash one another's feet." (John 13:14)

- "Love one another." (John 13:34 and 35)

- "Love each other." (John 15:12 and 17)

- "Be devoted to one another in brotherly love." (Romans 12:10)

- "Honor one another above yourselves." (Romans 12:10)

- "Live in harmony with one another." (Romans 12:16)

- "Love one another." (Romans 13:8)

- "Stop passing judgment on one another." (Romans 14:13)

- "Accept one another." (Romans 15:7)

- "Instruct one another." (Romans 15:14)

- "Greet one another with a holy kiss." (Romans 16:16)

- "When you come together to eat, wait for each other." (1 Corinthians 11:33)

- "Have equal concern for each other." (1 Corinthians 12:25)

- "Greet one another with a holy kiss." (1 Corinthians 16:20)

continued . . .

those who belong to the family of God (Galatians 6:10). In fact, I (Ken) think one of the most effective evangelistic strategies in the New Testament has been largely ignored by the church. Read Jesus' command in John 13:34-35: "A new command I give you: Love one another. As I have loved you, so you must love one another. By this all men will know that you are my disciples, if you love one another." It is this kind of love that will reach and heal the hearts of young adults.

As we noted in chapter 3, many young adults were raised in broken homes and felt the effects of being reared in an antichild society. Many felt that they were deprived of the one thing they needed most: love. The need for love is the heart cry of this generation. Psychologist Henry Cloud notes the human need for love:

God created us with a hunger for relationship—for relationship with Him and with our fellow people. At our very core we are relational beings. Without a solid, bonded relationship, the human soul will become mired in psychological and emotional problems. The soul cannot prosper without being connected to others. No matter what characteristics we possess, or what accomplishments we amass, without solid emotional connectedness, without bonding to God and other humans, we will suffer sickness of the soul.[4]

Yet this love that young adults need to mature and develop into whole and healthy people is often blocked by their two greatest fears: abandonment and rejection. The brokenness they

---

The "One Anothers" of the New Testament, continued . . .

- "Serve one another in love." (Galatians 5:13)

- "Let us not become conceited, provoking and envying each other." (Galatians 5:26)

- "Carry each other's burdens." (Galatians 6:2)

- "Be patient, bearing with one another in love." (Ephesians 4:2)

- "Be kind and compassionate to one another, forgiving each other." (Ephesians 4:32)

- "Speak to one another with psalms, hymns and spiritual songs." (Ephesians 5:19)

- "Submit to one another out of reverence for Christ." (Ephesians 5:21)

- "In humility consider others better than yourselves." (Philippians 2:3)

- "Do not lie to each other." (Colossians 3:9)

- "Bear with each other and forgive whatever grievances you may have against one another." (Colossians 3:13)

- "Admonish one another." (Colossians 3:16)

continued . . .

The "One Anothers" of the New Testament, continued . . .

- "May the Lord make your love increase and overflow for each other." (1 Thessalonians 3:12)

- "Love each other." (1 Thessalonians 4:9)

- "Encourage each other." (1 Thessalonians 4:18)

- "Encourage one another and build each other up." (1 Thessalonians 5:11)

- "Encourage one another daily." (Hebrews 3:13)

- "Spur one another on toward love and good deeds." (Hebrews 10:24)

- "Encourage one another." (Hebrews 10:25)

- "Do not slander one another." (James 4:11)

- "Don't grumble against each other." (James 5:9)

- "Confess your sins to each other and pray for each other." (James 5:16)

- "Love one another deeply, from the heart." (1 Peter 1:22)

- "Live in harmony with one another." (1 Peter 3:8)

- "Love each other deeply." (1 Peter 4:8)

- "Offer hospitality to one another without grumbling." (1 Peter 4:9)

- "Each one should use whatever gift he has received to serve others." (1 Peter 4:10)

- "Clothe yourselves with humility toward one another." (1 Peter 5:5)

- "Greet one another with a kiss of love." (1 Peter 5:14)

- "Love one another." (1 John 3:11)

- "Love one another." (1 John 3:23)

- "Love one another." (1 John 4:7)

- "Love one another." (1 John 4:11)

- "Love one another." (1 John 4:12)

- "Love one another." (2 John 5)

have experienced, and the rejection from both family and society, have deeply wounded their souls and damaged their ability to trust. This pain and fear has caused many to protect themselves by living behind a hard emotional shell. Inside, they long for relationship and crave intimacy. But on the outside they push it away because they're afraid of being hurt. So how do we create safe relationships where this generation can heal and come to know and experience the love of God? The answer lies in creating transformational communities.

FROM SMALL GROUPS TO TRANSFORMATIONAL COMMUNITIES

Young adults need a safe place to be real, a place where they can take off their masks of self-sufficiency and composure and allow their fears and failures to come into the light. Christian psychologist John Powell says:

> We need to be able to express ourselves, to talk ourselves out, without fear of rejection by others. Too often the problems that we keep submerged within us remain, in the darkness of our own interior, undefined and therefore destructive—we will very likely "act out" the problems that remain submerged within us if we refuse to "talk out" these problems. . . . Our real fear is that we would be rejected.[5]

> Human beings . . . crave connectedness and meaning, we seek lasting and deep relationships, we grow by sharing and not by keeping secrets, and we need to trust and be trusted in order to feel safe enough to dare.[6]

The only place this can happen is within transformational communities patterned after the "one another" commands in the New Testament. These transformational communities are similar to traditional small groups, but with some important additions. Traditional small groups tend to be more content-driven, where doing homework and discussing questions related to the homework become the main focus of the group meeting.

A traditional small group typically looks like this: The group usually meets at someone's house during the week or on a Sunday morning in a traditional Sunday school format. After a little small talk among members, they drink some coffee, eat a few doughnuts, open the study up in prayer, and work through the lesson. Most of the time is spent discussing the content of the lesson, and group members rarely, if ever, get around to sharing much that is going on in their personal lives. Typically, the format of the meeting just doesn't allow for that.

A transformational community looks different. It involves the discussion of biblical content just as a traditional small group does. But its focus is more on group members connecting than on getting through a certain amount of material. Transformational communities are small groups of people who share each other's burdens. They are safe places where people take off their masks without fearing rejection. They are places where the needs of each person are of deep concern. In transformational communities, group members rejoice with each other, mourn with each other, accept each other, confront each other in love, listen to each other, pray together, and study the Bible with a desire to live out what they learn in the context of their relationships with each other.

Whether your ministry calls them small

groups, cell groups, or (adopting our fancy label) transformational communities, groups conducted with these objectives in mind create an incredible environment for spiritual/personal growth and emotional healing. Psychologist Scott Peck makes note of the incredible things that happen within this type of true community:

> It takes a great deal of work for a group of strangers to achieve the safety of true community. Once they succeed, however, it is as if the floodgates were opened. As soon as it is safe to speak one's heart, as soon as most people in the group know they will be listened to and accepted for themselves, years and years of pent-up frustration and hurt and guilt and grief come pouring out. And pouring out ever faster. Vulnerability in community snowballs. Once its members become vulnerable and find themselves being valued and appreciated, they become more and more vulnerable. The walls come tumbling down. And as they tumble, as the love and acceptance escalates, as the mutual intimacy multiplies, true healing and converting begins. Old wounds are healed, old resentments forgiven, old resistances overcome. Fear is replaced by hope.[7]

Transformational community groups are an absolute necessity for ministering effectively to young adults. In order to build these groups in your church, we'd like to suggest nine steps for you to take.

CREATING TRANSFORMATIONAL COMMUNITIES (TCs)

STEP 1: MAKE TCs A CORE VALUE IN YOUR MINISTRY.

The first step in creating TCs is to move them from being just another program to becoming a core value. The whole focus of your ministry should revolve around helping people develop healthy relationships. For this to happen, you as the leader must be convinced that relationships are the key to life change. You have to be willing to model vulnerability and your own need to be connected with others.

> Core values are the basic elements of your ministry that define what is uniquely important to your ministry. Your core values never change; they are the constant and enduring tenets, the guiding principles that determine what you do and why you do what you do.

To get people started in TC groups, talk up the benefits of being in community with each other. Tell stories of how existing groups work. Better yet, bring group members to the front of the larger group and have them tell their story of how their group has helped them. People will catch the excitement of what is happening in the lives of others, but you have to make it a core value and you have to emphasize it in everything you do.

HOW TO BIRTH NEW TC GROUPS

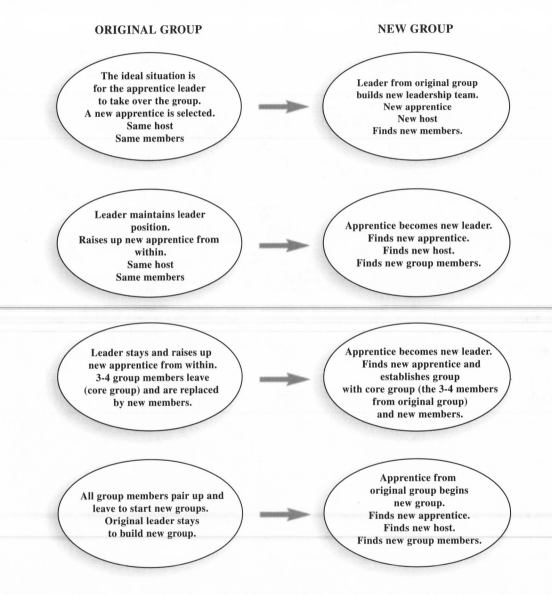

ORIGINAL GROUP

NEW GROUP

The ideal situation is
for the apprentice leader
to take over the group.
A new apprentice is selected.
Same host
Same members

Leader from original group
builds new leadership team.
New apprentice
New host
Finds new members.

Leader maintains leader
position.
Raises up new apprentice from
within.
Same host
Same members

Apprentice becomes new leader.
Finds new apprentice.
Finds new host.
Finds new group members.

Leader stays and raises up
new apprentice from within.
3-4 group members leave
(core group) and are replaced
by new members.

Apprentice becomes new leader.
Finds new apprentice and
establishes group
with core group (the 3-4 members
from original group)
and new members.

All group members pair up and
leave to start new groups.
Original leader stays
to build new group.

Apprentice from
original group begins
new group.
Finds new apprentice.
Finds new host.
Finds new group members.

STEP 2: DETERMINE THE PURPOSE OF TCs.
The next step in creating transformational communities is to understand the types of relationships that are involved. The Great Commandment (Luke 10:27) outlines four primary relationships that are to be emphasized in the life of each believer: (1) Love the Lord your God with all your heart and with all your soul and with all your strength and with all your mind, and (2 and 3) love your neighbor ("neighbor" has two components: loving other believers represented in the diagram as "one another" and loving unbelievers represented in the diagram as "world") as (4)

Leadership Terms and Position Descriptions

- *Ministry Leader:* The pastor, director, or key layperson in charge of the entire young adult ministry.
- *TC Leader:* This person is the leader of a transformation community group of ten people.
- *TC Apprentice Leader:* This person assists the TC group leader.
- *TC Host:* This person organizes and administers the various details of the transformational community group.
- *TC Coach:* This person oversees up to five TC Leaders and helps them with their groups.

See Appendix 1 for detailed job descriptions.

yourself. These four relationships make up the four purposes of TCs. The diagram on page 127 outlines these relationships.

> I believe that the smaller group within the whole is a crucial but underdeveloped resource in most churches. It is, I contend, the most strategically significant foundation for spiritual formation and assimilation, for evangelism and leadership development, for the most essential functions that God has called for in the church.[8]

Relationship with God: The first purpose of a transformational community is for each person to develop a growing and healthy relationship with God. That means each comes to know God in a personal way; it goes beyond just knowing facts about Him. Group members come to know God through studying the Bible, praying with others and alone, and practicing spiritual disciplines such as fasting, solitude, silence, and sacrificial giving.

This type of group interaction will have several results: members will understand God as He reveals Himself in the Bible; they will experience the love and grace of God as He works and reveals Himself through other group members; and people will use this knowledge to live a life of worship where everything that is said and done reflects their desire to honor and please God. These are the elements that involve loving God with all our heart, soul, mind, and strength.

Relationships with one another: The second

purpose of a TC involves group members living out their relationship with God in the context of their relationships with each other. This entails putting the various "one another" commands into practice.

Safe people are "individuals who draw us closer to being the people God intended us to be. Though not perfect, they are 'good enough' in their own character that the net effect of their presence in our lives is positive. They are accepting, honest, and present, and they help us bear good fruit in our lives."[9]

Relationship with self: The third purpose of TCs has to do with the group members gaining a healthy biblical perspective of themselves. As we begin to understand how God sees us, we gain a sense of security that enables us to confess our sins to each other, and as a result experience the freedom of forgiveness. As we begin to see ourselves from God's perspective and experience His love and grace through other believers, we in turn are able to love ourselves in a healthy way. When people begin to understand their identity in Christ, they begin to feel totally different about themselves.

Each one should use whatever gift he has received to serve others, faithfully administering God's grace in its various forms. (1 Peter 4:10)

Serving others: The fourth purpose of TCs is for every believer to realize that he or she is gifted to serve both within the church as well as among unbelievers in both the local and global community. This is primarily done through service evangelism projects and global mission trips where people influence unbelievers for Jesus Christ. Serving is loving your neighbors both locally and abroad.

True community involves "a group of individuals who have learned how to communicate honestly with each other, whose relationships go deeper than their masks of composure, and who have developed some significant commitment to 'rejoice together, mourn together,' and to 'delight in each other, make others' conditions our own.'"[10]

STEP 3: DEVELOP A PLAN THAT BUILDS TCS.
The church is the body of Jesus Christ. A body is a living organism composed of many cells. Think of biblical communities as the cells that make up the body. Within each cell, or community, each person plays a vital role, as Paul said in Romans 12: "So in Christ we who are many form one body, and each member belongs to all the others. We have different gifts, according to the grace given us" (Romans 12:5-6).

Think of a TC as a cell that makes up the greater body of the church. These cells are typically composed of about ten people. Ten is not a magic number, but it is about the maximum number of people for healthy group dynamics. If you have more than ten, the group loses its sense of intimacy; if you have fewer than ten, too few people show up on any given night when other members cannot attend for some reason. Each of these ten people makes up the cell and each has a vital role to play among the others. Note the following diagram for the different roles that each group member plays.

The leadership team: The leadership team is comprised of three people with specific roles. The *host* is the administrator of the group, overseeing all the other teams within the group and helping make sure details do not fall through the cracks. The *leader* is the group facilitator, who helps keep group dynamics healthy. The group leader is also the trainer of the *apprentice leader*, whose goal it is to take over leadership of the group when the leader leaves to birth another group. The apprentice leader facilitates the discussion half of the time as well as assists

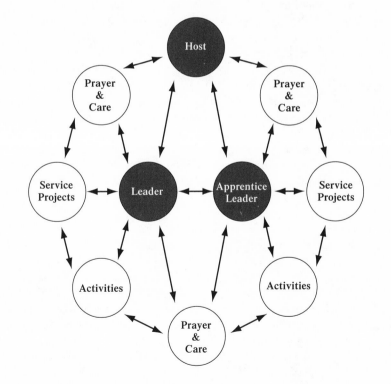

123

the group leader in maintaining healthy group dynamics. Typically within eight to twelve months, the group leader will birth another group and the apprentice leader will take over the existing group.

Cell teams: The remaining seven people join teams inside the group to help facilitate the various needs of group members as well as involve the group in ministry-wide service projects and events. People on the *outreach team* have gifts of evangelism and helps. They aid other group members in reaching people for Christ and bringing new people into the group when a "birth" happens. People on the *service project team* help to coordinate quarterly service projects that the group does together within the local community as well as within the church. The *activities team* helps organize monthly activities that the group does together as well as coordinates events with other small groups within the overall ministry. The *prayer and care team* makes sure that other group members are aware of anyone in the group who has an emergency or need: money, food, hospital visitation, and so on. Members of this team also facilitate group prayer requests.

Within a healthy group, everyone plays a part. As they do this, relationships are strengthened among group members, needs are meet, and lives are changed.

STEP 4: RECRUIT TC LEADERS.

For some reason, finding leaders always seems to be one of the greatest challenges for every min-istry. But it doesn't have to be if you keep a couple of things in mind. The following is a good process for identifying potential leaders:

Pray. This seems obvious, but it's critical to finding the right leaders. Jesus went away and prayed before He selected the disciples (Luke 6:12), and so must we. Ask God to bring you the leaders you will need to develop healthy groups.

Watch people. The best way to determine the people skills of any potential leader is to observe him or her over time. Look for individuals who have the ability to endear themselves to others. The best leaders are sensitive to the needs of others as well as warm and approachable.

Take your time. Don't rush people into leadership and don't feel like you have to force things to happen. God is in control and He will bring the right people at the right time. Remember, it's easier to wait for the right leader than to have to let go of the wrong one.

With these things in mind, approach the potential leader. How you approach anyone is critically important. You don't want to use an apologetic tone and say, "Hi, John. I know you're really busy, and you probably have better things to do. But do you think you might be just a little bit interested in becoming a TC group leader? Would you please think about it and see if it fits into your schedule, and then get back to me when it's convenient for you?" That type of approach is sure to fail.

Instead, approach John and say, "Hi, John. I've been watching you for the last few weeks and I've noticed that you really have a way with people. I have been praying for God to lead me to some people who have the potential to become community leaders, and I think you have great potential. Would you pray about it and get back to me in a week?" With this approach, John will feel honored that you have been noticing him as well as praying for him.

Now, to be honest, most of the time you will find that the potential leaders you approach like this will be reluctant at first, not because of their schedule, but because they don't feel qualified or worthy. Most people don't see themselves as leaders. You need to assure them that, if they feel God leading them to become a group leader, you will equip them thoroughly. You will also need to help them understand that being a group leader does not require them to have mastered all the content of the Bible. Certainly they don't need to have the answers to all of life's difficult questions. Help them see that their primary role is to be a facilitator who models an authentic life and who encourages this in the lives of others in the group. We also suggest that you give them a copy of the leader position description so they have some specific information to help them make their decision (see Appendix 1).

After you have asked potential leaders prayerfully to consider the position, the next step is to have them fill out the leadership questionnaire (see Appendix 1) before you commit to them. This questionnaire is important because it helps you get to know each person better, assess any previous experience, as well as assure you that this person is a believer.

STEP 5: BUILD THE LEADERSHIP TEAM.

The TC leadership team is the nucleus of the group. This nucleus includes the leader, apprentice leader, and host. We have already looked at the roles and expectations of the leader; now let's examine the roles and expectations for the rest of the leadership team.

The first task of the newly appointed leader is to recruit an apprentice leader and a host. This is an important first step because if the leader cannot adequately recruit two people to join him or her in leading a group, the leader's suitability for leadership should be questioned. This initial task for the new leader is a good litmus test of his or her motives, gifts, skill, and overall potential. Another thing to consider is explaining the importance of having a leadership team in the first place.

As we have noted earlier, young adults like to know the "why" behind most everything. It's important to be able to express to them the validity of a leadership team by answering the question "Why do I need a leadership team?" The answer is actually quite simple. Young adult ministry should be about doing ministry together in teams. We have already talked about the importance and benefits of teams in regards to accomplishing ministry tasks, and the same reasons apply to building TC groups. This team approach also prevents the group from polarizing around one charismatic leader, which greatly hinders birthing new groups. (We will look at the importance of birthing new groups later in this chapter.)

STEP 6: UNDERSTAND THE NUTS AND BOLTS OF THE LEADERSHIP TEAM.

Building a leadership team is a very straightforward process. First, the newly appointed leader begins looking for someone to become his or her apprentice by applying the same guidelines of prayer, watchfulness, patience, and approach that you used to recruit him or her. Once identified, the potential apprentice leader should be given the apprentice position description in Appendix 1 and asked to pray about God's leading.

As you can see from the apprentice position description, there are many similarities in both the requirements and expectations of the leader and apprentice leader. This is important to note because the ideal goal is for the apprentice leader eventually to assume leadership of the group when the leader leaves to birth a new group. It is critical that both the leader and apprentice buy in to the birthing process at the beginning to ensure that it happens. The more groups you have, the more people you can care for in a healthy way. These groups are one of the most effective ways to grow your ministry, facilitate life change, and truly care for people.

The next step in building the leadership team requires both the leader and apprentice leader to work together to find a host. They find the host by following the same pattern of prayer, watchfulness, patience, and approach as we've outlined throughout the recruiting process. Once a potential host has been identified, the candidate should be given the host position description (Appendix 1) before making a decision.

As you can see, the host position description is much different from both the leader and the apprentice leader positions. The primary role of the host is to oversee the various teams within the group that we have already outlined as well as help administer the overall group details. Don't assume or even expect the leader or apprentice leader to have strong administrative gifts. It's best that they have strong people skills and the ability to manage conflict and troubleshoot issues within the group because these are the tools they will need to create healthy group dynamics.

With the addition of the host and the apprentice leader, the leadership team is now complete. However, before they launch the group, there are a few final things they need to decide.

1. What day of the week and time of day is the group going to meet?

2. Where is the group going to meet? Often group members will take turns having the meeting at their house or apartment, but initially the leadership team needs to decide.

3. What will we study? In order to determine the area of study, the leadership team chooses one of the four relational purposes of TCs (see following diagram). Each area of study involves a three-month time period. The ultimate goal of the group is to complete the full cycle every twelve months. Each area involves specific study materials that will help facilitate the relational goal. The leadership team determines all of these things up-front because it's much easier for three people to agree than for ten people to reach a consensus.

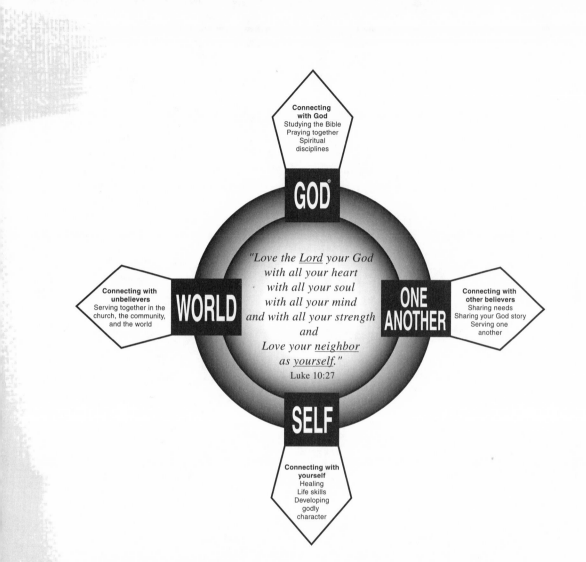

Connecting with God
Studying the Bible
Praying together
Spiritual disciplines

GOD°

Connecting with unbelievers
Serving together in the church, the community, and the world

WORLD

"Love the <u>Lord</u> your God with all your heart with all your soul with all your mind and with all your strength and Love your <u>neighbor</u> as <u>yourself</u>."
Luke 10:27

ONE ANOTHER

Connecting with other believers
Sharing needs
Sharing your God story
Serving one another

SELF

Connecting with yourself
Healing
Life skills
Developing godly character

STEP 7: UNDERSTAND THE BIRTHING PROCESS.
The birthing process keeps the TC-group ministry healthy. It facilitates the health of the current group because it lets new people in. It helps the overall ministry stay healthy because more groups create the ability to care for more and more new people. It's important to note that the birthing process does not mean the mother group disbands! Instead, the leader or apprentice leader and one other person leave the mother group and

127

establish another leadership team to begin a new group. Remember, one of the primary goals of TC groups is to build community. If more than two group members leave, it can break down the intimacy you worked so hard to establish. There are several ways to birth new groups, depending on what you want to accomplish. The diagram below shows various birthing methods that have proven to be effective.

From the diagram,[11] it's easy to see the process that takes place when either the leader or the apprentice leader leaves the original group.

To get groups going quickly, consider the "turbo birthing" option. This works very well

TURBO BIRTHING PROCESS

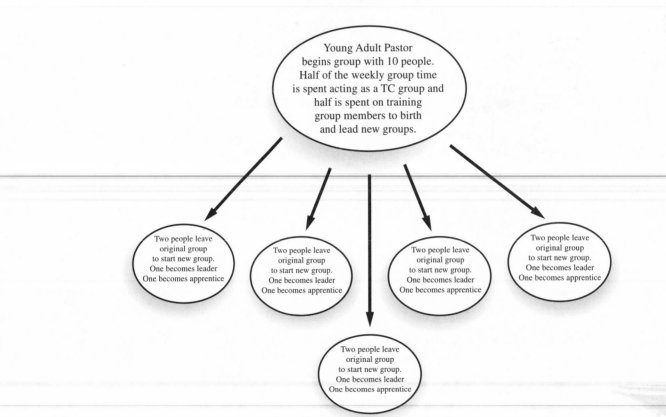

Young Adult Pastor begins group with 10 people. Half of the weekly group time is spent acting as a TC group and half is spent on training group members to birth and lead new groups.

Two people leave original group to start new group. One becomes leader One becomes apprentice

Two people leave original group to start new group. One becomes leader One becomes apprentice

Two people leave original group to start new group. One becomes leader One becomes apprentice

Two people leave original group to start new group. One becomes leader One becomes apprentice

Two people leave original group to start new group. One becomes leader One becomes apprentice when you are first beginning your TC-group ministry and find it difficult to recruit potential leaders. A turbo group consists of nine potential group leaders who meet with the pastor or ministry director and go through one of the three-month relational areas of study. During these three months, the leader spends half the weekly meeting time facilitating the group as if he or she were the leader and the other half of the time training the group members in how to lead, facilitate, and create healthy group dynamics. Turbo birthing provides hands-on training and works extremely well. At the end of the turbo birthing cycle (three months), a number, if not all, of your turbo group members will be ready to build their own leadership teams to launch new groups. If some aren't ready to start their own groups, they can team up with other leaders and become apprentices.

STEP 8: CREATE A HEALTHY SPAN OF CARE FOR GROUP LEADERS.

As groups mature, conflict happens, leaders get tired, and members realize that being in relationship with each other is sometimes as difficult as it is rewarding. In order to maintain healthy group dynamics, you need healthy leaders, and that requires what we call "a healthy span of care."

Be careful not to assume that one paid staff person will be able to care for all group leaders. If the staff person tries to do it all, he or she will bottleneck the process and limit the number of groups that can develop. A

more effective approach is to develop a coaching system that adequately distributes the span of care. A healthy span of care consists of three to five leader/apprentice pairs for each coach. The coach's primary role is to care for the needs of these leaders by providing feedback during crisis times, to offer regular encouragement, and to assist them in maintaining healthy group dynamics. When the leaders have problems they cannot handle, their first course of action is to contact the coach. You can find the coach's position description in Appendix 1.

The coaching position is the most difficult one to fill because it requires a certain amount of experience and maturity. Sometimes the most effective coaches are older adults who have a desire to minister in this capacity. However, the best-case scenario is when a group leader chooses to move into a coaching position. This is ideal because the leader has firsthand knowledge of the entire TC-group process and is committed to building transformational communities.

With the coach in place, the last element in creating an effective group system is to provide a monthly training and encouragement time for the leaders, apprentice leaders, and their coaches. Carl George refers to this as VHS (Vision, Huddle, Skill).[12]

STEP 9: EQUIP YOUR GROUP LEADERS AND COACHES.

Building and maintaining relationships among the leaders is a difficult but critical element in an effective group system. Each group leader must maintain the balance of seeing the young adult TC as a cohesive, autonomous entity and as a critical part of the young adult ministry and church. Leaders who lose contact with the vision and values of the overall ministry and their critical connectedness with other leaders and TCs will find their own group becoming more isolated, more difficult, and less fulfilling. Group leaders who are isolated and out of regular fellowship with other group leaders will eventually drop out. A VHS meeting is the right place to keep leaders encouraged, equipped, and connected. The monthly VHS meeting is a place where all the coaches, group leaders, and apprentices gather together. The meeting is divided into three main sections:

Vision casting: In order to keep each group aligned with the larger ministry vision and values (see chapter 7), people need to hear the overall vision every twenty-eight days. This is especially true for leaders. This is known as the Nehemiah principle. Nehemiah kept the people of Israel focused on the task of building the wall around Jerusalem despite intense opposition. This same focus is needed for TC coaches and leaders; they need a regular time to be "pumped up" with the vision. Vision casting can involve things like stories from other group leaders about life changes they are seeing in their group members, telling about the impact of a recent service project, and so on. When people hear what God is doing within other groups, it builds excitement and generates a sense of connectedness.

Huddle: During each VHS meeting, it is critical for leaders to gather together, preferably with their coaches, to share what is going on in their lives and to pray and encourage each other. During the huddle time, the leaders will share what is working and what is not working. They will teach and mentor each other in the art of TC-group leadership. It is important for you to devote as much time as possible to your huddle groups. If your leaders feel connected, they will continue to come with excitement month after month.

Skill: The final element of the VHS meeting involves a time for instruction. It is important for the leaders to sense that they are moving forward and growing in their knowledge and competence. Some will be struggling with how to address a difficult group member. Others want to know how to keep their group fresh week after week. It is important that the topics selected address the issues your leaders have on their hearts. A good way to ensure this is to have a different leader or coach lead this skill time each month. These people are in the trenches week after week, they know what works and what doesn't work, and they have a keen awareness of all the stress points.

These are the primary elements of every VHS meeting, but there are a few other things to consider; the most important is meeting time. It is important to find a time that works best for your particular ministry. Setting the time for the meeting when your leaders will already be at the church is often the best way to go because it doesn't add another meeting during the week. Providing food is often a helpful means to increase your attendance. You may want to recognize the leaders whose groups began most recently, or choose a leader of the month for going above and beyond the call of duty. You may choose a particular book you recommend, giving leaders ideas for areas of personal study and growth. These and many other options help to keep your groups moving forward for the long haul because the long haul is difficult.

Maintaining an ongoing VHS meeting can be very difficult. It must be a priority. You must creatively work to make it happen, for in so doing you will ensure the health of your leaders and ultimately the health of the entire ministry.

These are the steps necessary to build intentional and effective groups that foster life change and provide your ministry with healthy growth. If you want a healthy ministry to young adults, you have to care for their needs, and small groups are the best means of doing that. One young adult put it well when he said, "My generation hungers for friends who will be loyal and genuine. We long to belong to a community of acceptance and affirmation. We hunger for models of authenticity, integrity, and transparency. We are searching for people who are like us and who will build a relationship with us so that we don't have to feel we are alone."[13]

GETTING REAL YOURSELF

1. If you're familiar with traditional small groups, do you think what we call transformational communities are all that different? Make your own list of the similarities and differences between traditional small groups and TCs.

2. Look at the job descriptions in Appendix 1. Can you think of people in your church or ministry that can be group leaders, apprentice leaders, and coaches? Make a list and start praying for these people, even if you know it might be a long time before you get to the point of starting TCs. Also, ask God to bring new people who can fill in gaps.

3. What do you think is the single most important reason to have transformational communities in young adult ministry?

PROGRAMS THAT WORK

Okay, we've said many times that ministry is about people, not programs. But now, for lack of a better word, we are going to use the p word: *programs*.

Programs are a vital part of any young adult ministry. Programs are the strategic ways you implement your core values. The effectiveness of your programs is determined by how well they implement your core values. For example, if you are planning a ski retreat, you must ask how that retreat fits in with your core values. Is it going to be a retreat where people bring their unchurched friends? Is it going to be a retreat that builds community among group members?

Your core values determine the type and content of your programs. It's futile to copy another ministry's programs because they may exist for an entirely different reason. Their goals won't necessarily line up with yours because they will have started with different core values. "Programs make sense only when they are applied to an adequate foundation."[1]

PROGRAMMING PURPOSES

The following funnel diagram is based on a people-driven model of ministry that we mentioned in chapter 5. It's a helpful tool that will enable you to keep your programs aligned with your core ideology and vision statement. The diagram outlines four basic programming purposes and answers four basic programming questions that will help you achieve your vision with your programs.

Attracting (Q1): The purpose of the programs within the first quadrant is to attract young adults to your ministry. The specific types of programs will depend on a number of factors: your target audience, the type of church you are in, the city and state you live in, and the flexibility and freedom you have within your church policies and structures. Quadrant one answers the question *"Why do people come to our programs?"*

Involving (Q2): The purpose of second quadrant programs is to connect people into the ministry. We've observed that 25 percent of the people who come to your ministry will never come back no matter what you do, and another 25 percent will never leave no matter what you do. The other 50 percent of the people in your ministry are the ones you need to be the most intentional about involving in ministry in order to keep them. Quadrant two programs are designed to help you answer the question *"Why do people stay?"*

Reproducing (Q3): The purpose of programs in the third quadrant is to facilitate the maturity process among believers. Equipping, discipling, mentoring, and leadership development are all core elements within quadrant three. Quadrant three helps you answer the question *"How do we develop mature believers?"*

Multiplying (Q4): Finally, the purpose of quadrant four programs is to grow your ministry through outreach. Reaching unchurched young adults—through service projects, mission trips, and a variety of outreach-oriented programs—is the core element of quadrant four. Through these programs, you answer the question *"How do we multiply?"*

A program will be effective only as long as it fulfills its stated purpose. Programs must stay flexible and adapt readily to change. The danger exists that programs will become "sacred cows" and exist after they are no longer effective. Remember, your programs serve your ministry, not the other way around.

Next, let's take a look at some specific programs that are working with postmodern generations.

PROVEN PROGRAMS

ATHLETIC CLUBS

Find a large park in your area that is fairly central

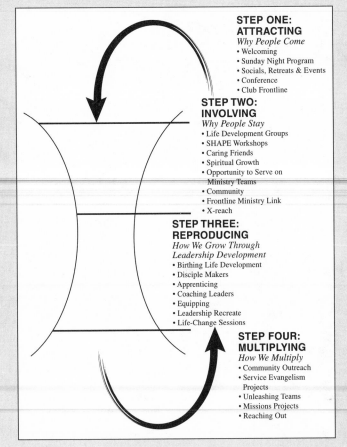

STEP ONE:
ATTRACTING
Why People Come
- Welcoming
- Sunday Night Program
- Socials, Retreats & Events
- Conference
- Club Frontline

STEP TWO:
INVOLVING
Why People Stay
- Life Development Groups
- SHAPE Workshops
- Caring Friends
- Spiritual Growth
- Opportunity to Serve on Ministry Teams
- Community
- Frontline Ministry Link
- X-reach

STEP THREE:
REPRODUCING
How We Grow Through Leadership Development
- Birthing Life Development
- Disciple Makers
- Apprenticing
- Coaching Leaders
- Equipping
- Leadership Recreate
- Life-Change Sessions

STEP FOUR:
MULTIPLYING
How We Multiply
- Community Outreach
- Service Evangelism Projects
- Unleashing Teams
- Missions Projects
- Reaching Out

to a majority of your young adults and meet there every week at a set time, say from 10 A.M. to noon. Organize team sports like flag football, volleyball, ultimate frisbee, and softball, or sponsor mountain bike trips, backpacking hikes, or even a citywide 10K run. Another effective means of outreach is to have a team from your group join a city softball, soccer, or basketball league. It's a great way for the team to build community and share Christ with other teams after the games at the local pizza place.

TURKEY OUTREACH

Over the past few years the Frontline young adult ministry and the rest of our church have teamed up to distribute complete Thanksgiving meals to a variety of people in need throughout the Washington, D.C. area. Boxes are prepared with a frozen turkey, a roasting pan, a sack of potatoes, a can of cranberries, a box of stuffing, a pumpkin pie, dressing, gravy, and a copy of the gospel of John from *The Message*. Each box will feed a family of four to six people and can be assembled for $25.

In 1997 we collected enough money to feed 2,500 families. We assembled the packages on a Saturday morning with hundreds of volunteers working together. We then loaded the boxes onto rental trucks and sent teams out into the community to distribute the meals to preselected churches, homeless shelters, and other organizations. The *Washington Times Magazine* even called for an interview. They asked us why we were doing this, and we responded, "We were just sharing the love of God in practical ways." They ran a huge article in the paper that weekend. TV crews showed up at a number of drop-off spots to capture the moment on film.

How to Do Your Own Turkey Outreach

Suggest to a couple of key people the idea to reach your community for Christ by providing boxed dinners. Then have them start influencing people in the group; let it be their idea. From that point, there will be many who want to get involved. Let them put together a team, and you just cheer them on.

Contact local grocery stores and ask if they are willing to donate turkeys or any of the box contents. Sometimes they will give away dented cans that they cannot sell. Next, locate trucks to help with delivery of the packages. Many times, truck rental companies will donate the trucks for a few hours to show their support.

Have the people in your group share the plan among friends and at work so individuals and corporations will have the chance to volunteer time or money.

Contact other churches in your area to see if they would like to network with you in reaching out to the community.

Contact a variety of organizations within your city or town that would be able to distribute the boxes to people in need. Many inner-city churches will love to work with you. Homeless shelters are also a great place to donate boxes. There will probably even be people in your own church who would be grateful for a free dinner.

SUNDAY NIGHT LIVE

At Frontline we have learned that the best time to take young adults deeper in their faith is when they are already at church. Because of this, we established a Sunday night discipleship program that includes four different modules for further equipping our young adults.

Module 1: X-Reach. X-reach is a repeating, three-week series that helps new believers and unbelievers explore the beginning steps of a spiritual journey. The lessons are focused on Up-Reach (stressing that God wants a relationship with them), In-Reach (focusing on the things that God wants to change in us to give us a more healthy way of life), and Out-Reach (which emphasizes that God wants us to share our story with others).

Module 2: Changed Lives. This is a nine-week module that focuses on the elements of becoming a fully devoted follower of Christ.

Module 3: Sharing Without Fear. This is a five-week module that helps people learn how to share their faith in a postmodern context.

Module 4: Open Forum. Each month we have an open meeting where people can come in and ask any questions they want about Christianity. We have found that this process is very effective in helping young adults on their spiritual journey.

LEADERSHIP DEVELOPMENT

Having a process by which you recruit and develop leaders is a key component of an effective ministry with young adults. Every three months at Frontline we have an all-day seminar called Leadership Summit. The people we invite are those people our current leaders have identified as potential leaders in all areas of ministry. The summit is composed of a number of sessions aimed at educating as well as equipping prospective leaders about the elements of spiritual leadership.

Session 1: Becoming an Effective Leader. This session outlines the new leadership styles that are most effective in today's world. In this session we talk about character and the seven secrets of effective leaders.

Session 2: Living Out Leadership in Ministry. This session focuses on the critical tasks of leading a team: how to empower others, how to plan and set goals, how to monitor progress and give feedback to team members. We teach participants how to build community within their team, how to manage conflict in constructive ways, and how to understand differences in individual personality and styles of teammates.

Session 3: Empowering Your Team. Here we have the summit attendees break into smaller groups to work through a case study that helps them apply what they have learned. The case study helps them think through the most effective ways to build teams, manage conflict, reach goals, and care for each other. We take them through a six-stage process that equips them to become effective leaders.

Session 4: Reproducing Leaders. Every leader is equipped and expected to develop an apprentice leader. In session four we go over all the training necessary for each leader to effectively choose and mentor other leaders. We outline all the ministry team structures, review the team position descriptions, show them what to look for in potential leaders, and give them a basic overview of each of the ministry teams. We also help them define their own team values and purposes.

SERVICE EVANGELISM PROJECTS

We have already looked at the basic philosophy behind service evangelism in chapter 4. Remember that the concept is to do acts of kindness that demonstrate the love of God to people in your community. Here are some examples of service evangelism projects that are inexpensive and fairly easy to pull off.

At each of these events, participants can distribute cards that list your church name and address, ministries that you offer, and times of regularly scheduled services.

Let the ideas on pages 138-139 start the creative juices flowing in your group members to come up with their own projects. Then go out and serve God together!

PARTIES WITH A PURPOSE

Most young adult ministries have any number of parties each year. Parties are great, but you can also use them to implement your core values. Ask this question in the planning stage of every party: What core value are we implementing with this party? Is this an event for believers, or is it better suited as an event where people can bring their unchurched friends? Below are a variety of ideas for parties and events that have worked well for us.

• Our annual Christmas party, held at a popular restaurant, features a DJ, catered food, and semiformal attire. The purpose and elements of the party are such that people can bring associates from work as well as unchurched friends to have a great time and mingle with Christians their age.

• Each year in Washington, D.C., there is a huge Fourth of July celebration on the Mall between the Capitol building and the Lincoln Memorial. About half a million people gather to watch a spectacular fireworks show. With so many people in one place, we have taken the opportunity to share Jesus Christ with the crowd. We set up a huge stage and rotate a variety of bands through the day for thirty-minute sets. After each concert, we have a speaker share a five-minute message or testimony. We also provide refreshments: one year we gave out ten thousand cups of water; another year we gave away popsicles. After each speaker, we tell people that we will pray with them in an adjoining tent or answer any questions they have. Each year, many people pray to receive Christ as well as come in for counsel on a number of issues. We use a follow-up card to help plug each person into a local church in the area.

GETTING YOUNG ADULTS INVOLVED IN MINISTRY

We use our SHAPE workshop to plug young adults into meaningful ministry by helping them discover their unique spiritual gifts, passions, abilities, personality traits, and life experiences. The workshop is an all-day seminar that integrates a variety of learning elements to help each young adult discover his or her unique calling. When we show people how they fit into the overall picture of our ministry, it creates a sense

PROJECT	CONCEPT	EQUIPMENT	PEOPLE NEEDED	COST
Ice Cream Gift Certificates	Go to a busy summer area in the evening and hand out free gift certificates for one scoop of ice cream.	Gift certificates. Make sure the store owner knows when your group is going to do this so he or she can staff appropriately.	Five or more	Approximately $2 per certificate. Ask the store owner for a bulk discount.
Free Car Wash	Go to a local gas station and ask to put up a sign that says, "Free Car Wash, No Kidding." Also ask if you can use their water source.	Buckets, sponges, towels, chamois, mild soap, and hoses	Five or more	Approximately $1 per car
Leaf Raking	Go around the neighborhoods and ask people if you can rake their leaves.	Rakes and trash bags	Two or more	Rakes run about $10 each. Trash bags in bulk are about $5. Dump costs vary. Ask the dump manager to donate the space.
Snow Shoveling	Go around the neighborhoods and shovel snow from driveways, walkways, and stairs.	4 x 4 vehicles, snow shovels, snow melt for stairs	Two or more	Snow shovels are about $10 each, and snow melt is about $5 per bag. Again, ask the store manager to donate any or all materials.
Rainy Day Grocery Escort	Help shoppers to cars with packages.	Golf umbrellas	Two or more	Minimal
Outdoor Window Washing	Wash first-floor windows of residences or businesses.	Professional squeegees and window cleaner, short ladder, buckets, towels	Two or more	Onetime purchase of squeegees, about $10 each

PROJECT	CONCEPT	EQUIPMENT	PEOPLE NEEDED	COST
Smoke Detector Batteries	Go door-to-door and give out 9-volt replacement batteries.	Reminders with date, 9-volt batteries	Two or more	In bulk, 9-volt batteries cost about $1.25 each.
Gutter Cleaning	Clean gutters of houses, removing leaves, sticks, and debris.	Gloves, ladders, trash bags	Teams of two	Trash bags in bulk cost about $5.
Popsicle Giveaway	On hot days, set up tables outside of sporting events or at store exits and give away popsicles.	Table, ice chests, ice, signs that say, "Free Popsicles, No Kidding"	Three or more	Minimal
Windshield Washing	Wash the windows of every car in a parking lot at stores and shopping centers.	Window cleaner, towels	Two or more	Minimal
Balloon Giveaway	Go to a park and give balloons to kids and cards to their parents.	Rented helium tanks, balloons	Two or more	Balloons and helium run about 10 to 15 cents per balloon.
Address Painting	Paint address numbers on curbs.	Stencils, spray paint	Two or more	$1 to $2 per house
Bird Feeder Giveaway	Share God's love with shut-ins by giving free bird feeders to convalescent hospitals.	Bird feeders, birdseed	Two or more	Birdseed, initial investment of bird feeder

of excitement and motivation that really makes an impact when harnessed for the kingdom of God. (See Appendix 5 for SHAPE materials.)

OPERATION MENTOR

Single-parent families are on the increase and usually consist of a single mom with her kids. Operation Mentor is Frontline's response to these families. Young men and women spend time with the kids of single parents in a variety of activities: going shopping, out for ice cream, to ball games, or just for a drive. It's great for the kids and it gives the parents a needed break.

Programs are an essential part of any ministry as long as you use them in the right way. When each program is a part of implementing your core values and ministry vision, you have an effective means of keeping everything in alignment. Remember, these program ideas are intended to get you started and encourage you to be even more creative in designing your own.

GETTING REAL YOURSELF

1. Take some index cards and make a list of the program/outreach ideas mentioned in this chapter. Alone or with your ministry leaders, spend some time thinking of how you could adapt the idea in your own ministry, or use these ideas as starting points for your own programs. Write your ideas on the back of the cards.

2. List the activities, programs, and projects your ministry has done in the past year. As you think about your ministry's purpose and values, evaluate how well each program "fits." In other words, did each project help you accomplish your purpose? Did it fit with one of your core values?

CHAPTER THIRTEEN

EMPOWERING PEOPLE

Recently, while helping a church start a young adult ministry, I (Rich) was amused to see the reaction by the church staff to the results of our efforts. A small group of leaders met all summer and planned and strategized what they wanted to do. After going through all the steps we have recommended in the earlier chapters of this book, the result was a great first meeting of a lay-led ministry. The team of lay leaders was amazed and delighted at what God did. The church staff seemed genuinely surprised at the large crowd that gathered for the first night's meeting, and at the apparent effectiveness of the group's hard work. This struck me as funny—and a little ironic— because it was the staff itself that had empowered this leadership team to pursue its dream.

We need to create "permission-giving" systems that free and empower people to explore their spiritual gifts individually and in teams on behalf of the body of Christ.[1]

Nothing is more important or powerful in the world
than a soul on fire.
—George Fox[2]

What every man wants is someone to inspire him
to be all he can.
—Emerson[3]

We are constantly on a stretch, if not a strain, to devise new methods, new plans,
new organizations to advance the church. This trend loses sight of the man and sinks him
into the plan or organization. God's plan is to make much of man, far more of him than
anything else. Men are God's methods. The church is looking for better methods;
God is looking for better men.
—E. M. Bounds[4]

A MINISTRY OF EMPOWERMENT

If you could take all the concepts discussed in this book and apply them, what would it look like? How do you empower people to dream and see those dreams realized? The steps in this chapter are still just suggestions that provide a starting point. It takes hard work and a commitment to empower people. It is also messy and at times very frustrating. But the result is worth it.

A ministry of empowerment has these elements:

ENCOURAGE PEOPLE TO BE THEMSELVES

Bruce Larson told me a story about a rabbi named Zosia. Rabbi Zosia said, "When I die, God will not ask why I was not Moses! But He may ask, why were you not Zosia?"

What does it mean to accept people where they are, to allow them to be in process? I (Rich) tell people all the time: "God will accept you just as you are, but He loves you too much to leave you that way." We need to love people and allow them to be in process. "Accept one another, then, just as Christ accepted you, in order to bring praise to God" (Romans 15:7).

Let me give you an example. Seth is a great leader. He is in his early twenties and has already built a strong ministry. But he has a hard time keeping his commitments. It would be easy to give up on Seth. But instead we have learned how important it is to work with the individual differences of every young adult leader.

The command in Romans is to "accept one another." This isn't an option. The verb "accept" is an imperative in the Greek. Paul doesn't say to accept one another if you feel like it, accept one another if it's convenient, accept one another if they deserve it. Paul is clear: accept one another, period. Paul even tells us how to accept each other: as Christ accepted you, so should you accept one another. God accepts us totally and unconditionally; He takes you just as you are. You don't need to change a thing for God to accept you!

Creating an environment of acceptance is not a license for someone to be irresponsible. People need to be held accountable, but you can't expect everyone to behave the same. Acceptance is life-giving; it is a powerful motivation for involvement. Another word for acceptance is *grace*. Grace motivates people; it empowers them in ways that nothing else will.

BUILD RELATIONSHIPS, NOT JUST PROGRAMS

Have you heard this before? Ministry is about relationships; it is about interacting with others to facilitate change in their lives. This is a far cry from pressuring people to staff the programs you want to create.

Good relationships with your leaders go a lot further in getting things done than do the most comprehensive job descriptions. There's no replacement for giving personal time to leaders—but not to check and see how they are doing at accomplishing the tasks of ministry. I've found the most important questions are not "Have you taken care of . . . ?" or "I gave you a job assignment; did you get it done?" but rather "How are you doing?" and "What's going on in your life that you'd like to talk about?"

One night I (Rich) met with several young adult leaders for dinner. Not too long after we ordered, they asked, "Okay, you wanted to meet. What do you want us to do?" They were so conditioned by their past experience that, when a pastor met with them, they thought it meant he or she wanted them to do something.

"Let's make a deal," I said. "Let's not talk about business tonight; let's talk about how we are doing in our personal and spiritual lives." We had a great evening, and they later said they felt cared about in a different way from any they ever had before in ministry.

Effective ministry isn't the result of getting everyone involved in our events but rather of asking the questions "How can we help all the leaders know they are important not for what they do but for who they are? What kind of people do we want to produce? What types of changes would we like to see in their lives as a result of being in the young adult ministry?"

I have always liked the mission of Willow Creek Community Church in the Chicago area: "We want to produce fully devoted followers of Christ." Simply put, when you know what you want to produce, you're a lot closer to knowing what to do and what not to do.

DEVELOP WORLD CHRISTIANS

Our goal is to produce world Christians, not "pew bunnies." But what is a world Christian? Remember, the first words of Jesus' public ministry were "The time has come . . . the kingdom of God is near" (Mark 1:15). And throughout Jesus' entire ministry, He relentlessly proclaimed

the kingdom of God. In fact, He even told His followers to make the kingdom their first priority. World Christians are those who put God's priorities for the world first. Building the kingdom of God has always been the objective; the church is the vehicle, not an end in itself. The church exists here on the earth to accomplish the objective of building the kingdom of God.

With that in mind, young adult ministry is just the vehicle as well, not the objective. The temptation is to think you are building a program. But your program is just the vehicle. Think of it this way: Your car exists to take you places. It's not your destination; it's your vehicle. Your young adult ministry exists to help you take people to new places in their faith and service for God.

There are various ways to help this happen, but among those some seem to be most effective. Short-term mission and service projects are some of the best ways to develop kingdom perspective. These projects create an awareness of others' needs and help participants develop more sensitive hearts.

THINK BEYOND THE WALLS OF THE CHURCH

The Bible teaches us that we are believer-priests. It teaches that each of us who has a relationship with Christ has been given a ministry. As a leader, you need to be convinced that your role is to equip those in your care to accomplish their own ministry.

Paul reminds us, "It was he who gave some to be apostles, some to be prophets, some to be evangelists, and some to be pastors and teachers, to prepare God's people for works of service, so that the body of Christ may be built up" (Ephesians 4:11-12). But how do you act on this? How do you make room in your church for everyone to have a place in ministry? After all, there are only so many openings for ushers and Sunday school teachers.

> If God loves you, why are you still tap dancing for everyone else?
>
> —From a conversation with John Westfall

The answer is this—think beyond the walls of the church. Matthew 28:18 is a passage known as the Great Commission. It is not the Great Invitation. Jesus didn't say, "Invite everyone to come to your church and make disciples of them." He said go. "Go into all the world . . . and make disciples."

Ask young adults this question: "If you could do anything for God without the fear of failure, what would it be?" One young adult said, "Perhaps many of us are attracted to service for precisely this reason: we hunger to know the reality beyond our cool, elegant cynicism—the truth behind the hip and humble distractions of kooky, modern America."

Many of today's young adults are tired of giving lip service. They want to get out there and do something. They want to make something happen that will mean the difference in the life of another person.

In a 1996 issue of *Christianity Today*, in an article titled "Elizabeth Dole's Fishbowl Faith," Mrs. Dole was asked about her plans for after her husband's presidential run. The interviewer asked, "You have said that after the election, no matter what happens, you are still planning to return to your position as president of the American Red Cross. Why?"

She replied, "It's a mission field for me, an opportunity to make a difference for people with dire human needs. Most First Ladies choose some overarching humanitarian mission or goal. The Red Cross is perfectly suited to that. I also want to lead a movement in the country to increase charitable giving."[5]

If you create an environment where people are encouraged and empowered to move out and do something for God, watch out! Things will begin to happen.

CHALLENGE PEOPLE TO ASSUME AUTHORITY

For lay leaders truly to take ownership of their ministries, they must understand that the ministry stands or falls with them. Surprisingly, this puts a burden on you. You must make sure the person responsible for a program gets the authority to do it.

At one church where I (Rich) served, we started a program called X-Cafe. It was meant to be a coffee and discussion time after one of our church services. The idea had come from a group of young adults who were very excited about something in their church for people their age. We met for weeks, prayed, and laid out a strategy. Each week different leaders would run into roadblocks as they prepared for the kick-off week. (The church was so staff-driven that if a staff person was not involved in a particular program, it never got off the ground.)

The leader of the program was volunteering hours and hours of time. She was a very talented and creative person, and even had a seminary degree. She finally came to me and said, "I cannot get anything done in this church. You gave me the job to get the X-Cafe set up, but honestly, there is no way to get anyone to cooperate with me. I have no authority, so no one listens to me."

Nothing is more frustrating than to have a job to do and not have the authority to do it. One of the most paralyzing experiences in the church today is to want to do something for God and not feel empowered to do it.

We have continued to encourage you to listen to people's dreams, but if you don't follow up by giving young adults the power or authority to take action on those dreams, you might as well not listen.

DON'T FORCE ANYTHING

If God wants something to happen, He will provide the right person who has the right passion and set of abilities to do it. Launch only those ministries that someone has the passion to launch. And be willing to allow for some chaos. William Easum writes, "Chaos is disorder in the source of new order instead of something to be avoided. Chaos is desirable because it is the start of something new. Organizations, over time, do not have to wind down and go out of existence

if they embrace chaos and learn new ways to achieve old things."[6]

Now, there are certain times when you have to recruit people. Face it, certain things have to be done. But the most effective way to do this with young adults is to help them see how these things fit into the larger picture. When you can help someone see how his or her gifts and abilities line up with the accomplishment of the overall vision of your ministry, you have a win-win situation that is extremely motivating and empowering.

It was just before the Passover Feast. Jesus knew that the time had come for him to leave this world and go to the Father. Having loved his own who were in the world, he now showed them the full extent of his love.

The evening meal was being served, and the devil had already prompted Judas Iscariot, son of Simon, to betray Jesus. Jesus knew that the Father had put all things under his power, and that he had come from God and was returning to God; so he got up from the meal, took off his outer clothing, and wrapped a towel around his waist. After that, he poured water into a basin and began to wash his disciples' feet, drying them with the towel that was wrapped around him. (John 13:1-5)

HELP THEM LEARN TO NETWORK

Recently, I (Rich) was in a city conducting a seminar put on by four different churches. There was a great spirit of cooperation at the event. Apparently, the prior year just one church held the conference, but it had since decided to network with other churches. The result was a great conference, great relationships built with leaders from other churches, and a great outreach event. On the other hand, I recently watched as two different young adult ministries in a major city held separate leadership training events. Neither one was very effective in reaching people, and both groups were disappointed.

> If you have raced with men on foot, and they have worn you out, how can you compete with horses? If you stumble in safe country, how will you manage in the thickets by the Jordan? (Jeremiah 12:5)

The principle of networking holds true for the people in your young adult groups as well. Here is one example. Matt is Frontline's Homeless Ministry Coordinator. He came to Ken about six months ago and said he was burning out and wanted to step out of this leadership role. Well, no one had stepped up to the plate to take over the leadership of it. So instead of forcing it, Ken let the program die. He embraced Matt, told him how much he appreciated all his hard work and how he had made a difference in many lives. He didn't throw guilt on him or punish him. Ken showed that he cared more about Matt as a person than about what Matt could do for the ministry.

But as a leader, Ken learned something very important in the process. It is absolutely necessary that each leader have an apprentice, someone of his or her own choosing. That way, if the leader wants to move on, the program doesn't die.

Granted, some programs need to be buried and laid to rest. But others tend to define your ministry. So, unless you want the character of your ministry to change without your control, you need to develop an apprentice system to keep these defining programs alive!

> That evening after sunset the people brought to Jesus all the sick and demon-possessed. The whole town gathered at the door, and Jesus healed many who had various diseases. He also drove out many demons, but he would not let the demons speak because they knew who he was.
>
> Very early in the morning, while it was still dark, Jesus got up, left the house and went off to a solitary place, where he prayed. (Mark 1:32-35)

PRINCIPLES OF EMPOWERMENT

As you empower people, let us remind you of some helpful principles:

A LEADER KNOWS TO WHOM HE OR SHE BELONGS.

Jesus was able to have compassion on others because His identity was not dependent upon His ministry. If we are unsure who owns us, then we will spend vast amounts of time trying to impress people. And all of us need to make a decision in leadership: Do we want to impress people or influence them? You impress people from a distance; you influence people up close, by being a part of their lives. You can't do both.

A LEADER TAKES PERSONAL GROWTH SERIOUSLY.
Jesus could care for others because He took care of Himself. He had "boundaries," we might say today. Do you have good boundaries? Can you answer these three key questions?
- Where am I being nurtured?
- Who is my sounding board?
- Where is my source of affirmation?

> Now I am glad to boast about how weak I am; I am glad to be a living demonstration of Christ's power, instead of showing off my own power and abilities. Since I know it is all for Christ's good, I am quite happy about "the thorn," and about insults and hardships, persecutions and difficulties; for when I am weak, then I am strong—the less I have, the more I depend on him.
> (2 Corinthians 12:9-10, TLB)

A LEADER IS A WOUNDED HEALER.
We all have a need to be strong, to be above any suspicion of weakness. The irony is that God's grace is reflected through those who have experienced brokenness, forgiveness, and renewal. We are all broken people affected by and infected with sin. We are all trophies of God's grace. A good leader has a healthy sense of his or her own fallibility and brokenness. He or she

is not morbid about it and not paralyzed by it. A healthy leader uses personal brokenness to connect with others. The apostle Paul was a great example of this; he continually mentioned his own weaknesses, and at the same time, pointed out Christ's sufficiency.

> They are God's servants, not yours. They are responsible to him, not to you. Let him tell them whether they are right or wrong. And God is able to make them do as they should. (Romans 14:4, TLB)

A LEADER CREATES AN ENVIRONMENT OF NURTURE.
How we treat others is an important issue. We need to realize that there is no hierarchy in God's kingdom. We are all equals standing side by side in ministry. When a leader displays an attitude of servanthood rather than superiority, he or she begins a process of nurture that eventually spreads to every member of the group. The leader nurtures groups of leaders who each reach out to a group of people, who reach out to others.

A LEADER KNOWS HOW TO PLAY.
Healthy leaders know how to have fun. They don't take themselves too seriously. Play is contagious. Caring is contagious. You can't teach involvement; you can only catch it. It must be infectious. It won't happen when you try to keep score. Henri Nouwen says, "When we start being too impressed by the results of our work, we slowly come to the erroneous conviction that

life is one large scoreboard where someone is listing the points to measure our worth."[7] Tim Hansel said, "My kids know I love them not when I take them places or buy them things, but when I play with them."[8]

> This book, being about work, is, by its very nature, about violence to the spirit as well as to the body. It is about ulcers as well as accidents. About shouting matches as well as fist fights. About nervous breakdowns as well as kicking the dog around. It is, above all (or beneath all), about daily humiliations. To survive the day is triumph enough.
>
> —Studs Terkel, in *Working*

Gordon Dahl says, "Most middle-class Americans tend to worship their work, to work at their play, and to play at their worship. As a result, their meaning and values are distorted. Their relationships disintegrate faster than they can keep them in repair, and their lifestyles resemble a cast of characters in search of a plot."[9]

A LEADER SEES BEYOND THE IMMEDIATE TO THE POTENTIAL.
Jesus gave people the freedom to grow. He always saw beyond the immediate to what people could become.

Vince Lombardi is recognized as one of the greatest football coaches ever. One day his team wasn't doing well. Coach Lombardi was upset, especially with one of his guards who was not "putting out." Lombardi called the player aside and said, "Son, you are a lousy football player.

You're not blocking, you're not tackling, you're not putting out. As a matter of fact, it's all over for you today. Go take a shower."

The big guard dropped his head and walked into the dressing room. Forty-five minutes later, Coach Lombardi walked in and saw the big guard sitting in front of his locker still wearing his uniform and sobbing quietly.

He walked over to the player, put his arms around his shoulders, and said, "Son, I told you the truth today. You are a lousy football player. You're not blocking, you're not tackling, you're not putting out. However, in all fairness to you, I should have finished the story.

"Son, inside of you there is a great football

> The apostles gathered around Jesus and reported to him all they had done and taught. . . .
> Then Jesus directed them to have all the people sit down in groups on the green grass. So they sat down in groups of hundreds and fifties. Taking the five loaves and the two fish and looking up to heaven, he gave thanks and broke the loaves. Then he gave them to his disciples to set before the people. He also divided the two fish among them all. (Mark 6:30, 39-41)

player, and I'm going to stick by your side until the great football player inside of you has a chance to come out and assert himself."

With these words Jerry Kramer went on to become one of the all-time greats in football. A few years ago he was named as the best guard in the first fifty years of professional football.[10]

Good coaches can see things in their players that the players seldom can see in themselves. The coaches' job is to inspire them to use the talent they have, to help them correct their mistakes, and to celebrate with them in their victories.

If you see others as having worth and value, if you see the good in them and the potential they have, and if you help them achieve it, they will soar. A lot of people have gone further than they thought they could because someone else thought they could.

A LEADER IS WILLING TO GIVE MINISTRY AWAY.

A strong leader has no need to hoard all the credit; he or she is willing for someone else to get it. A good leader knows his or her job is to help people succeed, to remove barriers and empower people. Jesus gave the ministry away to the disciples; He could have done it better Himself, but He chose to work through them.

GETTING REAL YOURSELF

1. Think about your own leadership style. Do you recruit people to fulfill your ministry ideas, or do you seek other leaders who will excitedly implement their own ideas? The difference between the results of the two seems obvious, doesn't it?

2. As a leader, do you take care of yourself? Do you look for ways to be nurtured, to be held accountable, to be affirmed? Do you work at having fun? Take a few minutes and list ways to care for yourself in the coming months.

3. Do you make sure that those you lead also are nurtured, held accountable, and affirmed? Do you make sure they have fun in the leadership roles? List what you can do for each of those you lead.

4. Think of three ways you can affirm the leaders you work with. Make sure you do at least one of those this week!

CHAPTER FOURTEEN

COMMON QUESTIONS

Those who minister in the emerging postmodern context have many challenges before them. Over the last few years, people have asked us many things about ministry to postmoderns. We've boiled these down to eight common questions.

While this may seem like like an unusual way to wrap up the main portion of the book, we can't think of a more appropriate way to answer the most pressing questions you'll face as you start a new young adult ministry or work to rebuild an existing one.

1. WHAT ARE THE VERY FIRST STEPS I SHOULD TAKE BEFORE I START A YOUNG ADULT MINISTRY?

The first thing to consider before beginning a young adult ministry is to define your target clearly. You need to decide who you are going to reach and who you are *not* going to reach. The reality is that you are not going to be able to meet the needs of every young adult—and if you try, you will fail. We talked about targeting in chapter 8, but here are a few things to remember:

• *Identify the demographics around your church.* To reach any people group effectively, you must begin by gathering some basic information. The most expedient way to do this is to go to your local library or log on to the Internet and do some demographic research using a radius of fifteen to twenty miles around your church as a guide. If you want to build a ministry to young adults, you have to know which subcultures (see chapter 3) of young adults are in your area.

• *Organize a focus group.* After assessing some basic demographics, gather a group of five or six young adults to educate you. Tell them you want to make an impact on this generation but you don't know how. Ask *them* to tell *you* how to reach their friends for Christ. Ask them to give you ideas of what a young adult ministry could look like at your church, what they would like to see done, and whether you should even try to build a young adult ministry. Have them evaluate the knowledge you have acquired by reading this book and doing other research, and see if they agree with your insights. Rely on their input; use what they agree with and discard the rest. The goal is to let them teach you.

• *Make sure your church leadership wants a young adult ministry.* This is a critical issue because if your senior pastor and church leadership are not willing to support the ministry, it will never get off the ground. There are two important things to remember at this stage: people resist what they do not understand, and process is everything. Keep church leaders in the loop on everything you learn from the focus groups. Make copies of articles, tapes, and so on. Have church leaders read specific chapters in this book that you think will be helpful. Remember that your senior pastor is extremely busy. Go through the articles and highlight key points for him so that he can get the main ideas. Don't expect him to have the same passion for this as you do. But if you do not have the support of the senior leadership of your church, it just will not happen, no matter how badly you want this ministry.

2. How do I get the senior leadership of my church to support a young adult ministry?

The first thing you need to do is expose them to all the information about postmodern generations you can: books, tapes, magazine articles, newspaper articles, and so on. Many senior pastors don't understand some of the forces that have shaped Generation X and the Net Gen. Have yours read chapters 1, 2, and 3 for a basic understanding of postmodernism and a general overview of the differences within these post-

modern generations. It's important to get senior pastors involved in the process and get their input on it as much as possible. Expose them to other ministries across the country that are doing what you want to do. One of the fears for many senior pastors is that young adults will be a financial black hole. Help them see that young adults will support financially what they are a part of.

Also, help your pastor see the benefits of having a lot of young adults in your church. Their vitality and availability to help in a variety of other ministries are two very real benefits for any church. Young adults can fill the church with a lively and energetic spirit. Help your senior pastor see their passion for serving in the community as well as in the world through short-term mission trips. Show that young adults are not whiny, apathetic, angry slackers; they want to be involved in something that makes a difference in their lives as well as in the lives of others. Be patient and remember that process is everything.

3. After I've got the support of the pastor and the senior leaders of the church, what's the very first thing I should do?

When Ken was in high school, he went to a John Wooden basketball camp one summer. Coach Wooden is a legend in the basketball community. He led the UCLA Bruins to a number of national championships during his heyday as head coach.

Each morning as Ken would get up at camp,

he would notice Coach Wooden walking around the campus, deep in conversation with various men—each of whom was enormous! He later found out that those huge men were NBA basketball players who were in a slump. Coach Wooden took these professional athletes back to the basics, the fundamentals of the sport, and helped them get their game back.

The same is true in ministry. No matter how small or large your young adult group is, there are certain nonnegotiable fundamentals that serve as the foundation of your ministry. These fundamentals include establishing a clear purpose and determining a set of core values. These two elements are not just words; they are the shaping force of what you believe.

Your core ideology is unique to your ministry. It will help you answer two important questions: "What do we do?" and "Why do we do it?" When you can answer these two questions, you are well on your way to building an effective ministry. Establishing your core ideology is the foundation for building your ministry if you are starting from scratch, and it's the most important next step in making your current ministry more intentional.

4. HOW DO I GET THE YOUNG ADULTS THEMSELVES MOTIVATED AND INVOLVED?

One of the most important concepts to remember in doing young adult ministry is that motivation is directly connected to ownership. The more young adults are involved in dreaming, planning, and implementing ministry strategies, the more excited they will be about being involved. Your job as the leader is not to think of everything that needs to be done, create job descriptions and goals, and then recruit people to get involved. Instead, you need to let your young adults build the ministry while you encourage them and remove any barriers that might inhibit their success.

> Like the fundamental ideals of a great nation, church, school, or any other enduring institution, core ideology in a visionary company is a set of basic precepts that plant a fixed stake in the ground: This is who we are; This is what we stand for; This is what we're all about.[1]

For example, a group of young adults was coming to Frontline who really didn't want to get involved in anything currently going on. So, they came to a person on our ministry staff with the idea to start a club. As they talked excitedly about their dream of building a dance club that was safe and fun, it occurred to me that they didn't realize our church's view of dancing. Knowing that the senior pastor and the elders would most likely not support this program, I made it my mission to do everything I could to remove this barrier. After some lengthy discussion (and with the senior pastor really going to bat for us), the elders consented with the following conditions: no slow dancing, the event must be held off-site, and the club must be closely supervised by ministry staff. We agreed and Club Frontline was born.

The club team went out and found a local restaurant, rented it for a Friday night, put black light bulbs in every light socket, hung beads from all the doorways, put some lava lamps on the tables, and moved some other tables and chairs out of the way to make room for five or six couches. They set up TV monitors to play music videos and hired a Christian DJ. The slogan: "No Smoking, No Alcohol, No Macarena." The club was an absolute hit! About eight hundred people showed up, many of whom would never come to our church services.

At about 12:30 A.M. a group of young people came to the door. They wanted to come in to smoke a cigarette and have a beer. When we told them that this event was non-smoking and alcohol-free, they looked inside at all the people, heard the music playing, and asked what was going on. We told them we were from a church down the street. They said, "Wow! How long will you be here?" We said, "Until 2:00 A.M." So they went and got their friends and then came back and had a great time.

The club taught me a valuable lesson: One of my main jobs as the leader is to listen to the dreams of our young adults and then do everything I can to remove barriers and help make those dreams happen in such a way that Jesus Christ is glorified and people are exposed to the gospel. If you want to motivate and involve young adults in ministry, you have to give them the freedom to do ministry in their own, often unconventional, ways. Now, I realize that many churches would never consent to sponsoring something like a dance club, but the point is to push the status quo as far as you can without dashing yourself against the rocks. My encouragement to you is to take a risk. It never hurts to ask!

5. WHAT ARE SOME OBSTACLES I WILL HAVE TO OVERCOME IN DOING YOUNG ADULT MINISTRY?

Two of the biggest obstacles that many people have to overcome are (1) comparing yours with other ministries, and (2) having unrealistic expectations.

Be careful about comparing yourselves to other ministries: bigger is not better; healthy is better. It's fairly easy to draw a crowd. The hard part is to build a relational ministry that is healthy and facilitates life change. Unrealistic expectations are very common in starting new ministries. It's easy to think, *If I just develop this really cool program, or if I can just pull off a few awesome events, then young adults will come en masse.*

Realistically, that's probably not going to happen. No matter what you do, no matter how good your programs are, it will take time to build a vital young adult ministry. Once you launch your ministry, people will come one time and then you won't see them for two or three months. This will occur even if they go on and on about how much they liked it. They'll come back after a few months, say the same thing, and you won't see them again for several more weeks. Eventually, if you keep things consistent and have some type of system to plug people into relationships and service, they will start to stick.

But it can take up to six months for someone to become a regular attendee.

The danger is to think you're doing something wrong and keep trying to change everything while you're looking for the right combination. There is no right combination! You need to determine your core ideology, identify your target (see chapter 8), and then commit yourself to it for twelve months before you start evaluating your whole structure. If you take the time in the beginning to lay the foundation we've talked about here, you shouldn't have to make very many major adjustments in the first twelve months.

One of the most liberating things I've learned in ministry is that when I stop trying to be the general manager of the universe, things go much easier. Here is one thing to remember: *you* build *people;* leave the growth of the group to God. If it's healthy, it will grow numerically.

6. HOW DO I KEEP MY MINISTRY FOCUSED ON YOUNG ADULTS WHEN OLDER SINGLES WANT TO GET INVOLVED?

It won't be long after you get your young adult ministry off the ground before you'll have to develop a response to older single adults who want to become part of your group. This is important, because in order to meet your goals, you need to keep the ministry focused on people in their twenties. Young adults, for the most part, don't want to hang out with older adults. A twenty-two-year-old thinks that a thirty-six-year-old is ancient. Young adults want to hang out with other young adults. I'm not saying this is right, but it's a reality. If you violate this principle you'll watch your young adults begin to trickle away.

At Frontline we had to learn this the hard way. Not long ago we started to notice a sizable group of older single adults wanting to attend our services and get involved in ministry teams. Our services have always been open to everyone, but we limit involvement in other aspects of the ministry to young adults in our target age range. This policy hurt many people and caused a fairly large number of older single adults to leave the church. I regret both of these things very much.

To help solve the problem, we launched another ministry to meet the needs of the older single adults. We didn't force anyone out of our young adult ministry, but now that we have something else for the older adults, they are making the transition on their own. The process is working very well. Most people will not have a problem with being redirected to other ministries, provided that you have something else for them.

After starting Frontline for young adults five years ago, we have launched three other communities: a young married couples community, a younger adult community for people in their early twenties, and a community for single adults in their thirties and early forties. When building your young adult ministry, you might think you have enough to worry about just getting it off the ground. However, if you don't think through this issue, you are putting yourself in a position that will ultimately hurt people, your ministry, and the reputation of your church.

7. How is a young adult ministry different from a singles ministry?

Most young adults do not consider themselves to be single. Instead, they see themselves as never married. The term "single" can carry with it a negative stereotype: not committed, lonely, and so on. Of course, we know that these stereotypes are not accurate, but the perception remains. So it's important that leaders don't play into singleness stereotypes.

For example, I (Ken) never teach singles-related series because I don't think single adults have spiritual needs different from those of anyone else. Nor do they have the corner on the market of emotional struggles. I do teach an annual dating/marriage series at the request of many people. But again, I talk about issues in relationships that are not exclusively singles-related.

People's perception is probably the single greatest difference between a singles ministry and a young adult ministry.

8. Aren't young adults the same from one generation to the next? Why are today's young adults different?

It's true that developmental stages for young adults don't change. The difference is that every generation goes through these developmental stages within a different cultural context. It's our contention that, although developmental stages are no different for today's young adults than they were for preceding generations, they have experienced circumstances in their upbringing that merit special attention (see chapter 2 for more details). Of course, this happens with every generation.

Take divorce, for example. As we have already noted, during their formative years, today's young adults experienced a dramatic increase in the divorce rate of their parents. The effects seem to have been severe. Gen X and the Net Gen are similar in many ways to all other young adult generations that have preceded them. But churches must understand certain distinctions related to the tumultuous cultural context of their childhood in order to minister effectively to them—or to any generation.

TRANSFORMATIONAL COMMUNITIES TOOLS

(see chapter 11)

GROUP LEADER
Position Description

Time Commitment: About eleven hours per month (two hours per week for TC meetings, two hours per month to attend Leadership Community, one hour per month to meet with your coach).

Length of Commitment: A minimum of six months.

Reporting Relationship: You report to your assigned coach.

Spiritual Gifts: Any combination of leadership, teaching, exhortation, administration, and encouragement.

Goal: To build a leadership team that consists of an apprentice and a host. The ideal is to equip your apprentice to become the next leader when you go out and birth a new group within eight to twelve months.

Expectations:
   1. That you will demonstrate an attitude of encouragement and support toward group members, others within your reporting relationship, and the church and pastoral staff.
   2. That you have a desire to birth new groups every eight to twelve months.

3. That you will develop your own leadership team consisting of an apprentice and host. The apprentice is to facilitate at least half of the group meetings and share in any other leadership decisions and responsibilities.

4. That you will attend the monthly Leadership Community Meeting.

5. That you will talk with your coach weekly.

6. That you will read through the ministry's vision and values and be in agreement with the doctrinal statement of the church as well as the overall philosophy and methodology of the church.

7. That your group will serve together in a service project at least once per quarter.

Spiritual Expectations:

1. That you have a personal relationship with Jesus Christ and can clearly communicate your conversion experience.

2. That you are growing in your ability to love others and are submitting to the Holy Spirit's work in your life.

3. That you are living a life of integrity and are an example to others.

COMMUNITY GROUP LEADER/APPRENTICE QUESTIONNAIRE

Name: Phone (H):
Address: Phone (W):
                                   E-mail Address:

This questionnaire is for those interested in being either a leader or an apprentice leader of a community group.

Please print clearly and return to the director of Young Adult Ministries when complete.

1. Where do you attend church on a regular basis?

2. Are you currently a member of a church? If yes, which church?

3. What is your current involvement with our church? How long have you been coming to our church or young adult group?

4. Have you ever been in a small group?

   a. If you answered yes to question 4, was your experience in that group positive or negative? Please list the specifics of either.

5. Have you ever led or facilitated a small group before?

   a. If you answered yes to question 5, what did you learn from that experience about yourself and the people in the group?

6. Please share your conversion experience (God story) and how it has impacted your life. Please be as specific as possible.

7. What do you consider to be your personal strengths?

8. What do you consider to be the main area of growth that God is currently developing in your life?

9. Do you love to work with people?

10. Why do you want to be a community leader or apprentice leader?

11. If someone in your group were to ask you to explain salvation, how would you respond? (If you don't know, that's okay. Just say so and we will train you.)

Please feel free to use additional paper if you need to. Thanks for taking the time to fill this out! It will be very helpful in our placement process.

GROUP APPRENTICE LEADER
Position Description

Time Commitment: About eleven hours per month (two hours per week for TC meetings, two hours per month to attend Leadership Community, one hour per month to meet with your coach).

Length of Commitment: A minimum of six months.

Reporting Relationship: You report to your group leader.

Spiritual Gifts: Any combination of leadership, teaching, exhortation, administration, and encouragement.

Goal: To learn how to facilitate a community group so that you can either take over the leadership of your current group or leave to birth your own group in eight to twelve months.

Expectations:
1. That you will demonstrate an attitude of encouragement and support toward your group members, others within your reporting relationship, and the church and pastoral staff.

2. That you have a desire to begin a new group within eight to twelve months or assume leadership of your existing group as the leader leaves to birth a new group.

3. That you demonstrate three essential attributes:
   * Faithful—You take your position seriously and you show commitment to your group and coaching staff.
   * Available—You're willing to make time for people in your group.
   * Teachable—You cooperate with the group leader in learning the various skills necessary to become an effective group leader.

4. That you facilitate 50 percent of the group meetings and help create a healthy group environment.

Spiritual Expectations:

1. That you have a personal relationship with Jesus Christ and can clearly communicate your conversion experience.

2. That you are growing in your ability to love others and are submitting to the Holy Spirit's work in your life.

3. That you are living a life of integrity and are an example to others.

COMMUNITY GROUP HOST
Position Description

Time Commitment: About nine hours per month (two hours per week for TC meetings, one hour per month to meet with your coach).

Length of Commitment: A minimum of three months.

Reporting Relationship: You report to your group leader.

Spiritual Gifts: Administration, hospitality, and/or helps.

Expectations:

1. That you will demonstrate an attitude of encouragement and support toward group members, others within your reporting relationship, and the church and pastoral staff.

2. That you will oversee the prayer and care team and make sure that three-by-five-inch cards are given to each of the group members at the beginning of each meeting for prayer requests. Each person is then to exchange cards at the end of the evening to pray over during that week.

3. That you will oversee the activity team within your group to help organize the monthly activity. Each month your group should go out and do something fun. You are to poll the group to see what you're going to do and make sure that everyone is informed.

4. That you will oversee the service project team and help them in scheduling and coordinating the various service projects for your group. Once per month your group will help out with a church-related need and once per quarter your group is to serve in a community service project.

5. That you will complete the weekly report sheet and make sure it gets to the group leader, who will in turn give it to your coach.

6. That you will keep all group members informed as to meeting places, times, monthly activities, service projects, and so on, as well as any changes that come up on a weekly basis.

Spiritual Expectations:

1. That you have a personal relationship with Jesus Christ and can clearly communicate your conversion experience.

2. That you are growing in your ability to love others and are submitting to the Holy Spirit's work in your life.

3. That you are living a life of integrity and are an example to others.

COMMUNITY GROUP COACH
Position Description

Time Commitment: About eleven hours per month (two hours per week for TC meetings, two hours per month to attend Leadership Community, one hour per month to meet with your group leaders).

Length of Commitment: Twelve months.

Reporting Relationship: You report to your ministry staff person or equivalent.

Spiritual Gifts: Any combination of leadership, teaching, exhortation, encouragement, and discernment.

Goal: To support and encourage your TC group leaders and their apprentice leaders by providing instruction, encouragement, and support in times of need.

Expectations:
1. That you will assist ministry staff in recruiting and training leaders for TC groups.
2. That you will encourage, guide, and affirm small-group leaders through weekly meetings either in person, through e-mail, or by phone.
3. That you will provide spiritual care for your leaders by praying with and for them weekly.
4. That you will model servant leadership.
5. That you will help TC group leaders aid their hosts in implementing service projects within the community each quarter.
6. That you will visit each group under your care occasionally (ideally, one group each week) to encourage and to assess any needed changes that might make the group more effective.
7. That you will facilitate the birthing process of new groups every eight to twelve months.
8. That you will recruit and train one apprentice coach during your term.
9. That you will meet with your group leaders and their apprentice leaders each month at the Leadership Community Meeting.

Spiritual Expectations:

1. That you have a personal relationship with Jesus Christ and can clearly communicate your conversion experience.

2. That you are growing in your ability to love others and are submitting to the Holy Spirit's work in your life.

3. That you are living a life of integrity and are an example to others.

SAMPLE MESSAGES

This section contains outlines for a number of messages you can use in a variety of ways: as Sunday school lessons, TC group curriculum, or to preach. Each message is also available on audiocassette complete with outlines. Full manuscripts of each message are also available on floppy disk for your convenience; contact Frontline Ministry Resources at (703) 421-8108 or www.frontline.to. Each message in this section contains a theme, (in most cases) video clip ideas, and a basic outline used for illustration purposes.

"REALITY CHECKS" SERIES

Series theme: It's easier to run from the harsh realities of life than to stand your ground and face them. So how do we do that? How do we deal with the inevitable realities that life throws our way? That is the purpose of this series, to equip young adults to deal with reality using principles from God's Word.

"WE CAN'T CHANGE THE PAST," REALITY CHECKS, PART 1

Theme verse: "There is now no condemnation for those who are in Christ Jesus" (Romans 8:1).

Video clip: *The Mission.* Show the scene where Robert DeNiro is using penance to try to absolve himself from the guilt of killing his brother in a fit of rage. Real freedom didn't happen in his life until the natives he was capturing and selling as slaves came and cut him free from his guilt. That is what God has done for us through Jesus Christ: He has cut away our guilt of sin and forgiven us, giving us true freedom.

Message outline:
"We Can't Change the Past"
  I. How to Respond to Sin in Our Lives (2 Corinthians 7:10)
     A. Option 1 is godly sorrow.

B. Option 2 is worldly sorrow.

II. The Results of Worldly Sorrow

    A. Guilt destroys our confidence.

    B. Guilt damages our relationships.

    C. Guilt keeps us stuck in the past.

III. Finding Freedom from Guilt (Psalm 32:1-2)

    A. Take a personal moral inventory (Lamentations 3:40; Psalm 139:23-24).

    B. Accept responsibility for our fault (Proverbs 20:27, TEV; 1 John 1:8).

    C. Ask God for forgiveness (1 John 1:9, PH).

        1. God's forgiveness is received through confession (1 John 1:9; Isaiah 1:18; Romans 8:1).

IV. Admitting Our Faults to Another (James 5:16)

    A. Who? What do we say? When do we do it?

V. Accepting God's Forgiveness and Forgiving Ourselves (Romans 3:23-24)

"FAITHLESS FEAR," REALITY CHECKS, PART 2

Theme verse: "Without faith it is impossible to please God" (Hebrews 11:6).

Video clip: *Jurassic Park*. Use the scene when the Explorer is thrown into the tree by T-Rex and the little boy is frozen in fear, not wanting to come out even with the help of the doctor. His fear paralyzed him, yet he had to place his faith in the doctor in order to be saved. The point: fear has a paralyzing effect on all of us. As we place our trust in Christ, the fear may not go away entirely, but at least we know that we are in good hands and that He won't let us fall.

Message outline:

"Faithless Fear"

  I. Four Types of Fear

    A. Fun fear

    B. Fight-or-flight fear

    C. False fear

    D. Faithless fear

  II. Facing Our Fears: How to Walk on Water (Matthew 14:23-32)

    A. Realizing our chance to step out of the boat usually comes during a storm.

    B. Realizing we are going to have to get out on our own.

    C. We have to be able to see Jesus (John 10:27; 12:46).

    D. We have to be willing to fail (Mark 10:29-30).

E. Remember, when we get out on the water, we are not alone (Matthew 14:30-31).

"GOOD GRIEF," REALITY CHECKS, PART 3
Theme verse: "In this world you will have trouble" (John 16:33).

Video clip: *Monty Python and the Holy Grail.* There's a scene where the knights approach a deep cavern guarded by an old sage who asks a series of questions. The idea is that there is a right way and a wrong way to answer his questions, just as there is a right and wrong way to process pain in life.

Message outline:
"Good Grief"
  I. Conventional Sorrow Management (Bad Grief)
     A. Bury our feelings.
     B. Replace the loss as soon as possible.
     C. Grieve alone.
     D. Time alone heals all wounds.
     E. Unfinished business stays unfinished.
     F. Never get close to anyone because we will get hurt.
 II. God's Approach to Sorrow Management (Good Grief)
     A. Feel our pain (John 11:35; Ecclesiastes 3:4).
     B. Review the loss.
        1. Talk about it openly.
        2. Review it deeply.
        3. Write about it reflectively.
        4. Pray about it thoroughly.
     C. Grieve in community (Romans 12:15; Job 2:11-13).
     D. Seek the comfort of the Holy Spirit (John 14:26).
     E. We don't have to live with regret (Romans 12:18).
     F. Put Christ at the center of our lives (Deuteronomy 31:6; Proverbs 14:12).

"YOU CAN'T CHANGE PEOPLE," REALITY CHECKS, PART 4
Theme verse: "Love one another. As I have loved you, so you must love one another" (John 13:34).

Video clip: *Les Misérables.* Play the scene where Jean Valjean steals the silver candlesticks from the bishop and gets caught by the police and they take him back to the bishop's house. The bishop welcomes him and dismisses the police, and Jean Valjean crumbles in tears at the unconditional love of the bishop. He then goes on to change and becomes an extremely good citizen.

Message Outline:

"You Can't Change People"

I. Two Types of Love (John 8:3-11; 1 John 4:7-11)
   A. One kind of love seeks value.
   B. Another kind of love creates value.
II. God's Love (1 John 4:8)
   A. God's love is sacrificial (1 John 4:10; John 15:12-13).
   B. God's love is unconditional (Romans 5:8; Titus 3:4-5).
   C. God's love is affirming (1 Thessalonians 5:11).
   D. God's love is corrective (Romans 2:4, MSG; Colossians 3:16; Ephesians 4:15; 1 John 3:18).

"YOU CAN'T DO EVERYTHING," REALITY CHECKS, PART 5

Theme verse: "You are worried and bothered about so many things; but only one thing is necessary…" (Luke 10:41, NASB).

Video clip: *Superman: The Movie.* Show various clips where Superman can do everything—leap tall buildings, dodge bullets, and so on. The idea is that he's not real; there is no Superman, only ordinary people.

Message outline:

"You Can't Do Everything"

I. Three Types of Rest We Need
   A. Physical rest (Psalm 127:2)
   B. Emotional rest (Matthew 14:23)
   C. Soul rest (Matthew 11:29)
II. Following the PACE of Jesus
   A. **P**urpose (1 Peter 4:10; Ephesians 2:10; Matthew 20:28)
   B. **A**lignment (John 5:30)
   C. **C**ontentment (Philippians 4:11-12)
   D. **E**ternal perspective (Matthew 6:19-20; Luke 10:27)

"CONTAGIOUS CHRISTIANITY" SERIES

Series theme: Our generation will not be drawn to Jesus Christ by a bunch of glib clichés and pat answers about life. They want to see the reality of our faith lived out in our day-to-day lives. They want to see the difference Christ has made in our lives. Therefore, we must be intentional about allowing the Spirit of God to continue to do the work of changing us more and more into the image of Jesus so that those of our generation will see the gospel fleshed out. To do that, we must make three virtues central to our lives in order to influence our generation for Jesus Christ.

"HANDLING THE HERD INSTINCT," CONTAGIOUS CHRISTIANITY, PART 1

Theme verse: "Do not conform any longer to the pattern of this world, but be transformed by the renewing of your mind" (Romans 12:2).

Video clip: *Crimson Tide*. Put together various clips showing Denzel Washington standing up for what he thought was right in spite of what the captain and most of the other shipmates thought. There are some very intense scenes that fit well together.

Message outline:

"Handling the Herd Instinct" (Virtue 1: Courage)

I. Biblical Insights About Not Conforming to the World (Romans 12:1-2)
   A. This truth is mainly for believers.
   B. Paul has a sense of urgency in his tone.
   C. Nonconformity involves sacrifice.
   D. This sacrifice is both inside and outside (Ezekiel 36:26-27).
   E. This sacrifice leads to a practical and radical decision to move in a new direction.

II. How to Stand Out from the Crowd (Six Principles That Will Influence People for Christ)
   A. Be an encourager (1 Thessalonians 5:11; Philippians 2:14-15).
      The world's system: Criticize, condemn and complain.
   B. Be enthusiastic of others (Proverbs 16:24).
      The world's system: Be negative, look for weaknesses to exploit in others.
   C. Be sensitive to others' needs (Philippians 2:3-4, MSG; Philippians 4:5)
      The world's system: Look out for yourself!
   D. Admit when you are wrong (1 Peter 2:12; Proverbs 13:10).
      The world's system: Defend yourself, rationalize, lie if you have to.

E.   Persevere during times of crisis (2 Corinthians 4:17-18).
    The world's system: Blame someone else, lash out at God, or just give up.
F.   Be content (1 John 2:16; Luke 12:15; Psalm 17:15).
    The world's system: Fortune is the goal; always want more; don't be satisfied.

"The Cost of Commitment," Contagious Christianity, Part 2
Theme verse: "If anyone would come after me, he must deny himself and take up his cross daily and follow me" (Luke 9:23).

Video clip: *First Knight.* Play the opening scene where Lancelot is fighting for sport and tells a would-be sword fighter that in order to be as good as he is you have to not care whether you live or die.

Message outline:
"The Cost of Commitment" (Virtue 2: Conviction)
 I. The Cost of Commitment (Mark 4:19)
    A.   "The attractions of this world . . ."
    B.   "The delights of wealth . . ."
    C.   "The search for success . . . "
    D.   "The lure of nice things . . ."
 II. Why Make a Total Commitment to God?
    A.   Because God knows best (Jeremiah 29:11)
    B.   Because Jesus died for us (John 3:16)
    C.   Because God promises to reward our commitment (Proverbs 3:6)
III. Four Questions/Commitments We Need to Make
    A.   What will be the center of my life (Matthew 22:37-38; Philippians 3:7)?
        Commitment 1: To loving God (John 14:15; 1 John 5:3; Philippians 2:13)
    B.   What will be the contribution of my life (1 Peter 4:10; Ephesians 2:10; Ephesians 4:12)?
        Commitment 2: To a community
    C.   What will be the character of my life (Romans 8:29; Ephesians 5:18; Galatians 5:22-23)?
        Commitment 3: To God's change process
    D.   What will be the communication of my life (Romans 10:14)?
        Commitment 4: To telling others

"Compassion," Contagious Christianity, Part 3

Theme verse: "What pity he felt for the crowds that came, because their problems were so great and they didn't know what to do or where to go for help. They were like sheep without a shepherd" (Matthew 9:36, TLB).

Video clip: *Leap of Faith.* Show the part where Steve Martin comes out of the tent after the boy seemingly has been healed and he looks at the hundreds of people camping out in the field, reading stories to kids, playing games, and so on, waiting for the healing service to begin the next day. The idea is that these people were looking for some type of hope, something to hold on to. If we are sensitive to the needs of others, it gives them hope—hope that someone really cares.

Message outline:
"Compassion" (Virtue 3: Hope)
  I. The Power of Hope
    A. Hope gives us confidence in the midst of uncertainty.
    B. Hope gives us endurance in the midst of difficulty.
    C. Hope gives us comfort in the midst of pain.
    D. Hope gives us courage in the midst of confusion.
  II. How to Instill HOPE in Others
    A. **H**elp people change their way of thinking (Proverbs 4:23).
       People need help rethinking:
       1. How they think about themselves (2 Corinthians 5:17; Hebrews 1:3)
       2. How they think about God
          • God is unreasonable.
            Truth about God: God is giving (Psalm 145:9).
          • God is unreliable.
            Truth about God: God is consistent (Romans 11:29; Psalm 59:10).
          • God is unconcerned.
            Truth about God: God is caring (Matthew 20:28).
          • God is unpleasable (1 Corinthians 6:11).
            Truth about God: God is gracious (Ephesians 1:4).
    B. **O**ffer your life as an example (1 Peter 3:15).
       Hope is a matter of security (Romans 15:13).
    C. **P**oint people toward the victory (1 Corinthians 15:54-55; 2 Corinthians 4:17-18; Romans 6:6-7; Philippians 4:13).
    D. **E**xpress God's concern for them (Luke 15:4-10).

"SPIRITUAL VIRUSES" SERIES

Series theme: A virus is a protein shell that contains genetic material. The shell that encases a virus is sticky and latches onto healthy cells and then begins to slowly inject its own genetic code into the healthy cell. Eventually it rewrites the code and takes over complete control. A particularly aggressive virus will transform a healthy cell into a factory that reproduces the virus and takes complete control of the way the healthy cell functions and reproduces.

In the spiritual world, aggressive spiritual viruses follow a similar pattern. If we allow these to creep into our lives, they will slowly destroy us. This series identifies these viruses and develops strategies for effectively eradicating them from our lives.

"Coming to Grips with Greed," Spiritual Viruses, Part 1

Theme verse: "Watch out! Be on your guard against all kinds of greed" (Luke 12:15).

Video clip: *Star Trek: First Contact.* Show some clips of the Borg and how they are relentlessly greedy not only to conquer all life-forms in the galaxy but also to assimilate them as their own. There is no mercy, only assimilation.

Message outline:

"Coming to Grips with Greed" (Spiritual Virus 1: Greed)

I. Our Two Primary Desires (James 4:1-3)
   A. The desire to survive.
   B. The desire to be happy.
      Greed: The insatiable desire for more of something we think will make us happy (1 John 2:15-17; Ecclesiastes 12:13).

II. How We Keep God's Commands
   A. Love (Matthew 22:35-40)
   B. Giving (1 John 4:21, MSG; Romans 13:9)

III. How to Break the Grip of Greed
   A. God wants us to give away our time (Ephesians 5:15-16, AMP; Ephesians 2:10).
   B. God wants us to give away our abilities (Romans 12:6-8; 1 Peter 4:10, TEV).
   C. God wants us to give away our money (Matthew 6:24; 1 Timothy 6:7,17-19, MSG; Proverbs 11:28; Matthew 6:19-20).
   D. God wants us to give away love (Romans 13:8; 1 John 3:17-18, TLB; Ephesians 5:1-2, MSG).

"The Trauma of Truth Telling," Spiritual Viruses, Part 2
Theme verse: "Stop lying to each other; tell the truth, for we are parts of each other and when we lie to each other we are hurting ourselves" (Ephesians 4:25, TLB).

Video clip: *Liar, Liar.* Show scenes of how hard it was for Jim Carrey's character to tell the truth.

Message outline:
"The Trauma of Truth Telling" (Spiritual Virus 2: Deceit)
  I. Why We Are Traumatized by Truth Telling
     A. Speaking truth causes conflict.
     B. Speaking truth causes pain.
     C. Speaking truth causes fear.
        1. We are afraid of others' anger.
        2. We are afraid of being rejected by them.
        3. We are afraid they will turn our truth back on us.
 II. How to Speak the Truth in Love (Ephesians 4:15, MSG; Ephesians 5:15;
     1 Corinthians 13:5, TLB)
     A. We should focus our feedback on the behavior, not the person (John 8:10-11).
     B. We should focus our feedback on observation, not assumptions (1 Timothy 5:19).
     C. We should focus our feedback on descriptions, not judgments (Romans 14:13).
     D. We should focus our feedback on ideas, information, and alternatives, not on advice and
        answers (Ephesians 4:29).
     E. We should express our feedback at the right time (Ecclesiastes 3:1).
     F. We should watch not only what we say but also how we say it (Ephesians 4:2).

"Putting Off Pride," Spiritual Viruses, Part 3
Theme verse: "Do not think of yourself more highly than you ought, but rather think of yourself with sober judgment" (Romans 12:3).

Video clip: None.

Message outline:
"Putting Off Pride" (Spiritual Virus 3: Pride)
  I. Healthy v. Unhealthy Pride (Galatians 6:4)
     A. Healthy pride: The feelings that come after we do a job well—satisfaction.
     B. Unhealthy pride: The feeling of superiority that comes when we compare ourselves to others.

II. Jesus on Pride (Luke 18:10-14; Matthew 23:23, MSG; Matthew 23:2-3, MSG)

III. The Bible and Pride (Proverbs 11:2; 13:10; 16:18; 29:23; 18:12)

IV. The Many Faces of Pride
   A. Self-Preoccupation (Proverbs 17:19, TLB)
   B. The Messiah Complex (Genesis 3:4-5)
   C. Stubbornness (Proverbs 29:1)

V. How to Put Off Pride
   A. Acknowledge our pride (1 John 1:8; John 8:32).
   B. Humble ourselves (Isaiah 66:2; Proverbs 3:34; Psalm 147:6; Psalm 25:9; Ephesians 4:2; James 4:10).

"HANDLING HURRY," SPIRITUAL VIRUSES, PART 4

Theme verse: "A relaxed attitude lengthens a man's life" (Proverbs 14:30, TLB).

Video clip: *Alice in Wonderland.* Show some clips of the rabbit always hurrying around everywhere, always late and never stopping to talk or enjoy life.

Message outline:

"Handling Hurry" (Spiritual Virus 4: Hurry, or anxious striving, Mark 4:18-19)

I. Jesus' Busy Lifestyle (Mark 1:32-33, MSG; Mark 3:20-21, TLB; Ecclesiastes 2:22-23)

II. Why We Hurry
   A. We mistakenly think that busy people are important.
   B. We are afraid that if we slow down, we'll crash.
   C. Staying busy is a way of avoiding intimacy with others.
   D. We just get stuck in a rut.
   E. We're afraid to say no.

III. How to Handle Hurry (Exodus 20:8, TLB; Mark 2:27, TEV; Ecclesiastes 10:15, TEV)
   A. Use a day to rest our bodies (Psalm 127:2, TLB).
   B. Use a day to recharge our emotions.
      How to Recharge Emotions:
         1. Include time for solitude (Mark 1:35; Luke 9:10; Mark 6:31, TEV; Psalm 23:2-3).
         2. Include time for friends (Proverbs 17:22, TEV).
         3. Include time for fellowship (Hebrews 10:25; Psalm 122:1).
   C. Use a day to refocus our spirits (Psalm 95:6; Matthew 6:32-34, MSG).

Theme verse: "Jealousy is more dangerous and cruel than anger" (Proverbs 27:4, TLB).

Video clip: *The Bodyguard.* Put together various clips showing the jealousy Whitney Houston's sister had toward her and how it destroyed her life and almost the life of her family.

Message outline:
"Juggling Jealousy" (Spiritual Virus 5: Jealousy)

  I. Jealousy Summed Up

    A. It's resenting God's goodness in others' lives.

    B. It's ignoring God's goodness in my own life.

  II. Why We Should Avoid Jealousy

    A. It distracts us from our life's purpose (Luke 9:62, TLB).

    B. It causes conflict in our relationships (James 4:1; Ecclesiastes 4:4, TLB).

    C. It leads to other sins (James 3:16; Matthew 5:21-22; 1 John 3:15).

    D. It makes us miserable (Proverbs 14:30; Luke 12:15).

  III. Getting Rid of Jealousy

    A. God's Antidote to Jealousy: Contentment (Philippians 4:12, MSG)

      1. We should resist comparing ourselves to others (2 Corinthians 10:12; Galatians 6:4).

      2. We should recognize our uniqueness (Psalm 139:13, TEV; Psalm 139:15, TLB).

      3. We should rejoice in what we do have (Ecclesiastes 6:9; Luke 12:15).

      4. We should respond to others in love (1 Corinthians 13:4; Romans 12:15).

      5. We should refocus on pleasing God (Colossians 3:2; Psalm 119:37, TLB; John 4:13-14).

"GOD'S BLUEPRINT FOR DATING AND MARRIAGE" SERIES

Series theme: Relationships are our generation's greatest fear and greatest need. No matter where you go or what you do, you will interact with people. Most of us can handle ourselves fairly well in superficial relationships. But when we begin to get close to others, within the context of either dating or marriage, things start to go wrong. This series focuses on a set of biblical skills that will enable you to have more lasting and rewarding relationships with others, especially those you're closest to.

"Picking the Right Partner," God's Blueprint for Dating and Marriage, Part 1

The first question people ask when dating: How do I know if he/she is "the one"?

Message outline:
"Picking the Right Partner"
  I. Be Careful Whom You Pick (Proverbs 21:9,21,19; 27:15; 31:10; 12:4)
 II. Who God Says to Pick as a Partner (1 Corinthians 7:39; 2 Corinthians 6:14)
     The primary principle when choosing a marriage partner is spiritual compatibility.
III. Why God Requires Spiritual Compatibility
     A. So that you as married partners can share a common goal (Matthew 13:44-46; Galatians 6:7-8, TLB; Proverbs 14:12)
     B. To ensure that you build your marriage with a common blueprint (Mark 3:25; Matthew 7:24-27, TLB)
     C. To ensure that you each possess a common power and perspective in the face of adversity (1 Corinthians 1:7, TLB; 2 Corinthians 4:16-18; Hebrews 12:2-3)
     D. To ensure common values when raising children (Deuteronomy 6:6-9)

"Before You Say, 'I Do,'" God's Blueprint for Dating and Marriage, Part 2

Theme verse: "Share each other's troubles and problems, and so obey our Lord's command" (Galatians 6:2, TLB).

Video clip: *Groundhog Day.* Play the scene where Bill Murray is in a coffee shop with Andie McDowell and he asks her what she wants in a man. She rattles off a list. The banter is very funny.

Message outline:
"Before You Say, 'I Do'"
  I. Six Things You Need to Know About Potential Marriage Partners
     A. What are their issues (John 8:32; Galatians 6:2, TLB)?
        Key question: Are they willing to be honest?
     B. What are their personality weaknesses (Ephesians 5:18, TLB; Ephesians 3:16, MSG; Galatians 5:22-23, TLB)?
        Two parts of us:
          1. Real self
          2. Ideal self
        Key question: Are they willing to admit their character weaknesses and submit them to Jesus Christ?

C. What are their expectations of you?
Key question: Are they willing to serve you (Philippians 2:5-7)?
D. Do you share common interests?
Four differences that destroy:
1. Energy level
2. Personal habits
3. Use of money
4. Verbal skills and interests
Key question: Are they willing to be flexible (Colossians 3:13; Philippians 2:4, TLB)?
E. Can they communicate?
1. Barrier to communication: fear.
2. The critical skill to develop in communication: empathy (James 5:16, TLB).
F. Are they safe (2 Corinthians 3:18; John 1:14)?
Three characteristics of safe people:
1. They can connect with you (Romans 12:15).
2. They will accept you (Romans 15:7).
3. They will speak the truth in love (Galatians 6:1).

"WHAT A WOMAN NEEDS FROM A MAN," GOD'S BLUEPRINT FOR DATING AND MARRIAGE, PART 3
Theme verses: "Don't be selfish; don't live to make a good impression on others. Be humble, thinking of others as better than yourself. Don't just think about your own affairs, but be interested in others, too, and in what they are doing.

"Your attitude should be the kind that was shown us by Jesus Christ, . . . taking the disguise of a slave and becoming like men" (Philippians 2:3-5,7, TLB).

"A man should fulfill his duty as a husband, and a woman should fulfill her duty as a wife, and each should satisfy the other's needs" (1 Corinthians 7:3, TEV).

Video clip: None.

Message outline:
"What a Woman Needs from a Man"
I. A Woman's Five Basic Needs
A. A woman needs affection (Colossians 3:19).
How to show affection:
1. By words (Ephesians 4:29, MSG; Proverbs 31:31; Proverbs 31:30)
2. By actions
3. By focused attention

B. A woman needs conversation (Philippians 2:2, PH).
   To a woman, conversation is verbal attention (Proverbs 13:17, TLB).
C. A woman needs to trust her man.
   Things that break down trust:
   1. Looking at other women
   2. Lack of vulnerability
   3. Being judgmental (Matthew 7:1-2)
   4. Dishonesty (Ephesians 4:25, TLB)
D. She needs family commitment.
   1. Be faithful to her (Matthew 5:28; Proverbs 6:32-33).
   2. Share the parenting responsibilities (Ephesians 6:4, TLB).
   3. Share the household responsibilities.
   4. Provide financially for the household (1 Timothy 5:8).
E. She needs spiritual leadership (Ephesians 5:25, PH).
   Spiritual leadership is about men taking initiative.
   1. You take the initiative when forgiveness is needed (Romans 5:8).
   2. You take the initiative to meet her needs first.
   3. You take the initiative for the spiritual climate in your home.

"WHAT A MAN NEEDS FROM A WOMAN," GOD'S BLUEPRINT FOR DATING AND MARRIAGE, PART 4

Theme verses: "A man should fulfill his duty as a husband, and a woman should fulfill her duty as a wife, and each should satisfy the other's needs" (1 Corinthians 7:3, TEV).

"Don't be selfish; don't live to make a good impression on others. Be humble, thinking of others as better than yourself. Don't just think about your own affairs, but be interested in others, too, and in what they are doing.

"Your attitude should be the kind that was shown us by Jesus Christ, . . . taking the disguise of a slave and becoming like men" (Philippians 2:3-5,7, TLB).

Message outline:
"What a Man Needs from a Woman"
I. A Man's Five Basic Needs
   A. He needs physical intimacy (Ephesians 5:31; 1 Corinthians 7:3-5, PH).
   B. A man needs support, not suggestions.
   C. Men need to be accepted, not changed (Ephesians 3:20, TLB).

Three things men want women to accept about them (Ephesians 4:2-3):
1. Most men are dreamers.
2. Most men come home disconnected.
3. Most men need cave time.
D. Men need to be appreciated, not apprehended.
E. Men need respect, not resistance (Ephesians 5:33, TLB; Proverbs 31:12).

"Moving from Conflict to Connection," God's Blueprint for Dating and Marriage, Part 5
Theme verse: "Know the whole truth, and tell it in love" (Ephesians 4:15, MSG).

Video clip: None.

Message outline:
"Moving from Conflict to Connection"
  I. Five Things That Cause Conflict
    A. Misunderstandings cause conflict.
    B. Uncommunicated needs cause conflict.
    C. Assumptions cause conflict.
    D. Buried hurt causes conflict.
    E. Truth causes conflict.
 II. How to Deal with Conflict
    A. We need to "care-front" (John 1:14; Ephesians 4:13; Romans 12:9,16, NEB;
       1 Corinthians 3:5; Galatians 5:14-15, NEB).
      1. Caring is about grace.
      2. Care-fronting is about truth.
III. Why We Don't Communicate Our Needs
    A. One word: FEAR.
      1. Fear of rejection.
      2. Fear of abandonment
      3. Fear of hurting another's feelings
IV. How to Care-Front Effectively
    A. Focus your feedback on the behavior, not the person (John 8:10-11).
    B. Focus your feedback on observation, not assumption (1 Timothy 5:19).
    C. Focus your feedback on descriptions, not judgments (Romans 14:13).

D. Focus your feedback on ideas, information, and alternatives, not on advice and answers (Ephesians 4:29).

E. Express your feedback at the right time (Ecclesiastes 3:1).

V. After You Care-Front (Five Questions to Ask)

A. Did you care-front constructively (1 Thessalonians 5:11)?

B. Did you care-front with care (2 Corinthians 7:8-9)?

C. Did you care-front gently (Ephesians 4:2)?

D. Did you demonstrate acceptance to the person (Romans 15:7)?

E. Did you care-front clearly (Matthew 5:37)?

"Breaking Up with Grace," God's Blueprint for Dating and Marriage, Part 6
Theme verse: "Be kind and compassionate to one another" (Ephesians 4:32).

Video clip: None.

Message outline:

"Breaking Up with Grace"

I. Why Dating Relationships End

A. Incompatibility over Major Issues

Three important elements you need:

1. Faith (2 Corinthians 6:14)

2. Focus—Your values and mission in life

3. Fun—Do you enjoy doing similar things together?

B. Getting Too Close Too Soon (Hebrews 13:4, MSG)

C. Undealt-with Hurt from the Past (Ephesians 4:26-27; Hebrews 12:15)

II. Four Ways to Process Pain and Loss

A. Remember that God is in absolute control (John 15:2).

B. Remember, God uses pain for good, not evil (Romans 8:28-29).

C. God uses the pain in our lives to help us relate to others (Hebrews 2:17-18, TLB; 2 Corinthians 1:3-4).

D. Pain helps us maintain an eternal perspective (2 Corinthians 4:17-5:1).

III. How to Break Up with GRACE (Colossians 3:12-15)

A. **G**entle (Ephesians 4:2; 1 Peter 3:8)

B. **R**espectful (James 3:6; Galatians 5:15, TLB; James 4:11, MSG)

C. **A**pologetic (Ephesians 4:3; Romans 12:18)

D. **C**lear (Colossians 3:16)

E. **E**mpathetic (Matthew 7:12)

GEN X WOMEN

by Melissa Fulfer

en X women were born in the middle of the feminist movement, and that has created some interesting needs for us. Here's a quick overview and some ideas for ministering to this segment of the young adult population.

Whether or not our mothers were involved in the feminist movement, all women were certainly influenced by the cultural implications of the feminist movement. Women everywhere were deserting the roles of their predecessors and were taking up different types of roles, mainly ones in the workplace. Divorce rates increased as our parents continued to separate as a result of this new search for freedom. We watched as our single mothers had to take on multiple roles of conducting a professional life, parenting, and providing for our needs.

The new independence that women gained wasn't so great after all. They may have been making money independently of men, but they were still making considerably less money for the same tasks men were doing. For those of us whose parents remained together, our mothers stepped into new territory as more opportunities opened to them. No longer did they have to stay home with us. They could now find jobs other than teaching and nursing as the workplace doors opened. The freedom obtained was addicting, as was the flow of extra cash.

The feminist movement afforded us the trappings of materialism. The more we had, the better off we were, so we thought. We didn't own just one Barbie; we had the whole collection of dolls, the dream house, and the dream cottage. We were raised on *General Hospital, Dallas, The Love Boat,* and *Dynasty.* These shows have had an impact on how we view relationships with men. Many of us were taught that we didn't need a man to take care of us— we could do anything we wanted to, on our own. Yet we still had a natural desire to be in relationship with others.

Not only do we desire to work, but we want to own our own company and run it the way we want. We want to be financially independent and yet madly in love. It is not that we want to run the relationship with the man; we simply want to be trusted, honored, and loved. Yet the reality is that we don't need men. We don't need their paycheck to live on, and with reproductive technology, we don't even need them to have babies. This creates an interesting ideology to work through.

We are beginning to see the effects on women who bought into the feminist movement. Many of these women are realizing that their devout commitment to the cause may have cost them a marriage and maybe the opportunity to have children during their childbearing years. There are women who have great careers but no family ties, creating a void in their life and a sense of regret. This forces us to take a careful look at the feminist movement. While many of us embrace the basic definition of feminism—the belief that women should be granted the same rights and privileges as men—we are skeptical of those who bash men and are still fighting for rights that we already have.

The major question we need to ask is, "How do we minister effectively to Gen X women?" With all of the choices and options women face, it is important to have a place to talk about the meaning of life and the world we must be a part of. The changing of the family dynamic has left us without a consistent place to work through our thoughts and feelings about the world we live in. Many of us live in states far from our parents or have strained relationships with them, yet we still need the guidance and interaction that parents often provide.

We also need the influence of Christ in life, in areas including politics and technology, and everything from cloning to Internet ethics. We are becoming a global society and we wonder how we will fit into this ever-changing world.

Women realize that friendships are the key to getting through life. We desire to have friendships with women who will be committed to us through thick and thin. This sounds easier than it is. By nature, women tend to be more collectivistic than men. With society becoming more and more isolated, making friendships can be difficult, especially with women who share common ground in Christ. Providing a healthy arena for this to take place will be an effective way to minister to women.

Women and children make up the highest percentage of those considered below the poverty level. Even though many of us are not in poverty situations, we need help with our own monetary situations as well. Many of us are in debt, and we need to learn or relearn about finances and spending. The financial resources we had growing up are now limited by our vocations.

One of the best ways to minister to women is to involve them in service. Serving others creates a worldview that may not be obtained without such service. This will also help to develop community among women.

Even in the midst of AIDS, STDs, and other infections, Gen X women still desire to express sexuality in our lives. To some, it means being sexually active; to others, it can simply mean being embraced or holding hands. Nevertheless, we desire to be loved. We don't need to have sex outside of marriage, but we need to understand our sexuality. We need a way to express who we are as sexual beings. We know that having sex isn't the answer to understanding our sexuality. A few years ago, a small book containing "rules" for women to live by became a best seller, not because it is a scholarly endeavor, but because we need help in many aspects of relationships. The authors gave practical advice on how to deal with men and be in relationships with them. Though the book has some good tips on dating, we still need Christ's influence on this part of our lives. We also need role models and other women to work through the tough issues surrounding the relational choices in our lives.

Some Gen X women have other relational issues that stem from having had babies as teens and becoming single moms. The church needs to recognize this societal trend and focus energy on ministering to these women. They do not fit into traditional college and career groups, and many don't fit into older singles groups. These women have desires similar to those of non-mothers, but they face some challenges and choices that they need guidance on.

With all of these factors and needs, women often fall through the cracks of the traditional church. However, with the right leadership and opportunities, young women can play a productive role as the church faces a new millennium.

OVERVIEW OF METRO MINISTRY

by Todd Phillips

Austin Metro is different from other Generation X ministries because it is a true parachurch ministry. It is designed to walk alongside the local churches of the community to reach out to the unchurched singles between the ages of eighteen and thirty. Its official purpose is to "stand in the gap between the local churches and the unchurched singles, providing a comfortable atmosphere where they can experience God." Metro is aggressively evangelistic, providing Christians a place where young people can feel comfortable bringing their unchurched friends so that their friends might get "in the path of the gospel."

Metro began as an in-home Bible study with six single young men who desired simply to learn more about their relationship with God. We chose to use the *Experiencing God* Bible study as our guide. We had no idea that God would use our small group to launch a citywide ministry in the months to come. We assumed that we would finish the twelve-week course and it would end there. You know what they say about assumptions.

As we came together to dig into the Word of God over those three months, we watched in amazement as God moved in the life of one of the men who began a new relationship with Christ five weeks into the study. We were truly taken aback by the growth of each person in the group and decided we would continue with the study even after the last chapter was completed. We prayed about inviting others and agreed that we should give others an opportunity to join the study. The next day, each of us went to our offices and e-mailed many friends and coworkers, expecting only a marginal response. By the end of the week, we received more than fifty confirmations from those who planned to attend. Several problems surfaced immediately: Where will we put all these people? Who is going to teach them? What study will we use as our guide?

I called my singles minister and asked him if we could use a large room in the church on Sunday nights for this new group, and he agreed. So, we had a place to put our new members. But what would we teach them and who would be the teacher? I was put in charge of finding another study guide during the week, but I never got around to finding our new material. So, there I was on Saturday night in my apartment, with no study guide and no one to teach the class and less twenty-four hours to solve both problems.

I sat down with my roommate and put together a "message" on the fall of man using Genesis as my Scripture. (I thought I would start there because it was the first book of the Bible—I didn't want to give away the ending.) I decided that I would teach the first night or until we could work out some other arrangements. The next evening we were astonished to find fifty-three people gathered in our assigned room, anxiously awaiting the beginning of the study. I preached (or talked) that night for thirty minutes and closed in prayer. We decided to give the group a name. We called it "The Bottom Line: A Citywide Bible Study." I am still amazed that we were confident enough in God to call our get-together a citywide *anything!*

Over the next several months, the study fluctuated wildly in attendance and in vision. Many who attended the first night weren't there any longer, and four of the six men who started the Bible study had decided to move on to other things. Mark Wolf and I found ourselves involved with a group of people eager to learn about God yet needing leadership. We felt completely inadequate for the task. My teaching was marginal at best, but God was developing in me a deep desire to share His truth with others, so I continued to develop new lessons each week.

In just over three months we were averaging about twenty people in attendance, less than half of our original number. We were moved to three different rooms within the church, and we had no formalized leadership group. Yet we were still convinced that God was going to use us to develop a citywide ministry to reach out to the unchurched singles of Austin. Nothing we saw at that time even suggested that it might actually happen, but we pressed on toward that goal. At times I wondered if we were just talking ourselves into believing that God would use us. But the conviction ran deep and we were diligent in prayer. God would bring it to fruition.

Meanwhile, there was a man in Houston who had in the past several months experienced the power of God in his life. His name is Aldie Warnock, and he was attending a singles ministry in Houston called Metro Bible Study. Through his attendance there, he recommitted his life to Christ and then God began to heal his broken marriage. He was a lobbyist who spent a lot of time in Austin and knew many people there who, in his opinion, desperately needed God. He was surprised to find that there was nothing in Austin like the ministry he attended in Houston, and became compelled by the thought that there should be an Austin Metro.

The first place he called was Hyde Park Baptist Church. He chose Hyde Park only because the Metro Bible Study in Houston was located in a large Baptist church, so he thought it reasonable to call a large Baptist church in Austin to discuss the idea of Metro. He was directed to John Walters, who was my singles minister. John introduced Aldie to me in March of 1995 and we began a relationship that, with the blessings and guidance of God and the help of countless others, took our small Bible study and turned it into "Austin Metro: A Young Singles Sort of Get-Together Thing."

We decided to clearly define the ministry as an interdenominational Bible study for people with any church background or no church background at all. It would be an independent ministry, not supported financially by any one church or denomination. The finances, direction of the ministry, and all other variables would be managed internally by those involved in the ministry. This proved to be invaluable in the months and years to come as churches desired to control various aspects of the ministry at different times. We didn't waver in our commitment to these basic core decisions.

Metro moved from the main building at Hyde Park Baptist Church to a small building across the street that housed around a hundred people. Hyde Park agreed to allow us the use of their facilities without them having any direct involvement in the ministry. Housing the ministry in a Baptist church, however, became a concern for several people in leadership. They felt that if we were going to define Metro as an interdenominational ministry, we needed to be sensitive to the fact that I was the speaker of Metro and I was also a member of Hyde Park. They felt that some might see Metro as less autonomous than it actually was. I agreed, and we moved to First Evangelical Free Church in June of 1995. Due to increases in attendance

and the sale of a building we were using, Metro moved a total of three times before ending up back at Hyde Park in June of 1996.

From June to August of 1996, Metro grew from 120 to 360 in attendance. A strong radio advertising campaign we ran during the late summer months was the catalyst for the growth we experienced. The concern about my membership at Hyde Park turned out to be unwarranted; the growth was phenomenal. We grew steadily during the fall of 1996 and the spring of 1997, until reaching five hundred people attending weekly by May. During the summer of 1997, again using secular radio advertising as our outreach tool, we watched as God increased our weekly attendance to more than one thousand in July. Seventy-six churches were represented in the ministry from many different denominations. We had truly become what God had given us a vision for—a citywide interdenominational evangelistic ministry for young singles. We were in awe!

WHY DOES IT WORK?

Why does this "singles sort of get-together thing" work? First of all, it doesn't work; God works! I mean that literally. All the leaders who have given their time to God's work through this ministry have come to one overarching conclusion: God is more concerned with building His relationship with His people than with using the "right" methods. With God there is no one right method for reaching a generation, but there is one right God. The Bible study, *Experiencing God*, that God used to ignite the vision for this ministry has within it some profound insights relating to this idea of relationship over method:

The Bus Ministry Parable
Once a church asked, "Oh, God, how do You want to reach our community through us and build a great church?" God led them to start a bus ministry to provide transportation for children and adults to come to church. They did what God told them to do, and their church grew into a great church.

They were flattered when people from all over the country began to ask, "What are you doing to grow so rapidly?" They wrote a book on how to build great churches through a bus ministry. Thousands of churches began to buy buses to reach their communities, feeling that the method was the key to growth. Later many sold those same buses, saying, "It didn't work for us."

It never works! *God* works! The method is never the key to accomplishing God's purposes. The key is your relationship to a Person. When you want to know how God would have you reach your city, start a new church, or whatever, ask *Him.* Then, when He tells you, don't be surprised if you can't find any church that is doing it just that way. Why? God wants you to know Him. If you follow someone else's plan, use a method, or emphasize a program, you will have a tendency to forget about your dependence on God. You leave the relationship with God and

go after a method or a program. I've heard this referred to as spiritual adultery.

God in Control
This is a perfect example of what has happened and is happening today in many churches. People are drawn in by methods as the answer to reaching a lost generation when in fact it is God who chooses and changes the methods by which He works as He sees fit.

We are to know the times and respond to them, changing methods as God directs. Hanging on to method is religion; changing methods as God leads is relationship.

None of this is to say that this or any other book, seminar, or course is invalid in helping determine God's will for your ministry. I wholeheartedly support seminars, books, and courses as agents for education and change in God's kingdom. However, I believe that God must first reveal to the individual or group His desires for them. Then He can reveal His methods to them by any number of avenues.

All of this is to say simply that God is truly in control. That may sound too simplistic when dealing with methodology in ministry. However, I am firmly convinced, in light of witnessing God's creative and diverse process relating to both Metro ministries, that God desires for us to rely on Him for all parts of ministry, including and probably specifically methodology.

SHAPE

The SHAPE assessment is a tool that will allow leaders to determine their calling, passion, and purpose in ministry. By completing this assessment, leaders will understand their gifts and strengths and will better understand the ways in which they are empowered for ministry.

S

Spiritual Gifts: "Each . . . has his own gift from God; one has this gift, another has that" (1 Corinthians 7:7). *What am I gifted to do?*

H

Heart: "It is God who works in you, inspiring both the will and the deed, for his own chosen purpose" (Philippians 2:13, NEB). *What do I love to do?*

A

Abilities: "There are different abilities to perform service" (1 Corinthians 12:6). "I [God] have filled him with the Spirit of God, with skill, ability, and knowledge in all kinds of crafts" (Exodus 31:3). *What natural talents and skills do I have?*

P

Personality: "No one can really know what anyone else is thinking, or what he is really like, except that person himself" (1 Corinthians 2:11, TLB). *Where does my personality best suit me to serve?*

E

Experience: "By this time you ought to be teachers yourselves, yet here I find you need someone to sit down with you and go over the basics on God again . . . (you are) inexperienced in God's ways." (Hebrews 5:12-13, MSG). *What life experiences have I had?*

SHAPE Summarized . . .

Your ministry will be most effective and fulfilling when you are using your *gifts* and *abilities* in the area of your *heart's desire* in a way that best expresses your *personality* and *experience*.

My SHAPE will determine my ministry!

What are the goals of SHAPE?

• I will discover my unique design (SHAPE) for ministry and commit to developing and using my God-given gifts and abilities in serving God and others.

• I will select and begin serving in the ministry God made me for.

• I will increase my awareness of how God can use me strategically in ministry.

• I will see that I am an integral part of what God is doing.

GIFTED TO SERVE

"Each one should use whatever gift he has received to serve others, faithfully administering God's grace in its various forms" (1 Peter 4:10).

GOD'S MISSION IS REACHING OUT

"He [God] longs for all to be saved and to understand this truth: That God is on one side and all the people on the other side, and Christ Jesus, himself man, is between them to bring them together" (1 Timothy 2:4-5, TLB).

"God put the world square with himself through the Messiah, giving the world a fresh start by offering forgiveness of sins. God has given us the task of telling everyone what he is doing. We're Christ's representatives. God uses us to persuade men and women to drop their differences and enter into God's work of making things right between them" (2 Corinthians 5:20-21, MSG).

GOD'S METHOD INCLUDES US

"He handed out gifts above and below, filled heaven with his gifts, filled earth with his gifts. He handed out gifts of apostle, prophet, evangelist, and pastor-teacher to train Christians in skilled servant work, working within Christ's body, the church, until we're all moving rhythmically and easily with each other, efficient and graceful in response to God's Son, fully mature adults, fully developed within and without, fully alive like Christ" (Ephesians 4:10-12, MSG).

1. It is God who gives the gifts.
   • "Every good and perfect gift is from above" (James 1:17).
2. There are specific gifts.
   • 1 Corinthians 12:1-31; Romans 12:3-8.
3. Using your gifts promotes unity.
   • "Your strong love for each other will prove to the world that you are my disciples" (John 13:35, TLB).
4. When everyone uses his or her gifts, we reach unbelievers.
   • "God did not send his Son into the world to condemn the world, but to save the world through him" (John 3:17).
   • "Make my joy complete by being like-minded, having the same love, being

one in spirit and purpose"
(Philippians 2:2).

5. Using your gifts results in spiritual
   maturity.
   • "You see that [Abraham's] faith and
     his actions were working together, and
     his faith was made complete by what
     he did" (James 2:22).
   • "As the body without the spirit is
     dead, so faith without deeds is dead"
     (James 2:26).
6. When we use our gifts we become fully
   alive.
   • "My purpose is to give life in all its
     fullness" (John 10:10, NLT).

Spiritual Gifts Survey

For your leaders to understand more fully their
calling and their unique place in ministry, it is
essential that they understand how their spiritual
gifts complement the gifts of others in the body of
Christ. There are a number of spiritual gifts surveys available that help people identify the combination of gifts they have received. We recommend
Gifts Survey by Rich Hurst, available for a nomi-
nal fee by calling Dreamtime Publishing at (888)
603-7326 or going to www.dreamtime2.com.

YOU HAVE HEART

Everyone has a passion for ministry. The "why"
of your ministry is determined by your heart,
your passion; "what" you will do is determined
by your spiritual gift(s); and the "how" grows
out of your personality.

Your ministry calling is important to God.
God has designed you for a special purpose.

You created my innermost being,
you knit me together in my mother's
    womb.
I praise you because I am fearfully and
    wonderfully made. . . .
My frame was not hidden from you
when I was made in the secret place.
    (Psalm 139:13-15)

*God has placed you in the twentieth and
twenty-first centuries.* "All the days ordained for
me were written in your book before one of
them came to be" (Psalm 139:16).

*God works in you, giving you the desire and
ability to pursue your ministry calling.* "Work out
your salvation with fear and trembling, for it is
God who works in you to will and to act according to his good purpose" (Philippians 2:12b,13).
God has designed you to have a dream for ministry. It may have to do with the church and it
may have to do with ecology, economics, pris-
ons, junior highers, or AIDS patients.

Your passion is important to you. You cannot
be the person God intended you to be unless
you pursue the ministry call that God has for
you. "Faith by itself, if it is not accompanied by
action, is dead. . . . Show me your faith without deeds, and I will show you my faith by
what I do" (James 2:17,18).

The key will be faithfulness, not success.
While success is nice, it is not guaranteed. God

decides what the effect of your ministry will be (1 Corinthians 12:6).

Your passion is important to your church. Every part of the church is important to and interdependent with the other parts. "The body is a unit, though it is made up of many parts. . . . God has arranged the parts in a body, every one of them, just as he wanted them to be" (1 Corinthians 12:12,18).

Your ministry passion determines your church's mission. The mission of the church should reflect and be shaped be the ministry passion, or heart, of all the people.

Your ministry passion is important to your culture. As we enter the twenty-first century, the world is in a cultural crisis with alarming rates of illiteracy, teenage pregnancy, prison failure, crime, divorce, drug addiction, and so on. Government is relinquishing its welfare role. The schools, medical field, and legal system are in a shambles.

Fill out the following "calling card." This will help you to begin to understand your heart (passion, dream) for ministry.

CALLING CARD

STEP ONE
Passion (What is your greatest passion in ministry? In simple language, what is your dream?)

STEP TWO
Price (There is always a price to pay if you commit to something. What is the price you will have to pay?)

STEP THREE
Persuasion (We believe you need a team to do any ministry. Who are some people who will work with you?)

Step 1. The first step is all about passion. What are the things that you feel passionate about right now? You have been given different passions from God. Some have a passion to do junior high ministry, single adult ministry, literacy ministry, or AIDS ministry. However, that passion is played out differently according to your "shape." I would like you to write down in one or two sentences the answer to this question: "If I could do anything for God, what would that be?"

Step 2. There is a price to be paid. This step is all about that price. If you are going to invest yourself in a ministry, you will have to pay some kind of price. Maybe you are like our friend Bob Williams, who was a doctor and decided to give up half his practice so he could have a half-time practice in the inner city. This involved a sacrifice of time, even time away from his family. So, everybody has to be willing to pay a price. If you were to do your passion, what is the price you think you would have to pay?

Step 3. Every one of us who wants to lead a ministry has to earn the right. One of the ways we know we've earned that right is that there are people who want to be involved with us or follow us in doing this ministry.

Many ministries are led just by one person, and that may be okay. However, the ideal situation is to have several people involved in a certain ministry.

It has been our goal to help you to create your own calling card, just like a card you might use to get some cash from the cash machine or to charge something. We hope this card will be a reminder to you of the three steps—passion, price, and persuasion—everybody has to fulfill before he or she can operate fully within his or her calling.

YOU HAVE ABILITIES AND INTERESTS

Do you know of a community service organization we should research? If so, please name the community service organization and briefly describe what they do.

What languages do you speak?
    American Sign Language
    German
    Spanish
    French
    Russian
    Other

Please circle your preferences:
Adult: 1. literacy 2. life-building skills 3. other
Infant: 1. AIDS/HIV babies 2. pediatrics ward, 3. other
Children: 1. mentoring 2. tutoring 3. outings 4. other

Teenagers: 1. mentoring 2. structured work activities 3. outings 4. other
Disabled: 1. outings 2. reading to the blind 3. physical therapy 4. shopping/errands 5. other
Crisis Pregnancy Center: 1. information 2. counseling 3. receptionist 4. other
Health Care: 1. AIDS/HIV 2. counseling 3. information 4. other
Elderly: 1. meal delivery 2. outings 3. group activities in a nursing home 4. reading 5. shopping/errands 6. other
Mentally Disabled: 1. teenager 2. adult 3. children 4. other
Criminal Justice System: 1. rehabilitation 2. Big Brother/Big Sister 3. mentoring 4. other
Homeless: 1. soup kitchen 2. rescue mission 3. street evangelism 4. other
Special Skills: 1. CPR 2. clerical 3. coaching 4. answering calls 5. computer 6. data entry 7. domestic violence 8. ESL (English as Second Language) instructor 9. first aid 10. newsletter 11. photography 12. music 13. transportation/driving 14. ushering 15. victims assistance 16. other
Additional comments welcome.

YOU HAVE PERSONALITY

1. We recommend the Keirsey Temperament Sorter. But remember, its results are personality *tendencies,* not absolutes!

2. There is no good or bad profile. All people are a composite of all the types, but some tendencies are stronger than others.

3. You are what you are. And that's good.

4. We all have particular strengths and weaknesses.

5. We are what we are, but successful individuals are those who (a) understand why and how they affect other people and how other people affect them, and (b) understand their strengths and weaknesses and develop positive attitudes about themselves.

You will discover your temperament style by doing the Keirsey Temperament Sorter. You can obtain one from PN Books, Box 2748, Del Mar, CA 92014; TEL (760) 632-1575; FAX (619) 481-0535 or (714) 540-5288. They are very inexpensive, so please buy one for each person you are working with. We strongly encourage you to read *Please Understand Me: Character and Temperament Types* by David Keirsey and Marilyn Bates, Gnosology Books Ltd., 1984.

HOW TO GET INVOLVED AT [YOUR CHURCH'S NAME]

Provide job descriptions on all the ministries and jobs inside and outside the church that you want to help people connect with.

Encouragement Team
This team sends cards and other special items to encourage people in difficult times (death in family) or to acknowledge times of special joy (college graduation, birthdays).

Liaison to Caring Ministry
This person plugs people into the appropriate caring ministry team or support group.

Care Card Callers
This team calls all first-time visitors the week after they attend, in addition to calling people who need special encouragement.

YOU HAVE EXPERIENCES

Tell us about your past volunteer experiences that were both rewarding and fun for you:

Did you have this experience at this church or another church?

What is your current time availability? (circle one)
Once per month   Twice per month
Once per week   Days   Evenings
Weekends only

Operation Mentor
This is a "Big Brother/Big Sister" outreach bringing Christ-centered love, guidance, and example to children of single parents.

Roommate Connection
This team publishes a roommate needed/housing available listing every two weeks.

Ride Connection
This team runs a shuttle to West Falls Church Metro station before and after your young adult ministry services.

MINISTRY TEAM
AREA DESCRIPTIONS

Your young adult ministry community outreach team

Inner-City Ministry Team

Be involved on a team that helps out with inner-city youth.

Homeless Ministry Team

Be involved on a team that reaches out in a physical and spiritual way to help the homeless on the streets of your city.

Youth Teams

Be involved on a team that helps out with inner-city Young Life.

Children with AIDS Team

Be involved in an ongoing outreach to children with AIDS at a local hospital in your city. Spend time ministering to the kids with gospel stories, games, outings, and so on.

Athletic Club

Be involved in this weekly ministry by using sports as an outreach to seekers.

SHAPE is a concept that Ken Baugh learned at Saddleback Community Church. We are greatly indebted for the name. We highly recommend *Please Understand Me* as your personality tool. All the rest of this material was created for our young adult ministries.

USING *GETTING REAL* AT A LEADERSHIP RETREAT

Note: Obviously, you cannot get through all the material in this book in one day without losing something. But because a one-day seminar may be the easiest for a group of leaders, we have mapped out a sample agenda. We suggest starting at 8:30 A.M. and ending at 4:30 P.M. because attention spans have a tendency to fade with more time than that.

8:30–9:30	Introductions and Overview of Agenda
	Do a journey of faith exercise. Have each person draw a picture of his or her faith journey and then share it with the group and tell his or her personal faith journey. Keep drawings simple. This could take longer if you have a large team. Break down into small groups if you need to.
9:30–10:15	What Is Postmodernism? Use *Star Trek* video clips to illustrate the points in chapter 1. Discuss how each element of postmodernism could affect your young adult ministry.
10:15–10:30	Break
10:30–11:30	Forces That Shaped a Postmodern Young Adult
11:30–12:00	Evaluation of Subgroups in Your Area
12:00–1:30	Lunch Break: Discuss Relational Ministry and Biblical Foundations
1:30–2:30	Vision, Targeted Ministry
2:30–3:15	Core Teams
3:15–3:30	Environment for Ministry
3:30–4:15	TC Group Ministry
4:15–4:30	Empowering Others
4:30	Prayer

RESOURCES

BIBLIOGRAPHY

Barna, George. *Baby Busters*. Chicago: Northfield, 1994.

Bell, Chip R. *Managers As Mentors*. San Francisco: Berrett-Koehler, 1996.

Blankenhorn, David. *Fatherless America*. New York: Basic, 1995.

Celek, Tim, and Dieter Zander. *Inside the Soul of a New Generation*. Grand Rapids, Mich.: Zondervan, 1996.

Cloud, Henry. *Changes That Heal*. Grand Rapids, Mich.: Zondervan, 1990.

Cohen, Michael Lee. *The Twenty-Something American Dream*. New York: Dutton, 1993.

Coupland, Douglas. *Microserfs*. New York: Regan, 1995.

———. *Generation X*. New York: St. Martin's, 1991.

Covey, Stephen R. *Principle-Centered Leadership*. New York: Simon & Schuster, 1990.

———. *First Things First*. New York: Simon & Schuster, 1994.

———. *The Seven Habits of Highly Effective People*. New York: Simon & Schuster, 1989.

Dalbey, Gordon. *Healing the Masculine Soul*. Dallas: Word, 1988.

Davis, Stan, and Christopher Meyer. *Blur: The Speed of Change in the Connected Economy*. Reading, Mass.: Addison-Wesley, 1998.

Dunn, William. *The Baby Bust: A Generation Comes of Age*. Ithaca, N.Y.: American Demographics, 1993.

Easum, William M. *Sacred Cows Make Gourmet Burgers*. Nashville: Abingdon, 1995.

Erickson, Millard J. *Postmodernizing the Faith*. Grand Rapids, Mich.: Baker, 1998.

Ford, Kevin Graham. *Jesus for a New Generation*. Downers Grove, Ill.: InterVarsity, 1995.

George, Carl F. *Prepare Your Church for the Future*. Tarrytown, N.Y.: Revell, 1991.

Grenz, Stanley J. *A Primer on Postmodernism*. Grand Rapids, Mich.: Eerdmans, 1996.

Grossman, David. "Trained to Kill." *Christianity Today*, vol. 42, no. 9: 30-39.

Hahn, Todd, and David Verhaagen. *Reckless Hope*. Grand Rapids, Mich.: Baker, 1996.

Hershey, Terry. *Go Away Come Closer*. Waco, Texas: Word, 1990.

Hershey, Terry, Karen Butler, and Rich Hurst. *Giving the Ministry Away*. Elgin, Ill.: Cook, 1993.

Holtz, Geoffrey T. *Welcome to the Jungle.* New York: St. Martin's Griffin, 1995.

———. *Young Adult Ministry.* Loveland, Colo.: Group, 1986.

Hurst, Rich. *Intimacy: The Search for Significance.* Colorado Springs, Colo.: Cook, 1998.

Koons, Carolyn A., and Michael J. Anthony. *Single Adult Passages.* Grand Rapids, Mich.: Baker, 1991.

Labovitz, George, and Victor Rosansky, *The Power of Alignment.* New York: Wiley, 1997.

Larson, Bruce. *No Longer Strangers.* Waco, Texas: Word, 1971.

Long, Jimmy. *Generating Hope.* Downers Grove, Ill.: InterVarsity, 1997.

Lopiano-Misdom, Janine, and Joanne De Luca, *Street Trends.* New York: Harper Business, 1997.

Mahedy, William, and Janet Bernardi. *A Generation Alone.* Downers Grove, Ill.: InterVarsity, 1994.

Maxwell, John C. *Developing the Leader Within You.* Nashville: Nelson, 1993.

McIntosh, Gary L. *Three Generations.* Grand Rapids, Mich.: Revell, 1995.

Murren, Doug. *The Baby Boomerang.* Ventura, Calif.: Regal, 1990.

Nelson, Rob, and Jon Cowan. *Revolution X.* New York: Penguin, 1994.

Peck, M. Scott. *The Different Drum.* New York: Simon & Schuster, 1987.

Perry, William G. *Intellectual and Ethical Development.* Orlando, Fla: Holt, Rinehart & Winston, 1968.

Powell, John. *Why Am I Afraid to Love?* Niles, Ill.: Argus, 1967.

Rainer, Tom S. *The Bridger Generation.* Nashville: Broadman & Holman, 1997.

Raines, Claire. *Beyond Generation X.* Menlo Park, Calif.: Crisp, 1997.

Regele, Mike. *Death of the Church.* Grand Rapids, Mich.: Zondervan, 1995.

Ritchie, Karen. *Marketing to Generation X.* New York: Lexington, 1995.

Rushkoff, Douglas. *The GenX Reader.* New York: Ballantine, 1994.

Sacks, Peter. *Generation X Goes to College.* Chicago: Open Court, 1996.

Schaeffer, Francis A. *The Church at the End of the 20th Century.* Downers Grove, Ill.: InterVarsity, 1970.

———. *He Is There and He Is Not Silent.* Wheaton, Ill.: Tyndale, 1972.

Senge, Peter M. *The Fifth Discipline.* New York: Doubleday, 1990.

Sheehy, Gail. *New Passages.* New York: Random House, 1995.

Sjogren, Steve. *Conspiracy of Kindness.* Ann Arbor, Mich.: Servant, 1993.

Strauss, William, and Neil Howe. *Generations.* New York: Morrow, 1991.

———. *13th Generation.* New York: Vintage, 1993.

———. *The Fourth Turning.* New York: Broadway, 1997.

Thau, Richard D., and Jay S. Heflin. *Generations Apart.* Amherst, N.Y.: Prometheus, 1997.

Tillapaugh, Frank, and Rich Hurst. *Calling.* Monument, Colo.: Dreamtime, 1997.

Tillapaugh, Frank. *The Church Unleashed.* Ventura, Calif.: Regal, 1982.

Tulgan, Bruce. *Managing Generation X.* Santa Monica, Calif.: Merritt, 1995.

Wadsworth, Barry J. *Piaget's Theory of Cognitive and Affective Development.* New York: Longman, 1989.

Warren, Rick. *The Purpose Driven Church.* Grand Rapids, Mich.: Zondervan, 1995.

Weil, Michelle M. *TechnoStress.* New York: Wiley, 1997.

Wesson, Vann. *Generation X Field Guide and Lexicon.* San Diego: Orion, 1997.

Wieners, Brad, and David Pescovitz. *Reality Check.* San Francisco: Hardwired, 1996.

Yukl, Gary A. *Leadership in Organizations.* Englewood Cliffs, N.J.: Prentice-Hall, 1989.

Zoba, Wendy Murray. "The Class of '00," *Christianity Today*, vol. 41, no. 2: 18-28.

Zustiak, Gary. *The Next Generation.* Joplin, Mo.: College Press, 1996.

GEN X-RELATED MAGAZINES

Echo
www.echomagazine.com
(800) 352-7225
"The only young adult discipleship magazine with an emphasis on the world. Our goal is to challenge Christians to worship God with all that we are."

Generation Lifestyle
203 North Wabash, Suite 1618, Chicago, IL 60601
(888) 782-3338
"A men's and women's lifestyle magazine for the current generation and each generation to follow. With real people, sharing their opinions and interests that reveal insights discovered as they evolve through their generation."

Spin
www.spin.com
"*Spin* will rock your world with coverage of the progressive music scene and in-depth investigative reporting on a slew of issues, from politics to pop culture. Reviews, essays, profiles, and interviews make up a package of pure rock energy with an alternative edge."

re:generation quarterly
www.regenerator.com
(800) 783-4903
"The purpose of *re:generation quarterly* is to equip the emerging generation to transform their world by providing commentary, critique, and celebration of communities and contemporary culture."

Wired
www.wired.com/wired/current.html
"*Wired* magazine is daring, compelling, innovative, courageous, and insightful. It speaks to those who see the landscape of the 21st century and think: possibility, hope, new opportunity,

and a wide-open frontier. Each month, *Wired* delivers authoritative stories that identify the driving forces reshaping our culture with an emphasis on technology and the information revolution."

OTHER MINISTRIES

The Next Level Church
Trevor Bron, pastor, tbron@ix.netcom.com
P.O. Box 260545
Lakewood, CO 80226
TEL (303) 422-3777

Metro Bible Studies
Todd Phillips
todphil@aol.com
1715 Hadbury Lane
San Antonio, TX 78248
TEL (210) 499-9492

Calvary Church, Newport Mesa
Tim Celek, pastor, Tcelek@sayyes.org
190 E. 23rd Street
Costa Mesa, CA 92627
TEL (949) 646-2151
FAX (949) 645-3547

Graceland at Santa Cruz Bible Church
Dan Kimball, pastor, dan@santacruzbible.org
TEL (831) 429-1162
FAX (831) 429-9575
http://www.santacruzbible.org/graceland/

MISCELLANEOUS ORGANIZATIONS

Planet X Ministries
Kevin Devires, director
2020 Hannan Rd.
Canto, MI 48188
TEL (734) 326-7717
planetxmin@aol.com

The Gospel and Our Culture Network
www.gocn.org

Young Leaders Network
Jason Mitchell, director, jason.mitchell@youngleader.org
2501 Cedar Springs LB-5, Suite 200
Dallas, TX 75201
TEL (800) 765-5323
www.youngleader.org

Frontline Ministry Resources
Ken Baugh, director, kenbaugh@erols.com
850 Balls Hill Road
McLean, VA 20165
TEL (703) 421-8108
FAX (703) 421-1541
www.frontline.to

Dreamtime
Frank Tillapaugh, director, Ftillapaug@aol.com
P.O. Box 1686
Monument, CO 80132
www.dreamtime2.com
TEL (719) 481-0281
FAX (719) 488-8721

NOTES

INTRODUCTION

[1] Heard in a lecture by Frank Tillapaugh, 1983.
[2] *USA Weekend* (August 19–21, 1988), p. 5.

CHAPTER ONE

[1] From a press release, The Associated Press, 1998.
[2] Francis Schaeffer, *The Church at the End of the 20th Century* (Downers Grove, Ill.: InterVarsity, 1970), p. 77.
[3] Thomas C. Oden, *Requiem: A Lament in Three Movements* (Nashville: Abingdon, 1995), p. 117.
[4] Leith Anderson, *A Church for the 21st Century* (Minneapolis: Bethany, 1992), p. 17.
[5] Thomas Oden as quoted by Christopher Hall, "Back to the Fathers," *Christianity Today* (September 24, 1990), pp. 28–31.
[6] Stanley J. Grenz, *A Primer on Postmodernism* (Grand Rapids, Mich.: Eerdmans, 1996), pp. 8–9.
[7] Kevin Graham Ford, *Jesus for a New Generation* (Downers Grove, Ill.: InterVarsity, 1995), p. 134.

[8] Thomas Oden, *After Modernity . . . What?: Agenda for Theology* (Grand Rapids, Mich.: Zondervan, 1990), p. 51.
[9] Stanley J. Grenz, "Post Modernism and the Future of Evangelical Theology: Star Trek and the Next Generation," *Evangelical Review of Theology* (October 18, 1994), p. 325.
[10] Grenz, "Post Modernism and the Future of Evangelical Theology," p. 325.
[11] Rich Hurst and Frank Tillapaugh, *Calling* (Monument, Colo.: Dreamtime, 1997).
[12] Bruce Larson and Ralph Osborne, *The Emerging Church* (Waco, Texas: Word, 1972), p. 47.
[13] Grenz, *A Primer on Postmodernism*, p. 174.

CHAPTER TWO

[1] Archibald D. Hart, *Healing Adult Children of Divorce* (Ann Arbor, Mich.: Servant, 1991).
[2] A. Carolyn Koons and Michael J. Anthony, *Single Adult Passages* (Grand Rapids, Mich.: Baker, 1991), p. 104.
[3] Matthew Kalman, "Children of Divorce

Inclined to Depression," *USA Today*, February 17, 1999, sec. 3, p. 1.

4 Holtz, p. 10.

5 Holtz, p. 15.

6 Holtz, p. 16.

7 Geoffrey T. Holtz, *Welcome to the Jungle* (New York: St. Martin's Griffin, 1995), p. 15.

8 William Strauss and Neil Howe, *The Fourth Turning* (New York: Broadway, 1997), p. 195.

9 Alan Axelrod and Charles Phillips, *What Everyone Should Know About the 20th Century* (Holbrook, Mass.: Adams, 1995), pp. 246–247.

10 Strauss and Howe, *The Fourth Turning*, p. 73.

11 Axelrod and Phillips, p. 265.

12 William Strauss and Neil Howe, *13th Gen* (New York: Vintage, 1993), p. 56

13 William Dunn, *The Baby Bust: A Generation Comes of Age* (Ithaca, NY: American Demographics), p. 16.

14 Koons and Anthony, p. 103.

15 Victor Bondi and Peter C. Holloran, *American Decades: 1970–1979* (Detroit: Gale, 1995), p. 348.

16 Paul D. Meier, *Christian Child-Rearing and Personality Development* (Grand Rapids, Mich.: Baker, 1977), p. 134.

17 Bob Loysk, "Generation X: What Are They Like?" *Current 392* (May 1997), p. 2.

18 Bondi and Holloran, p. 346.

19 Strauss and Howe, p. 61.

20 Strauss and Howe, p. 235.

21 Richard D. Thau and Jay S. Heflin, *Generations Apart* (Amherst, N.Y.: Prometheus, 1997), pp. 114–115.

22 Rob Nelson and Jon Cowan, *Revolution X: A Survival Guide for Our Generation* (New York: Penguin, 1994), p. 66.

23 Thau and Heflin, p. 65.

24 Lawrence J. Bradford and Claire Raines, *Twentysomething: Managing and Motivating Today's New Work Force* (New York: Master, 1992), p. 33.

25 Loysk, p. 10.

26 William R. Buck and Tracey C. Rembert, "Just Doing It: Generation X Proves That Actions Speak Louder Than Words," *E* (September–October 1997), p. 28.

27 Loysk, p. 10.

28 Buck and Rembert, p. 29.

29 David Blankenhorn, *Fatherless America: Confronting Our Most Urgent Social Problem* (New York: Basic, 1995), p. 1.

30 Gordon Dalbey, *Healing the Masculine Soul* (Dallas: Word, 1988), p. 13.

31 Blankenhorn, p. 19.

32 Blankenhorn, p. 222.

33 Loysk, p. 10.

34 Strauss and Howe, p. 40.

35 Michelle M. Weil and Larry D. Rosen, *Techno Stress* (New York: Wiley, 1997).

36 Meredith Bagby, "The X Factor: What Makes Generation X Tick?" *Entrepreneur* (August 1998), p. 42.

37 Richard A. Swenson, *Margin* (Colorado Springs, Colo.: NavPress, 1992), pp. 106–107.

38 Archibald D. Hart, *Adrenalin and Stress* (Dallas: Word, 1991), p. 31.

39 Joanne De Luca and Janine Lopiano-Misdom, *Street Trends* (New York: Harper Business, 1997), p. 7.

[40] Holtz, p. 208.

[41] De Luca and Lopiano-Misdom, p. 16.

[42] De Luca and Lopiano-Misdom, p. 15.

[43] Strauss and Howe, *The Fourth Turning*, p. 244.

[44] George Barna, *Generation Next* (Ventura, Calif.: Regal, 1995), p. 38.

[45] Chris Woodyard, "Generation Y," *USA Today* (October 6, 1998), p. 2A.

[46] Victoria Rainert, "Toward the Root of the Evil," *Time* (April 6, 1998), p. 23.

[47] Rainert, p. 23.

[48] David Grossman, "Trained to Kill," *Christianity Today* (August 10, 1998), p. 32.

[49] Grossman, p. 32.

CHAPTER THREE

[1] Rick Warren, *The Purpose Driven Church* (Grand Rapids, Mich: Zondervan, 1995).

[2] Warren, p. 165.

[3] "Transition to Adulthood Harder for '80's Youth," *Denver Post* (August 25, 1988), p. 6.

[4] Warren, p. 159.

[5] Kevin Graham Ford, *Jesus for a New Generation* (Downers Grove, Ill.: InterVarsity, 1995), p. 91.

[6] Marc Fienberg, "Adventures in Africa," *Generation Lifestyle Magazine* (April 1998), p. 9.

[7] Brendan I. Koerner, "Extreeeme," *U.S. News & World Report* (June 30, 1997), p. 56.

[8] Koerner, p. 57.

[9] Koerner, pp. 58–59.

[10] Wesson, p. 138.

[11] Vann Wesson, *Generation X Field Guide and Lexicon* (San Diego: Orion, 1997), p. 53.

[12] As quoted by William Dunn in *The Baby Bust* (Ithaca, N.Y.: American Demographics, 1993), p. 115.

[13] Mark Charlier, "Body Piercing," *Generation Lifestyle Magazine* (April 1998), p. 22.

[14] Tom Beaudoin, *Virtual Faith* (San Francisco: Jossey-Bass, 1998), p. 141.

[15] Wesson, p. 164.

[16] Wesson, p. 142.

[17] Beaudoin, p. 135.

[18] Charlier, p. 27.

[19] Douglas Rushkoff, ed., *The GenX Reader* (New York: Ballantine, 1994), p. 72.

[20] Beaudoin, p. 101.

[21] Strauss and Howe, *13th Gen* (New York: Vintage, 1993), p. 130.

[22] Bruce Tulgan, *Managing Generation X* (Santa Monica, Calif.: Merritt, 1995).

[23] As quoted by Rushkoff, p. 74.

[24] Rushkoff, p. 246.

[25] Strauss and Howe, p. 121.

[26] Rob Nelson and Jon Cowan, *Revolution X* (New York: Penguin, 1994), p. 1.

[27] Dieter Zander, "Life After God: Understanding Generation X," *WCA Monthly* (September–October 1995), p. 3.

[28] Randall Lane, "Computers Are Our Friends," *Forbes* (May 8, 1995), p. 105.

[29] Joanne DeLuca and Janine Lopiano-Misdom, *Street Trends* (New York: Harper Business, 1997), p. 34.

[30] Ted Polhemus, *Streetstyle* (New York: Thames & Hudson, 1994), p. 7.

[31] DeLuca and Lopiano-Misdom, p. 37.

[32] Rushkoff, p. 246.

[33] Wesson, p. 90.
[34] Wesson, p. 51.
[35] Wesson, p. 192.
[36] DeLuca and Lopiano-Misdom, p. 40.
[37] Zander, p. 3.

CHAPTER FOUR
[1] Gary McIntosh, *Three Generations* (Grand Rapids, Mich.: Revell, 1995), p. 9.
[2] McIntosh, pp. 26–28.
[3] McIntosh, p. 17.

CHAPTER FIVE
[1] Bruce Larson, *No Longer Strangers* (Waco, Texas: Word, 1971), p. 17.
[2] Larson, p. 16.
[3] Adapted from Bruce Larson.
[4] Kevin Graham Ford, *Jesus for a New Generation* (Downers Grove, Ill.: InterVarsity, 1995), p. 188.
[5] Larson, p. 30.
[6] Eugene Peterson, *Working the Angles* (Grand Rapids, Mich.: Eerdmans, 1987), p. 1.
[7] Larson, p. 50.
[8] Larson, p. 27.

CHAPTER SIX
[1] John Maxwell, *Developing the Leader Within You* (Nashville: Nelson, 1993), p. 53.
[2] Rich Hurst and Frank Tillapaugh, *Calling* (Monument, Colo.: Dreamtime, 1997), p. 73.

[3] Leighton Ford, *The Power of Story* (Colorado Springs, Colo.: NavPress, 1994), p. 13.
[4] Bruce Tulgan, *Managing Generation X* (Santa Monica, Calif.: Merritt, 1995), p. 8.
[5] Tom Beaudoin, *Virtual Faith* (San Francisco, Calif.: Jossey-Bass, 1998), p. 5.
[6] Kevin Graham Ford, *Jesus for a New Generation* (Downers Grove, Ill.: InterVarsity, 1995), p. 29.
[7] Chip R. Bell, *Managers As Mentors* (San Francisco: Berrett-Koehler, 1998), pp. 6–7.
[8] Leadership Network, "Large Churches, Consultants, and Global/Local Churches," *Net Fax* (August 17, 1998), p. 1.
[9] Robert McGarvey, "X Appeal: Secrets to Managing Generation X," *Entrepreneur* (May 1997), p. 2.
[10] Bill Easum, *Sacred Cows Make Gourmet Burgers* (Nashville: Abingdon, 1995), p. 25.
[11] William R. Buck and Tracey C. Rembert, "Just Doing It: Generation X Proves That Actions Speak Louder Than Words," *E* (September-October 1997), p. 29.
[12] Buck and Rembert, p. 29.
[13] Alister McGrath, *Intellectuals Don't Need God & Other Modern Myths* (Grand Rapids, Mich.: Zondervan, 1993), p. 175.
[14] Gustavo Gutierrez, *A Theology of Liberation* (Maryknoll, N.Y.: Orbis, 1988), p. 70.
[15] Beaudoin, p. 65.
[16] Jon R. Katzenbach and Douglas K. Smith, *The Wisdom of Teams* (New York: Harper Business, 1993), p. 27.
[17] Beaudoin, p. 70.
[18] Beaudoin, p. 70.
[19] Beaudoin, p. 55.

[20] George Barna, *Evangelism That Works* (Ventura, CA: Regal, 1995), p. 42.

[21] George Laboviz and Victor Rosansky, *The Power of Alignment* (New York: Wiley, 1997), p. 44.

[22] Rick Maurer, *Beyond the Wall of Resistance* (Austin, Texas: Bard, 1996), p. 65.

[23] Steven R. Covey, A. Roger Merrill, and Rebecca R. Merrill, *First Things First* (New York: Simon & Schuster, 1994), p. 206.

CHAPTER SEVEN

[1] J. Richard Middleton and Brian J. Walsh, *Truth Is Stranger Than It Used to Be: Biblical Faith in a Postmodern Age* (Downers Grove, Ill.: InterVarsity, 1995), p. 14.

[2] Max Depree, *Leadership Is an Art* (New York: Dell, 1989), p. 53.

[3] Robert C. Girard, *Brethren, Hang Loose* (Grand Rapids, Mich.: Zondervan, 1972), p. 120.

[4] C. S. Lewis, "Hamlet: The Prince or the Poem" in *Selected Literary Essays*, ed. Walter Hooper (Cambridge, U.K.: Cambridge University Press, 1967), p. 105.

[5] C. S. Lewis, *Of Other Worlds: Essays and Stories*, ed. Walter Hooper (New York: Harcourt, 1966), p. 25.

[6] Lewis, p. 26.

[7] As quoted in a lecture by Terry Hershey, University Presbyterian Church, 1988.

[8] Terry Hershey, Karen Butler, and Rich Hurst, *Giving the Ministry Away* (Colorado Springs, Colo.: David C. Cook, 1991), p. 92.

CHAPTER NINE

[1] Eugene Peterson, *Working the Angles* (Grand Rapids, Mich.: Eerdmans, 1987), p. 71.

[2] Frances Hesselbein, Marshall Goldsmith, and Richard Beckhard, *The Leader of the Future*, (San Francisco: Jossey-Bass Publishers, 1996), pp. 255–256.

[3] Robert C. Girard, *Brethren, Hang Loose* (Grand Rapids, Mich.: Zondervan, 1972), p. 119.

CHAPTER TEN

[1] John Maxwell, *Be a People Person* (Wheaton, Ill.: Victor, 1989), p. 53.

[2] Rich Hurst and Frank Tillapaugh, *Calling* (Monument, Colo.: Dreamtime, 1997), pp. 41–105.

[3] Studs Terkel, *Working* (New York: New Press, 1997), p. XXIV.

CHAPTER ELEVEN

[1] Steven Covey, *Seven Habits of Highly Effective People* (New York: Simon & Schuster, 1989), p. 241.

[2] Douglas Coupland, *Life After God* (New York: Pocket, 1994), p. 170.

[3] Henry Cloud, *Changes That Heal* (Grand Rapids, Mich.: Zondervan, 1990), p. 49.

[4] Cloud, p. 47.

[5] John Powell, *Why Am I Afraid to Love?* (Niles, Ill.: Argus, 1967), p. 68.

[6] Stephanie Pace Marshall, "Creating Sustainable Learning Communities for the Twenty-First Century," in *The Organization of the Future*, eds. Francis Hesselbein, Marshall Goldsmith, and

Richard Beckhard (San Francisco: Jossey-Bass, 1997), pp. 180–181.

[7]M. Scott Peck, *The Different Drum* (New York: Simon & Schuster, 1987), pp. 67–68.

[8]Carl F. George, *Prepare Your Church for the Future* (Tarrytown, N.Y.: Revell, 1991), p. 41.

[9]Henry Cloud & John Townsend, *Safe People* (Grand Rapids, Mich.: Zondervan, 1995), p. 11.

[10]Peck, p. 59.

[11]Bill Donahue, *The Willow Creek Guide to Leading Life-Changing Small Groups* (Grand Rapids, Mich.: Zondervan, 1996), p. 165.

[12]George, pp. 135–136.

[13]Kevin Graham Ford, *Jesus for a New Generation* (Downers Grove, Ill.: InterVarsity, 1995), p. 131.

[6]Easum, p. 25.

[7]Henri J. M. Nouwen, *Out of Solitude* (Notre Dame, Ind.: Ave Maria, 1974), p. 18.

[8] Tim Hansel, lecture, Seattle, Wash., 1987.

[9]Gordon Dahl, *Work, Play, and Worship in a Leisure-Oriented Society* (Minneapolis: Augsburg, 1972), p. 12.

[10] John Maxwell, "Criticism, The Act That Always Changes Us" (Lecture), Tape C5024.

CHAPTER FOURTEEN

[1]James C. Collins and Jerry I. Porras, *Built to Last* (New York: Harper Business, 1994), p. 54.

CHAPTER TWELVE

[1]Terry Hershey, Karen Butler, and Rich Hurst, *Giving the Ministry Away* (Colorado Springs, Colo.: David C. Cook, 1991), p. 173.

CHAPTER THIRTEEN

[1]Bill Easum, *Sacred Cows Make Gourmet Burgers* (Nasville Abingdon, 1995), p. 29.

[2]as heard in a lecture by Alan Loy McGinnis at Arrowhead Springs, CA, 1984.

[3]McGinnis lecture

[4]McGinnis lecture

[5]Kim A. Lawton, "Elizabeth Dole's Fishbowl Faith," *Christianity Today* (October 28, 1996), p. 69.

ABOUT THE AUTHORS

KEN BAUGH has a B.A. in Bible and Christian Education from Biola University in La Mirada, California. He earned a Master of Divinity from Trinity Evangelical Divinity School in Deerfield, Illinois. Over the last ten years, Ken has worked with young adults and has equipped pastors worldwide to be more effective in reaching Generation X for Christ.

Ken is the Pastor of Frontline Ministry, a young adult church within a church at McLean Bible Church near Washington D.C. Frontline began in 1994 and is currently reaching more than 1,200 young adults each week. The vision of Frontline is to reach the entire Generation X population by helping churches throughout the world to be more effective in reaching young adults. Ken's consulting has reached as far as Australia and includes both Military and Civilian consultation.

Ken has served as the singles pastor at North Suburban Evangelical Free Church in Deerfield, Illinois. He also was on the preaching team and was the young adult pastor at Saddleback Church in Mission Viejo, California. He is a popular conference and retreat speaker as well as a church consultant. He and his wife, Susan, are parents of two girls: Jessica and Ariella. Ken and his family live in Sterling, Virginia, near Washington D.C.

RICH HURST is a popular leader, encourager, and dynamic speaker who travels throughout North America teaching pastors and church leaders. He is a recognized authority on the topics of young adults, generational differences, and singles. Rich is also a national consultant for service ministries and organizations.

He has authored or co-authored several books including *Giving the Ministry Away: Empowering Single Adults for Effective Leadership,* which won two awards from the Network of Single-Adult Leaders; *Intimacy: The Search for Significance* (both David C. Cook Publishing); and the best-selling *Calling* (Dreamtime Publishing). Currently Rich is a part-time staff member of McLean Bible Church and serves on the board of The Next Level Church in Denver, Colorado, and oversees the National Gen X Conference, a ministry of Cook Communications International. Rich and his family live in Monument, Colorado.

LET STORIES CHANGE YOUR LIFE.

What's Your Story?

This interactive guide is designed to help people tell their stories
by recounting their experiences, feelings, values, and beliefs with others.
Start talking about—and listening to—the things that really matter.

What's Your Story?
(Toben and Joanne Heim) $10

Conversations with Jesus

Discover the relevance of Jesus' stories as Harold Fickett puts them
into today's terms and relates them to our everyday lives.
Begin a fresh investigation of Jesus' teachings and understand Him
better through *Conversations with Jesus.*

Conversations with Jesus
(Harold Fickett) $14

Piñon Press

Prices subject to change.